W9-BQS-235

PREFACE BY
# erica jong

# the new writer's
# HANDBOOK

## A PRACTICAL ANTHOLOGY OF BEST ADVICE FOR YOUR CRAFT & CAREER

## 2007

EDITED BY
## PHILIP MARTIN

The New Writer's Handbook 2007

# The New Writer's Handbook 2007

A Practical Anthology of Best Advice
for Your Craft & Career

EDITED by PHILIP MARTIN

PREFACE by ERICA JONG

SCARLETTA PRESS

MINNEAPOLIS

**Scarletta Press**

10 South Fifth Street, Suite 1105, Minneapolis, MN 55402, U.S.A.

Visit our website at www.scarlettapress.com

Publisher's Cataloging-In-Publication Data
(Prepared by The Donohue Group, Inc.)

The new writer's handbook : a practical anthology of best advice for your craft &
career / edited by Philip Martin.

v. ;  cm.

Annual
Includes bibliographical references.
ISSN: 1936-7104

1. Authorship—Handbooks, manuals, etc.—Periodicals. I. Martin, Philip, 1953-

PN151 .N49
808.02

ISBN 13: 978-0-9765201-6-0
ISBN 10: 0-9765201-6-8

Book design by Mighty Media Inc., Minneapolis, MN
Cover: Tracy Kompelien and Chris Long
Interior: Chris Long

First edition

10  9  8  7  6  5  4  3  2  1

Manufactured in the United States of America

# Contents

## Pitching & Proposals

## Marketing Your Work

## Internet Skills

## Literary Insights & Last Words

## Appendices

# All Writers Are Vain

*by Erica Jong*

ALL WRITERS *are vain, selfish and lazy, and at the very bottom of their motives there lies a mystery. Writing a book is a horrible, exhausting struggle, like a long bout of some painful illness. One would never undertake such a thing unless driven by some demon whom one can neither resist nor understand.*

So wrote George Orwell, who understood the process better than anyone. Later on the same page he says: "Good prose is like a windowpane." And I believe it is the journey from the miasma in one's head to that clear windowpane which makes writing so ultimately rewarding—and so painful. One comes to clarity through writing. And clarity is truth.

I called my writing memoir *Seducing the Demon*, in homage to the difficulty and mystery of the process. I was thinking of an Isaac Bashevis Singer demon rather than an Orwell demon, but maybe they are the same. The Singer demon is sexual, the Orwell political—yet the excitement the writer feels is indistinguishable. I believe it is the excitement of making order out of chaos.

If you are born to do this—poor you. And if you hope to get rich by it, double poor you. But if you understand that writing is about the possibility of altering, by one iota, the brains of people as yet unborn, then go for it. You may wind up poor, jailed or even assassinated for your ideas, but you will have spent your life in a gallant pursuit. I believe that nothing else matters.

Orwell understood better than any writer of the 20th century that a debased language makes for a debased political life. When we say the opposite of what we mean and tolerate others saying the opposite of what they mean, we are well on our way to totalitarianism. Language is that important. In 1984, the Ministry of Truth (Minitrue) disseminates lies; the Ministry of Peace (Minipax) makes war; and the Ministry of Love (Miniluv) maintains order—usually through violence. Surrounded by barbed war and gun turrets, the Ministry of Love has no windows and is heavily guarded at all times. The Ministry of Plenty (or Miniplenty) controls all economic life. How can there be poverty or deprivation when Miniplenty is in charge? You cannot even talk about such things. There are no words for them. But the people starve—for which newspeak has no word. No wonder the three mottoes of society are:

WAR IS PEACE

FREEDOM IS SLAVERY

IGNORANCE IS STRENGTH

Good writers are more needed than ever because our language has never been more debased. A debased language is more than a dirty windowpane (to continue Orwell's image). It is a windowpane that has become a funhouse mirror. Its purpose is deception. Your purpose is the opposite. Why do you think great writers are so often targets?

The world doesn't need another book! The world doesn't need another painting! These words are the Devil's counsel. You are not writing for "the world," but for yourself. Write for "the world" and you'll write only whiskey and cigarette ads. Write for yourself, above all, and the world will come to you because it needs your truth in exact proportion to how many whiskey and cigarette ads there are. The more "worldly" the world, the more it needs the solitary artist for its own spiritual health. Believe in yourself. You are the soul—and the conscience—of the world, even if the world doesn't yet know it.

I share these words with you because they are the words with which I encourage myself when I am most downhearted. And downheartedness is the curse of writing. Writing and depression go together. I think this is the case because human beings are social creatures and writing is so solitary. You cannot make order from chaos in the midst of chaos. You must find yourself a quiet place.

The basic rules of writing are so obvious that everyone has repeated them—from Orwell to Strunk and White. Don't use a long word where a short one will work. Avoid dead metaphors. Try to make your verbs carry images rather than resorting to adjectives. Choose active over passive. Be clear.

Most people cannot achieve this clarity in a first draft. Expect to rewrite. Clarity comes from polishing.

All writing problems are psychological problems. Blocks usually stem from the fear of being judged. If you imagine the world listening, you'll never write a line. That's why privacy is so important. You should write first drafts as if they will never be shown to anyone.

That's it. Those are my simple secrets. And one more thing. Expect to forget these rules with everything you write. You will need to relearn them with every new voice you invent.

Nobody said this was easy.

Erica Jong is the author of eight novels including *Fear of Flying, Fanny, Shylock's Daughter, Inventing Memory*, and *Sappho's Leap*, an odyssey about the greatest female lyric poet of all time, set in the ancient world. Several of her novels have been worldwide bestsellers. *Fear of Flying* (1973) is in print in 27 languages, with worldwide sales near 18 million copies. Her other books include nonfiction works *Fear of Fifty: A Midlife Memoir; The Devil at Large*, a study of Henry Miller; *Witches*; and *What Do Women Want*; and six volumes of poetry. Her book for writers, *Seducing the Demon: Writing for My Life*, was released by Tarcher/Penguin in March 2006.

In 1998, Erica Jong was honored with the United Nations Award for Excellence in Literature. In addition, she has received Poetry magazine's Bess Hokin Prize, the Deauville Award for Literary Excellence in France, and in Italy, the Sigmund Freud Award for Literature in 1975.

A graduate of Barnard College and Columbia University's Graduate Faculties where she studied 18th-century English Literature, Erica Jong has lectured and read her work all over the world. She lives in New York City and Weston, Connecticut.

Her website is www.ericajong.com.

# CREATIVITY, MOTIVATION & DISCIPLINE

# Writing Rhythms

*by Jane Yolen*

THOSE WHO KNOW ME have noticed that I work on more than one thing at a time. Well, to be honest, many more than one thing at a time. Perhaps you have wondered about that. Or marveled. Or though it odd, intriguing, or downright disgusting.

Here's the major scoop: it is simply the way I work. I can't envision writing any other way.

But how do I do it without …

1. Getting confused?
2. Losing track of things like voice and plot?
3. Becoming facile (well, that's a critical judgment call, isn't it?)
4. Missing deadlines?
5. Repeating characters/dialogue/ lines?

Here's how.

I read everything aloud, which is easier now that I am in the house alone. It makes for strange looks when I am sharing a household.

Everything is in a folder. Both a desktop computer folder *and* (usually) a printout. I go back over what I have done previously (if small enough) or just the last chapter (if a novel) before beginning that day.

If a project or piece of writing is being balky, threatening to block up, or otherwise shut itself down, this is what I do: I stand up, walk about, eat a chocolate chip cookie, have a cup of tea, watch a rerun of *Top Chef*, check email, read blogs like Miss Snark or Fuse #8 or BlueJo or Making Light, read magazines like *Newsweek* or *Style* 1900 or *Smithsonian*. If none of those distractions work, I turn to a different writing project. Since there are plenty of them around, I never have to worry.

Notice, I never settle into reading a novel. If I do, it will be many hours or days before I resurface, my own projects forgot, and the beat of the novelist's language in my head instead of my own voice.

I try not to work on two similar things at the same time. So I can be deep into a picture book, a book of poems, novel, short story, graphic novel, movie script, speech, and the latest installment of my online journal in the same day or week without confusion. But doubling up on any of these and even I run into trouble.

Please note, I will be in very different places with each of these (first paragraph, proposal, mid section, etc.), and not everything gets completed at the same time. Sometimes they are days, weeks, months, years apart. And some have *still* not been finished.

There are actually many projects I will never complete: *The Emily Sonnets* is a prime example. These are sonnets about Emily Dickinson's life. And while a few have been published (in *Horn Book*, in the Dickinson bulletin, elsewhere) I am pretty certain the book is something I will be working on forever. Though it goes months without my hauling it back into the light.

There are many other projects that will go really bad/sour/septic along the way. I simply stow them. Maybe I will pull one or two of them out again in the future. Maybe not. I may be able to turn a thwarted short story into a graphic novel. This happened with *Foiled*. Or a failed collection of poems into a picture book.

If I am lucky that happens. Usually it doesn't come that easily. My filing cabinets and computer desktop are quite the archeological dig.

Of course I have repeated lines, even repeated character traits. (For example, I believe I have at least three minor characters in novels and stories tagged with a wandering left eye, something an editor friend who has a wandering eye once pointed out to me.) With 287 published books out there, not to mention many uncollected stories, poems, essays, it would be more surprising if I never repeated myself.

I love what I do, so being at my desk writing is a pleasure. There is nothing else quite like it in my life. But remember—writing on many projects in the same day is simply what I do. I don't advise others to follow that path, but I don't discourage them either. One person may spend years on a single brilliant novel (Pynchon), others (Shakespeare, Dickens, Sir Walter Scott) only took months, and their novels or stories or plays are just as brilliant.

If you take any one thing away from this minor screed, it has to be this: Writing rhythms differ. Don't sweat it that you do not write the way I write. Do it your own way.

Jane Yolen, author of *Owl Moon*, winner of the Caldecott Medal, and the bestselling *How Do Dinosaurs Say Goodnight?*, writes for children and adults and is the author of over two hundred books, including novels, picture books, story collections, poetry, and nonfiction. She has been called "America's Hans Christian Andersen." Some of her other books include *Briar Rose, Sister Light, Sister Dark, White Jenna, The One-Armed Queen* (for adults); and *The Emperor and the Kite*, a Caldecott honor book, *The Devil's Arithmetic*, and the Young Merlin series (for children).

Her books have also won the Christopher Medal, the Golden Kite, the World Fantasy Award, and many other honors.

She divides her time between homes in western Massachusetts and St. Andrews, Scotland. This piece from December 2006 is from her online journal, Telling the True, found at her website, www.janeyolen.com.

# The Benefits of Messiness

*by Eric Abrahamson*
*interviewed by Michael McLaughlin*

**McLaughlin:** Is there really such a thing as a perfect mess?

**Abrahamson:** Yes. Your mess is perfect when it reaches the point at which, if you spent any more or any less time organizing, you would become inefficient.

If you devote all your time to organizing, you won't get anything done. If you don't spend any time organizing, the resultant mess bogs you down completely. When you find the 'sweet spot' between messiness and order, then you have a perfect mess.

**McLaughlin:** Why do you think people are so hung up about being organized and orderly?

**Abrahamson:** According to our research, two-thirds of people feel guilt or shame about their own messiness. And more than half think badly of someone else who is messy and disorganized.

Most people should just relax about the level of disorder and not be so worried about it.

There are many reasons people are biased toward being organized. We have deep-seated suspicions about mess and some people are very uncomfortable living with any level of disorder.

Then you have the moral lessons of thinkers like Benjamin Franklin, who admonished people to "Lose no time; be always employed in something useful; cut off all unnecessary actions." Many of us have been programmed to think this way.

Some of our conceptions about order come from the Industrial Revolution—the age of machination. The machine became a metaphor for organizational systems, with people as cogs.

After his book came out in 1911, Frederick Taylor's "scientific management" approach became extremely popular. He argued that companies had made great improvements in efficiency using machines but that the messy, unpredictable human worker was the weak link that needed to be brought into line.

Of course, now we have an entire industry devoted to personal productivity, including the National Association of Professional Organizers (NAPO). People eat it up, too—enough to support forty specialties within the field of professional organizing.

**McLaughlin:** What's right and wrong about the advice of all the productivity gurus out there?

**Abrahamson:** What's wrong about their advice is that frequently they extol the benefits of organization without counting in the cost of achieving those benefits.

When you're weighing the benefits of an organizational system, you need to do a cost/benefit analysis. Instead, people tend to just say organization is good ... we need more organization....

People have this weird tendency to look at the benefits of organization and just forget about the costs.

**McLaughlin:** So, being too organized has a downside?

**Abrahamson:** Organization can be limiting. And it's not just about spatial organization but also about time. Compare a messy schedule, with no clear times and places you have to be, to an extremely orderly schedule, which specifies exactly where you have to be all day. Well, the orderly schedule makes sense if nothing's going to change throughout your day.

But if new opportunities are going to pop up, you might miss them if you stick to your planned schedule.

Most of us can't be completely improvisational but we can find a balance between rigid planning and winging it all the time. It's not one or the other, but an optimal mix of the two. You should have a plan but be ready to junk the plan when appropriate.

Companies with strategic plans do as well as they do because they frequently ignore their plans.

**McLaughlin:** This Einstein quote leads into the first chapter of the book: "If a cluttered desk is a sign of a cluttered mind, of what, then, is an empty desk?" What does an empty desk reflect?

**Abrahamson:** An empty desk can reflect a person who is spending too much time organizing and not getting an appropriate return on that investment. Order has many costs, including setting up your system, filing, and changing the system.

Order also has opportunity costs. For instance, if you've got an important project to complete, but your desk is a mess, what should you do, clean up your desk or work on the project? The cost of your time at that point is huge.

Of course, order has its benefits. If you let ten items pile up on your desk, you can make one trip and file all ten things. If you're a clean-desk advocate then you make ten trips and file one thing at a time. But messiness does have efficiency benefits, like making that one trip instead of ten. There are also benefits of messiness with respect to creativity, power, and beauty.

**McLaughlin:** What are some of those other benefits of messiness?

**Abrahamson:** Mess can be ugly but it can also be very beautiful. Compare a Jackson Pollack painting to a representation work, or a Frank Gehry building to a set of row houses. There's no doubt about it that messiness can be pleasing to the eye.

In terms of creativity, messiness juxtaposes things that otherwise would be separated by order. For instance, let's say you're writing a proposal and you have many papers and documents on your desk. You can see all the relationships between the different documents and you can combine them in different, creative ways.

Creativity is spurred when things that we tend not to organize in the same category come together. When you allow some messiness into a system, new combinations can result. If you keep all your tools in the tool shed and all your kitchen utensils in the kitchen, you might never think of using a kitchen utensil as a tool or vice-versa.

**McLaughlin:** One last question: If you could give one piece of advice about being messy versus organized, what would it be?

**Abrahamson:** Two findings pop into my mind. First, too many people feel guilty about their messiness. Clearly if you're an unbelievable packrat or if you're schizophrenic, that's a problem. But most people should just relax about the level of disorder and not be so worried about it.

If you think about it, a lot of our systems have a fair amount of messiness in them and do perfectly well. And many highly successful people are very messy. We use Albert Einstein as our poster boy.

The other surprising finding is that people with orderly desks report spending 36 percent more time finding things. You might think that it's hard to find things in messy piles. But people who have elaborate organizing systems also have trouble finding things.

So I would emphasize those two points. Moderate messiness is completely acceptable and is, in fact, probably superior in a number of instances. And really put to the test whether a certain level of order is optimal, because more order is not necessarily better.

Eric Abrahamson is a professor at Columbia Business School and co-author with David Freedman of *A Perfect Mess: The Hidden Benefits of Disorder* (Little, Brown & Co., 2007), which challenges the accepted wisdom that neatness and organization are the keys to success. Abrahamson is also author of *Change Without Pain* (Harvard Business School Press, 2005), which won a Best Book of the Year award from *Strategy and Business* magazine.

Michael McLaughlin is co-author of *Guerrilla Marketing for Consultants*, with a website at www.guerrillaconsulting.com. He is also editor of *Management Consulting News*, www.managementconsultingnews.com, a monthly newsletter of articles that features the best ideas and tools from leading thinkers, consultants, writers, and marketers. This piece is excerpted from an interview in the March 2007 issue.

# Strange Fruit

*by Lynn Viehl*

As I stood in line at the pack-n-ship place in town, an elderly farmer came in. An instant character, raw-boned, scarecrow-thin, with a driftwood face and a jujube-size cyst on the edge of his left eyelid. Baggy, sun-faded denims with permanent dirt stains on the seat and a washed-out, long-sleeved gray shirt sagged on his clothesline frame. The wind had combed his pure white hair for him, and on his shoulder hung a homemade canvas fruit picking bag, as if he'd wandered in directly from a grove.

He seemed a bit antsy, and I had fifty pounds of books to ship, so I let him go ahead of me in line. He smelled of dirt and weedkiller, sunshine and old-guy sweat. He told the clerk he wanted to ship the grapefruit in his bag, which the clerk immediately informed him that he couldn't do. Florida currently prohibits private shipping fruit out of state to prevent the spread of citrus canker.

"It's goin'-a Washington D.C.," the farmer told the clerk. "They doan have no groves so they doan care 'bout the canker."

The clerk turned him down a second time and went to answer the phone. The farmer turned to me and asked if the post office would ship his fruit. I told him that, as far as I knew, no one would. While we were waiting for the clerk, the farmer took a grapefruit from his bag and held it out for me to admire.

I eyed what looked like a pale yellow cantaloupe, with faint rain-mold streaks on the rind (this is a sign of authentic homegrown; the streaks are always washed off commercially-sold fruit, which is sometimes also dyed and waxed.) I'm not exaggerating on the size, either—it had to be the largest grapefruit I've ever seen. The farmer told me his trees often produced eight pounders. I imagined he spent a lot of time shoring up his trees with cotton ties and two by twos to keep the weight of the fruit from snapping the branches.

I love grapefruit, and miss it terribly (I haven't been able to eat it for six months because it reacts with my medications) but that farmer's goliath specimen made me uneasy. He mentioned his grapefruit were very juicy and full of seeds, but what else was in them? What was he using as fertilizer? Had he planted his trees over some septic tanks? Why bring a bag of just-picked grapefruit directly from the grove to a shipper? Anyone even remotely involved with citrus knows the state law; I know it. And why so adamant to send it to Washington D.C.?

I never thought something as ordinary as a grapefruit could give me the creeps, but that one did.

The clerk finally got off the phone, and for the third time refused to ship the grapefruit for the farmer. The farmer asked if he brought in a box to the post office and didn't say there was grapefruit in it, would they ship it? I shrugged. The clerk said it was between him and his conscience. The farmer bought a big box from the clerk, paid for it in quarters and ambled out.

I may have acted non-committal, but I doubted the farmer would get his fruit past the folks at the post office. Grapefruit has a distinctive smell, very sharp-bitter, that is especially intense if the rind is bruised or scored. Unless he seals the shipment in plastic, the odor will give it away.

The encounter got to me, though. By the time I shipped my boxes and returned to my car, I had worked out in my head five different ways to explain the farmer and his strange fruit:

1.  A love gift to the farmer's old flame, who is dying of cancer in some hospital in Washington. A nurse will open the box for her and try to whisk it away, her rich husband will veto that, peel one and listen to her talk about the farmer as he feeds her the sections one by one.

2.  Shrapnel bombs disguised as grapefruit, being sent to a certain Congressional Committee that has pissed off that farmer for the last time.

3.  The final volley in a life-long feud between two brothers: one who got rich selling out the citrus industry as a lobbyist while his brother stayed home to farm the family groves (lobbyist brother has just been convicted in the Abramoff scandal, has lost everything, and is going to jail.)

4. Alien pods carrying something much worse than canker to Washington.

5. Grandpa's annual late-January, post-harvest box, sent as a gift to his son, daughter-in-law and grandkids, who will have to give half away to the neighbors, who will look at the size of them and wonder what the hell we have in the water here in Florida. One of the grandkids will dig out the designer tulip bulbs in her mother's windowbox and plant some of the seeds.

Or the whole thing could serve as the topic of a writer's weblog post on the method she uses to sketch out story ideas to get them out of her thoughts, onto paper and into a file so she can work on the WIP without mutant citrus dancing in her head.

How do you writers out there deal with your strange fruit?

Lynn Viehl is a pseudonym for Sheila Kelly, who lives in Florida and writes mostly novels in a variety of genres, including science fiction (as S. L. Viehl), romantic fiction (as Lynn Viehl, Gena Hale, and Jessica Hall), and Christian fiction (as Rebecca Kelly). This piece (January 2007) is from her blog, Paperback Writer, located at www.pbackwriter. blogspot.com.

# Where Do Ideas Come From?

*by Philip Martin*

*You don't build a story, you allow it to explode.*
—Ray Bradbury

Where do ideas come from?

If you are a writer, this oft-asked question easily becomes annoying. Some authors make up tongue-in-cheek responses: Poughkeepsie.

One of Neil Gaiman's favorite ploys was to credit a writing friend, Pete Atkins. Pete in turn agreed to say he got his ideas from Neil.

British fantasist Diana Wynne Jones recalled her favorite form of that question was asked by a 12-year-old: "Where do you get your ideas … or do you think of them for yourself?"

But the manner in which ideas are found lies at the heart of story-telling and writing. In *Dancing at the Edge of the World*, a collection of essays on writing and culture, Ursula Le Guin warns about misconceptions in that seemingly innocent question: where do ideas come from?

> *Writers do say things like "That gives me an idea" or "I got the idea for that story when I had food poisoning in a motel in New Jersey."*
>
> *I think this is a kind of shorthand use of "idea" to stand for the complicated, obscure, un-understood process of the conception and formation of what is going to be a story when it gets written down.*
>
> *The process may not involve ideas in the sense of intelligible thoughts; it may well not even involve words. It may be a matter of mood, resonances, mental glimpses, voices, emotions, visions, dreams, anything. It is different in every writer, and in many of us it is different every time.*

Robin McKinley, author of the Newbery Medal-winning novel, *The Hero and the Crown*, describes it as a process of accident plus recognition: "My stories happen to me; I bump into them like pieces of furniture; and they are clear and plain to me—like pieces of furniture."

Tolkien described the source of ideas as like leaf-mould. Poet Gary Snyder called this unconscious source of ideas a compost heap—perhaps even more accurate a term, as a compost heap is human-made, and should be turned on occasion with a garden fork to help the fermentation process. In either case, the source of ideas is jumbled and of uncertain origins. It is nutrient-rich with images, broken-down scraps of thought, scribblings, and real-life episodes from a writer's past.

The Hobbit, for instance, includes fragments of a youthful Alpine trek in 1911, plus the goblins of George MacDonald's books, plus an episode from Beowulf in which a cup is stolen from a sleeping barrow-dragon. For his battle scenes, Tolkien drew on memories of service as a signalman in the trenches in the First World War.

From that 1911 Alpine trek, Tolkien brought home a postcard. It showed a painting of the "spirit of the mountain": an old man with flowing beard, broad-brimmed hat, and long cloak, sitting on a rock under a pine. It later ended up in an envelope marked as the origins of Gandalf, the great wizard of Middle-earth.

Every intriguing item or curiosity is a starting point. The writer is always asking not "What is it?" or "What was it?" but "What could it be?"—perhaps if transferred to another context. Like rich compost, the origins of an idea are less important then the nature of the new growth that springs from it in the writer's garden.

From the imagination come fantastic ideas—at all hours of the day and night. The clever writer knows to jot them any promising idea down as soon as possible. Anne Rice admits that she has risen on occasion late at night to write down a half-dreamed idea on her room's wallpaper, so she could remember it in the morning.

When Tolkien started The Lord of the Rings, he did not know where the story would go. He only knew that it involved the magic ring carried over from his earlier tale, The Hobbit. So he started by writing a first chapter: a feast. Then, he started a trio of Bilbo's descendants out on a new journey ... not really knowing where or why. (In the initial draft their names were Bingo, Odo, and Frodo.) Only in writing those early scenes did Tolkien conceive in a blaze of inspiration the greater trilogy that sprang from that ring. To simplify, the trio, Bingo, Odo, and Frodo, became a duo—Frodo, now accompanied by his faithful servant, Sam Gamgee.

If Tolkien had not started writing and sent his threesome off on an unexplained journey, *The Lord of the Rings* might not have taken shape. The first idea became the next idea, and so on. The act of writing is its own story generator; a story underway creates its own surprises.

Some writers use a method to tap into the creative right side of the brain—the non-analytical, instinctive side. This is described by Dorothea Brande in her 1934 book on writing, *Becoming a Writer*.

> [T]o have the full benefit of the richness of the unconscious you must learn to write ... when the unconscious is in the ascendant.
>
> The best way to do this is to rise half an hour, or a full hour, earlier than you customarily rise. Just as soon as you can ... begin to write. Write anything that comes into your head: last night's dream, if you are able to remember it; the activities of the day before; a conversation, real or imaginary; an examination of conscience. Write any sort of early morning reverie, rapidly and uncritically. The excellence or ultimate worth of what you write is of no importance yet....

In *Zen in the Art of Writing*, Ray Bradbury tells how he used this same process. Upon awakening, he would get his creative juices flowing by writing down one or several words. "I would then take arms against the word, or for it," he said, "and bring on an assortment of characters to weigh the word and show me its meaning...." As he wrote further meditations on these words, a crystalizing idea or character would emerge, interesting enough to shape into a story.

In *Writing the Natural Way*, Gabriele Rico presents a related technique called clustering. This begins by placing one or several key words in the middle of a blank page. Then, associating freely with those central words, new words are jotted down, radiating outwards. Eventually the page is filled with words, a spider's web of far-flung words, ideas, and tenuous connections.

Often the key idea appears off in the margin, in an unexpected group of words, as spun strands of associations begin to weave their own images. While not every attempt at this will create a great story, it draws forth the imaginative powers that lurk in the non-rational hemisphere of your brain. And it may take only one brilliant, unexpected idea to spark a great story.

## The Writer's Notebook

A writer needs a place to keep random, unorganized ideas. A notebook is the perfect place. In a 1981 essay, "Escaping into Ourselves," on the creation of her fantasy stories (in *Dreams and Wishes: Essays on Writing for Children*), Susan Cooper wrote:

> A writer's notebooks are perhaps the best illustration ... of the way his mind works. Some consist of detailed blueprints for books or plays, set out with mathematical precision; some are filled with discursive examinations of character, building up backgrounds which may never appear in the story but which show the writer getting to know the people he has made.
>
> My own notes are mostly cryptic and random, full of images, scattered with quotations and ideas which often seem totally irrelevant to the book in hand—though they weren't at the time. Rereading them, I have always again the feel of what it is like to write fantasy....

She offers some journal entries for The Dark is Rising series:

> Names of fields in Hitcham: Great and Lower Cogmarthon; Upper and Lower Brissels; Homer Corner; Hogg Hill.

> The sword comes from the drowned land.

> The opening of doors. Wakening of things sleeping. Revealing of old things forgotten.

> Don't forget: "The mountains are singing, and the Lady comes."

> Bird Rock. The birds remember. It is their door.

> The Welsh word for "grass" is "glas-wellt" (lit. green straw).

> A sailor tattooed with a star between thumb and forefinger.

Ideas are everywhere. As Joan Aiken described in *The Writer* (May 1968), in an essay titled "Thought on Plots":

> Once you are in the way of noting down ideas for plots, they spring up everywhere: half-seen street signs, overheard remarks, dreams, news items. I used to find the personal ad columns very fertile sources. Sometimes, as an exercise, I set myself the task of combining two or three into a short story.

*Consider these: "Agile bagpiper with waterproof kilt wanted for party." ... "Model rhinoceros wanted." "Would exchange gentleman's library for Jersey herd." These are all genuine items from the London Times....*

## What If?

The phrase "What if ..." is the magic wand of the writer. Many ideas come from within, the ability to daydream and imagine. As Richard Matheson said, *The Shrinking Man* was researched by taking a chair and going to sit in his basement for hours.

Tolkien kept one scrap of paper, that he jotted down on the back of a student's paper, with a mysterious phrase that came to him unbidden: "In a hole in the ground there lived a hobbit." Years later, he returned to that scrap to begin his book, *The Hobbit*. His imagination had chewed on the obvious question behind that mysterious phrase: What is a hobbit? (And why had that popped into his mind when he was supposed to be grading papers?)

But it is also important to know how to move beyond initial ideas to stretch for more interesting ones. Learn to ask the next question. Neil Gaiman, playing the what-if game in an article, "Where do you get your ideas?"on his website, offers this example: "Well, if cats used to rule the world, why don't they anymore? And how do they feel about that?"

Writers needs to let ideas merge with other ideas as they molder in the compost. And some ideas just don't pan out when pressed into service. Others are too common and need to wait for some odder variant, more challenging or intriguing, to bring them to life.

One important skill is not to shy away from the difficult idea, to not be afraid to push into dangerous territory. As Murakami said in a 1997 *Salon* interview, when asked how he got the idea for *The Wind-Up Bird Chronicle*: "[T]he idea was very small, just an image, not an idea actually. A man who is 30, cooking spaghetti in the kitchen, and the telephone rings—that's it. It's so simple, but I had the feeling that something was happening there."

But he was willing to extend the story to face difficult ideas, to encounter scary places, putting his characters through hard and trying times, following Orpheus deep into the underworld.

*When I was writing [some difficult and dark] scenes, I was there. ... I can feel the darkness. I can smell the strange smells. If you cannot do that, you are not a writer. If you're a writer you can feel that in your skin.*

*When I was writing the scene of the skinning ... it was so horrible, and I was scared. I didn't want to write it, honestly, but I did it. I wasn't happy when I was doing it, but it was so important to the story. ...*

*You can't escape from that. There is a saying in Japan: "When you want a tiger's cub, you have to enter the tiger's den."*

Where ideas come from, then, is a combination of openness, constant seeking, and courage. If the writer is tuned to these, the serendipity of ideas coming unbidden can at times seen miraculous.

In a 2001 *BookPage* interview, Leif Enger told how creative inspiration came to him in the form of a child, bearing an idea, just as the boy's father was beginning to write *Peace Like a River*:

*I ... was working on it early one morning when my youngest son, John, got up and came toddling in in his pajamas. He said: "How's it going, Dad?" I said: "It's going pretty well." He said: "You got any cowboys in that book yet?" And I said: "No, not yet. But that's a fabulous idea. You think I should?" And he said: "Yes!"*

*I said: "Well, if you could give me a good name, I'll put a cowboy in the book." And he said: "Sunny Sundown." No hesitation ... He'd been thinking about Sunny, apparently, for a while.*

*... By the end of the day the first few stanzas of Sunny were written, and I just never looked back.*

With any luck, and with a readiness on your part, your story too might explode.

Philip Martin is director of Great Lakes Literary, which offers a range of development services for writers and their projects. He is editor of this anthology, *The New Writer's Handbook*, and previously was acquisitions editor for The Writer Books, where he edited guides for fiction and nonfiction writers, including works on crafting fantasy, romance, and mystery novels.

He is also author of a book about fantasy fiction, *A Guide to Fantasy Literature* (Crickhollow, 2007). He lives in Milwaukee, Wisconsin, and speaks at writing conferences around the country.

His website is www.greatlakeslit.com.

# Ingredients

*by Jonathan Carroll*

You know that feeling you have some mornings when first getting out of bed: your eyes are sort of blurry, joints ache, you're so stiff that you can barely bend over, etc? You're not sick though—just a bundle of sleepy knots, your whole system feels like it needs oiling, and all you can do is yawn for the first ten minutes as you get ready to meet the day.

I had that feeling last night when I tentatively began a new book. Unlike some writers, that's never been a big thing for me. The horror of the first blank page, the search for the "mot juste" as the French call it, etc. I've read about others experiencing that stuff. But I write for a living so when it's time to start a new book, I find a pen and start.

That doesn't mean the first words are any good or I end up going anywhere with them. But I don't superstitiously go out and buy a new Montblanc fountain pen each time as the playwright Athol Fugard used to do (and then retire the pen after the play had been written), a new swanky notebook, or a bottle of rare ink secretly mixed by an order of monks in the Carpathian mountains. I pick up a pen, the nearest paper (usually scrap) and just get to work.

But last night I felt as stiff and grumpy at it as if I'd just woken up one of those mornings when all you want to do is leap back into bed and pull the covers over your head. I had my first sentence, a picture in mind of who said it and where they were, but the rest was just bad mood slow going. When I was done, I looked at those first scribbles on the paper and spontaneously said out loud, "Are we going to be friends or what?"

It has always intrigued me how the ingredients for a new novel evolve. The title usually swims to the surface first. *Outside the Dog Museum* was a variation on the German title of a turn-of-the-century photograph of a circus midway in Dusseldorf I once saw in a photo magazine. *From the Teeth of Angels* came from mishearing a lyric in a John Hiatt song. *White Apples* was plucked from a line in a poem by the Russian Yesenin. Things like that.

While walking the dog last summer, I saw a child's chalk drawing on the ground in a park. A large horse with a small white house perched on its butt. Just that.

Because I was bored, I started playing with the wording. House on a horse. The horse's house. Eventually a variation of that sentence came to mind and I knew immediately that it would be the title of my next book. I had no idea what it meant and still don't, but that was definitely the title.

Some time later I wrote this down in a notebook and knew it would be the first line of that book: "Most men think they are good drivers. Most women think they are good in bed. They're wrong." More things came—a lonely man sledding by himself in winter, the metaphor of a Trojan Horse, etc.—and slowly, slowly, the disparate images and ideas begin to coalesce and take shape.

I have no idea what that shape will end up being, but while doing nothing in this fallow period after finishing *The Ghost in Love*, I can already feel the pieces gathering like those science demonstration films you see in school about how a magnet attracts iron filings.

Someone recently asked that familiar question "Where do you get your ideas?" Instead of giving the rote response, I thought about it a moment and realized the question is not so much where do you get your ideas for the books but what do you do with them after they come.

The British writer David Hare said, "write about what bites you." One of the things that has bitten me with the new book I am writing is this question (think about it in the tub this evening): However old you are, you have memories that belong in your personal hall of fame. Memories of times where you were happier than ever before. When you'd made that extraordinary one-of-a-kind business deal, kissed that person for the first time that you had been dying to kiss forever, saw your new baby born. You know—*those* memories.

You also know that for most of us, life is generally ho hum/same old/been there done that. The vast majority of our days are nothing special. Chances are they will continue to be like that till we die, with the rare exception now and then.

So the gods come down and offer you a choice: Go back and live (somehow) eternally in one of those golden memory moments. Or you can go on living as usual with the possibility of more and maybe even better golden moments in the future. Realistically speaking, the chances of those amazing experiences exist, but they are slim. We all want to be happy. You remember damn well when you were the happiest you have ever been. The gods give you a chance to go back and inhabit that time forever ... or take your chances on more but in the murky undependable future. Which will it be?

There's an apocryphal story about the American poet Robert Frost I have always liked and which I used to tell creative writing students. The story goes that someone asked Frost what advice he would give to the beginning writer. The great poet said if someone comes to him and says "I want to write because I have important ideas and stories that I want to tell the world," their chances are pretty slim of ever succeeding.

But if someone says "I want to be a writer because I love more than anything else to play with words and language," then that person stands a real chance of making it.

Jonathan Carroll is the author of many novels, including *Land of Laughs*, *Bones of the Moon*, *The Marriage of Sticks*, *Outside the Dog Museum*, *Kissing the Beehive*, *White Apples*, *The Wooden Sea*, and others. His widely acclaimed work has been called quirky and "infuriatingly hard to categorize," but often deals with some form of crossing back and forth between ordinary life and a twisted version of that, sometimes as magical realism. He currently lives and writes in Vienna. These thoughts are from entries across several months, from December 2006 to February 2007, of his blog, which can be found at his website, www.jonathancarroll.com.

# Choosing Words

*by Lu Chi*
*translated by Sam Hamill*


Shadowy thoughts are brought
    into the light of reason;
    echoes are traced to their sources.
It is like following a branch
    to find the trembling leaf,
    like following a stream to find the spring.
...

Calm the heart's dark waters;
    collect from deep thoughts
    the proper names for things.
Heaven and earth are trapped in visible form:
    all things emerge
    from within the writing brush.
At first, the brush
    parches our lips, but soon
    it grows moist from dipping.


This excerpt from the poem "Choosing Words" is from *The Art of Writing: Lu Chi's Wen Fu* (Milkweed Editions, 2000). This small graceful book is a poetic discourse on the art of writing by a soldier-poet, Lu Chi, who was born to a landed family on the Yangtse Delta in the year 261. Written in the 3rd century, it is one of the earliest Chinese works about the use of language. Sam Hamill is a poet, a founding editor of Copper Canyon Press, and translator of a number of works from the Chinese including *Crossing the Yellow River: 300 Poems from the Chinese*.

# The Cultivation of Mindstates

*by Gabriel Gudding*

HERE ARE SOME very basic, and I'm sure to some quite suspicious, thoughts about the prime and essential mental attitudes necessary to writing well, and how to cultivate them.

First, I begin with the radical premise that writing is a way to help myself and others to "wake up" and be happy. What this means politically is that writing is a way to change the world. What this means ethically is that writing is a way, ultimately, to remind others of wonder, determination, concentration, forgiveness, patience, tolerance, truth, renunciation, sympathetic joy, compassion, lovingkindness, generosity, courage, and equanimity.

But if we write daily and read widely, we soon run against a principal challenge common to writers: boredom with one's own mind and work, and the discouragement that stems from that. Know then that if we write daily (and it's a good idea to do that), we should understand that a lot of what we write will most likely bore us. And thus a fundamental skill to counteract this—and this is a skill that can be learned—is how to remain interested in one's own work.

It is important, in other words, to cultivate, husband, and maintain one's capacity to be surprised by one's own mind. Doing so will invite a wider sense of curiosity toward all things.

Take Whitman at his word when he says:

> *You must habit yourself to the dazzle of light*
> *and of every moment of your life.*

So, I try, when teaching, to disabuse students of the notion that the categories "mistake" and "craft" can have anything to do with writing. Lot of these kids come into our classrooms totally shut down. They don't need some teacher talking about mistakes. "Craft," though a great idea, is what German novelist and linguist Uwe Poerksen calls a plastic word: it has become more a tool with which to yield power and status and less a word that communicates, aids, and teaches.

In fact I tell my students to welcome the experience that they had initially labeled "error": do not try to avoid error; embrace it, use it, transform it. All rocks are broken rocks.

They do not need to be anything extra in order to write something that will surprise them and be surprising and useful to others. I have found that many of them need to hear that it's okay to toss work out, that it's okay that a lot of what they write might in fact bore them: my job is to help remove the pressure from them, not to increase it with notions like "mistake."

We don't write toward some distant aesthetic standard but for one another: we don't write for the ages, but for people we know. If there is a universal, said John Dewey, it is in the local. The attempt to write great poetry will probably only end in disaster.

Without exception they delight in hearing that poetry is not some kind of precious speech uttered by special beings. Once I realized that my whole life was more or less one continual mistake, I let go of the entire idea of mistake, or have tried to: and I encourage them to do so as well. To help with these modes of being and writing, we read essays by Epictetus, C. S. Peirce, Gertrude Stein, William James, Emerson, Baraka, and Bernadette Mayer, among others, on these matters. Also, we laugh a lot.

And as for attitudes necessary when entering this business (those being wonder, concentration, determination, forgiveness, patience, tolerance, truthfulness, renunciation, sympathetic joy, compassion, lovingkindness, generosity, courage, and equanimity), I find it effective to cultivate these attitudes by being kind and by thinking wholesome and positive thoughts about others.

Adopt, that is, the following as a daily mental training.

Hold in your mind warm and positive thoughts for each person in your social circle, then for each person on your continent, then for all people and animals in the entirety of history, also for each spherical object in the solar system, and finally for all those who will live in the variety of futures to come. Do this for a few minutes before and after writing each day. Begin by, one by one, "holding" the face and name of each person in your immediate life in your mind's eye, and think like this: "May [such and so] have a good day. May [she or he] not be upset today. May [she or he] have a really good day and be happy."

Rationale for this as a writing exercise: An earth, an animal kingdom, a star system, is a community. A history is a trans-temporal community. All healthy communities cannot be sustained without the active cultivation of goodwill and altruistic (empathic) ethics.

We are often encouraged in our public lives to maintain contemptuous and resentful attitudes toward one another (Rush Limbaugh anyone?), but we are rarely—as part of normal civic activity—encouraged to develop love and kindness for one another. That's really bizarre when you think about it. Love and empathy are not seen as productive, efficacious, or necessary for labor, nor are they things one normally associates with work and productivity.

Yet, though these mindstates and attitudes are difficult to cultivate, take mental effort, they have socially efficacious effects. They are in effect quite practical. Neuroscientists at Harvard, Berkeley, and UW Madison have noticed that attitudes of compassion and kindness have brain blood flow patterns and EEG patterns that are almost identical to patterns evinced by those holding mindstates of "courage" and "fearlessness."

Because writing is principally an act of generosity, cultivating an empathic mindstate, indeed an empathic temperament, will only enhance our desire and ability to write well.

Further, courage and fearlessness are essential in order to write in innovative ways and without immediate reward

Gabriel Gudding is the author of two books, *A Defense of Poetry* (Pitt Poetry Series, 2002) and *Rhode Island Notebook* (Dalkey Archives Press, 2007). The latter book he wrote entirely in his car during 26 roundtrips on the highways between Providence, R.I., and Normal, Ill. He is Assistant Professor of Literature and Creative Writing at Illinois State University, where he was hired to teach "experimental poetry." This piece is from Gudding's blog, with some additions from an interview by Angela Armitage with Gudding in June 2005 for *Mipoesias* magazine.

# How Many Writers?

*by Kristy Kiernan*

ONE TO DEVISE a breakdown of the steps necessary to change the bulb.

One to stare at the bulb hoping it will change itself.

One to explain why changing the bulb is futile, because the next one is just going to go bad too, and without co-op [publisher's marketing monies] we're all doomed to darkness anyway.

One to call their agent and publicist to make sure changing the bulb won't harm their reputation.

One to hold out for a bigger, better replacement bulb.

One to post "What's the best way to change a bulb?" on Backspace and wait for 36 answers.

One to extol the virtues of the old bulb, the golden glow of the light it gave, its soft, barely perceptible buzz when viable, the startling ping when it expired, the breadth of our loss, the depth of our grief.

One to edit the previous writer's bit whilst quoting Elmore Leonard.

One to bring the tequila. One to bring the beer. One to bring the wine.

And one to look around, call it a conference, and make it a yearly event.

So, that'd be 13? Yes, it takes 13 writers to change a bulb.

Kristy Kiernan is the author of *Catching Genius* (Berkeley, 2007), a debut novel that tells the story of two all-but-estranged sisters, Estella and Connie, who, in their forties, come together to clean out their childhood home on an island.

Kiernan lives in Florida. Her website is www.kristykiernan.com.

Backspace (www.bksp.org) is an online writers' community.

# The Three Cosmic Rules of Writing

*by Dennis Palumbo*

As a veteran writer and a licensed psychotherapist specializing in writers' issues, I know enough to know there aren't any rules when it comes to writing.

Except for the following, which I modestly call the Three Cosmic Rules of Writing. I'm serious. Learn these simple rules, then burn them into your hearts and minds. It couldn't hurt.

### The First Cosmic Rule: You Are Enough

It's a growth industry: there are dozens of seminars, how-to books and audio tapes promising to teach you to write better, faster, more commercially. And there's nothing wrong with most of these. I know; I teach some myself.

Because, frankly, there *are* things a writer needs to learn about craft, the traditions of storytelling and the reality of the marketplace. But for the writer just starting out, there's a hidden danger: namely, the belief that if you just take the right seminars, read the right books or pick the right guru, then you'll be successful. That the person you are right now just isn't enough.

It's a classic belief system ... writers who feel they have to be something more to succeed—smarter, better educated, funnier—with more interesting lives, more unique experiences. More something.

As a therapist who works with writers, I see this everyday. Writers who feel they're somehow not enough. Who believe all the *other* writers are more talented, more confident, less burdened by doubt.

It puts me in mind of that famous opening sequence of Woody Allen's *Stardust Memories*. A glum Woody sits in a dark, dingy train car, with other lost souls. Looking out the window, he sees another train car—shining, brightly lit. Inside, beautiful men and women laugh and drink champagne, a festive vision of wit and privilege out of a Noel Coward play. Woody despairs. Why isn't he in the sparkling car, with the sparkling people?

Once, when a writer client of mine made reference to this scene to explain his feelings, what emerged was not only his sense of himself as inadequate, but something else, more insidious and undermining. Namely, the idea that he'd been dealt a bad hand—"I'm in the wrong car"—because of intrinsic defects in himself. If he were a better writer—smarter, more talented, whatever—he'd be in the right car. Those happy, glittering people were in the shining train car because they *deserved* to be there while he did not.

Thereafter, in our work together, his self-sabotaging behaviors could be understood as a natural result of his belief in himself as basically defective. When this painful self-concept was successfully illuminated and challenged, things began to shift in his view of himself.

What this anecdote illustrates is the real danger to your writing in seeing yourself as less than, not enough. Admittedly, a very common, self-limiting belief. To which I offer this thought, which will save you thousands of dollars in therapy bills and trim years off your spiritual journey: everybody thinks the party's happening somewhere else.

But it isn't. It's happening right here, right now. With you.

You—with all your doubts and fears, joys and sorrows—are enough. You—the one reading these words at this very moment—have everything you need to become the writer you want to be.

"Me?" you may be asking. "Just as I am?"

Yes, you, who may, at this moment, be feeling scared, frustrated, blocked, discouraged. If so, join the club. Because so does every other writer in the world, even the most successful ones, who, after all, were once struggling writers themselves.

And now that they're successful, guess what? They still struggle. They have the same doubts, fears, longings, worries. They just don't give these feelings the same negative meanings you do. Smart writers recognize their feelings as important information about their inner lives, as the raw material of their writing craft. Just grist for the mill.

Which brings me to the second cosmic rule of writing:

## The Second Cosmic Rule: Work with What You're Given

One of my favorite *New Yorker* cartoons by George Booth depicts a tormented, obviously "blocked" writer sitting at his typewriter, crumpled paper strewn about, surrounded by literally dozens of dogs—napping, barking, hanging from the window sills, etc. The writer's wife stands in the doorway, glaring at him in weary disdain. "Write about dogs," she says.

Aside from its dark humor, the cartoon's truth is that the frustrated writer often doesn't see that a subject for his writing is right in front of him—the dogs; i.e., the obvious elements that actually inhabit his life.

In other words, work with what you're given. Writers have to practice *seeing*, really seeing the world around them. As a writer, your job is to do this consciously and artfully, using craft and imagination as well as memory and reflection. You have to pay attention.

Tolstoy said, "Love those whom God has put before You"; the Tao says, "Love the Ten Thousand Things." In short, love, that is—see— everything.

What do I mean by this? To "love" the totality of what we experience is to accept all our responses to it, to be enlivened by the variety of ways we experience events, good or bad, painful or joyful. The artist's task is to see every moment—and our reaction to it—as potentially interesting, challenging and worthy of our creative participation.

Viewed from this perspective, a writer is never bored, never longs for things in his or her life to be more exciting, more interesting, more something else than they actually are. Except, of course, when you DO feel that way, in which case you should write about that boredom or that longing. That's your grist for that particular day. It's working with what you're given.

## The Third Cosmic Rule: Writing Begets Writing

Which brings me to the Third (and, thankfully, last) Cosmic Rule of Writing ... namely, "Writing Begets Writing."

If you're stuck on a difficult scene, write it anyway.

Write it badly. Write it in verse. Write it as a journal entry, a Dennis Miller rant. If you're frustrated at being stuck, write about that. I don't care. But write.

If you have angry, self-critical feelings, give them to a character in your story. If there isn't a likely candidate, invent one. There *is* one, anyway: you. Your anguish, doubt, fears and frustrations are as vital and elemental to what you're writing as any character or plot point. Might as well make use of this fact.

Writing begets writing. Just as worrying begets worrying. Obsessing begets more obsessing. Pacing back and forth begets—well, you get the idea.

When you risk writing from where you're at, you set in motion a whole set of internal processes. The first rotten sentence you write has a life you can inhabit, evaluate, cross out. This first attempt can be replaced by a second, hopefully less rotten sentence—maybe a good piece of description or a sharp line of dialogue.

Then again, maybe not. But it doesn't matter. Just keep going. As William Goldman reminds us, some scenes you write are just going to be sludge, but they're important connective tissue. They keep things moving; they're links in a chain. Weak links, perhaps, but you can always go back and strengthen them later.

With what? The knowledge that you've written, for one thing, because writing doesn't just beget writing, it also begets—and reinforces—the reality that you can write; that pages will accumulate.

Look at it this way: Every hour you spend writing is an hour *not* spent fretting about your writing. Every day you produce pages is a day you *didn't* spend sitting at a coffee shop, bitching about not producing any pages.

Writing begets writing. Not writing begets … well … not writing. You do the math.

There you have it: the Three Cosmic Rules of Writing.
1. You Are Enough.
2. Work with What You're Given.
3. Writing Begets Writing.

Which all point to one rule, really. Write now. Don't wait. Write now. And keep writing.

Pass it on.

Dennis Palumbo, M.A., MFT, has been a Hollywood screenwriter whose credits include *My Favorite Year*. He is a licensed psychotherapist specializing in creative issues and a regular columnist for *Written By*, the magazine of the Writers Guild of America, West. His book *Writing From the Inside Out* (John Wiley and Sons, 2000) deals with the psychological issues of creative writing.

His website is www.dennispalumbo.com.

# Instructions

*by Neil Gaiman*

*Touch the wooden gate in the wall you never*
*saw before.*
*Say "please" before you open the latch,*
*go through,*
*walk down the path.*

*Remember your name.*
*Do not lose hope—what you seek will be found.*
*Trust ghosts. Trust those that you have*
*helped to help you in their turn.*
*Trust dreams.*
*Trust your heart, and trust your story.*

Neil Gaiman is the award-winning author of *American Gods*, *Stardust*, *Neverwhere*, *Coraline*, and other books, as well as short stories, comics, and screenplays. This is an excerpt from his poem, "Instructions," which first appeared in *A Wolf at the Door* (Simon & Schuster), an anthology edited by Ellen Datlow and Terri Windling.

His website is www.neilgaiman.com.

# Developing Intuition
*by Sheri McConnell*

SINCE EARLY 2001, I have been living a dream—a vision—that surfaced from using my intuition. When I first came up with the idea to start the National Association of Women Writers (NAWW), I was a suburban mother of three small children who had a somewhat bold dream to connect and support other women writers like myself.

Intuition can be defined as a quick and ready insight. This insight can steer you on a correct path, warn you of danger, and/or connect you to your creativity. In Shakti Gawain's book, *Developing Intuition*, she describes how "the most successful people are often very intuitive. Consciously or unconsciously, they follow their gut feelings. Following intuition puts us in the flow—a very alive, productive, and desirable state."

Accessing your intuition is like many other creative activities. As you string together words or put paint on a canvas, you must listen and pay attention to these mental insights. The more you trust these insights, the more your craft will improve.

Following are five suggestions for developing and accessing your intuition so that you may find, follow, and fulfill your dream! Continually use these techniques to make decisions and reach goals.

## 1. Reflect on Lessons Already Learned
In February 2000, I had just given birth to my third child and finished my M.A. in Organizational Management. At 30 years old, I was at a crossroad and in a position to finally pursue a career I loved. I just had to figure out what it was.

For seven months I read about and researched subjects that I was interested in: women's issues, writing, and business startups. I journaled a great deal during this time, reflecting on the past and looking towards the future. I came to understand through this process that I wanted to use my social work experience, my love of writing, and my organizational management skills.

Journaling helped me to document the insights and focus along the way.

### 2. Get Back to Nature

Developing intuition requires the absence of chaos. It is impossible to fully listen to this inner guidance with all the interruptions that occur in our lives. To tune in, you have to get away from the chaos.

For me, I jog or walk outside at least 30 minutes each day. Nature provides me with just the right sounds and scenery for my intuitive senses to come alive. I make this activity a priority in my life because this quiet time calms my soul, supports my creativity, and gives me the mental space I need to tune into my inner yearnings.

I have used my "getting back to nature" time for over five years to make crucial business decisions and to figure out many pivotal solutions to roadblocks in my personal and business lives. Experiencing the solitude that nature provides is a form of meditation that calms the soul and purges the stress from your life.

### 3. Trust Yourself

Most people usually act on impulses and societal cues. Those who slow down and pay attention to their own inner guidance find that they can think clearly and make difficult decisions. When my close friends and family were not supportive of my new dream, they would often say negative things. They weren't trying to be mean spirited, but simply could not visualize how I could possibly succeed at building an organization from scratch with three small children to care for.

But past lessons taught me I was on the right path. I had done enough research and my strengthened intuition faithfully guided me through the difficult times.

### 4. Block Out Negative Thoughts & People

Once you begin to trust yourself, you will inevitably have to start blocking out the negativity of others. Some of this negativity will come from loved ones. It is human nature for people to negate things and events they do not understand or have no personal experience with. Change causes stress, and many people subconsciously dismiss new ideas because it makes them feel more comfortable to do so.

Everyone who was close to me did not understand nor share in my dream in the beginning. Only after they started to see my dream materialize did they begin to support it. That is why it is essential to block out or at least filter the negativity.

Understanding the cause of these behaviors and reactions makes it easier to dismiss them and to follow your own thoughts instead.

## 5. Act

The last and most important suggestion is to be bold and act on the inner cues that are being sent to you as mental/emotional/spiritual signals or urges. Developing intuition is a cyclical process. Like any other innate talent, you must act on it to develop it.

When my intuitive side sent the messages of what to do to start the NAWW, I listened. I acted by researching my competition (other writing associations), by asking my customers (my women writer colleagues) what they wanted, and by building a website and starting the official weekly newsletter.

I acted quickly. In less than two months from the moment I conceived the idea of the National Association of Women Writers, the website and newsletter were born. My "baby" continues to grow and mature at a healthy rate.

When you continually use these five suggestions to develop your intuition and test your inner guidance, you will find it will become easier to make decisions and live peacefully with those decisions. Your life won't automatically become problem-free, but you will begin to trust in the ultimate outcome of events.

By filtering through the physical and subliminal cues inside and all around you, you will learn to develop your intuition and succeed.

Sheri McConnell is the President of the National Association of Women Writers (www.naww.org). She lives in San Antonio, Texas, where she helps women writers and entrepreneurs discover, create, and profit from their intellectual knowledge. Founded in 2001, the NAWW has over 3,000 members. Free reports for writers are available with subscription to NAWW Weekly.

This article is condensed from a longer version that appears on naww.org.

# The Treadmill Journal

*by Gregory Martin*

I ONCE MET A WRITER in Seattle who believed he could only write productively in small-town hotels. He wrote best in a hotel east of the Cascades, 100 miles away, in the town of Cle Elum, Wash. I said this seemed expensive. He shrugged, resigned. I suggested that he work at Microsoft to support his writing habit. That would never do, he said. He wouldn't have any time to write.

Jane Smiley has a wonderful phrase for the eccentric writing preferences we all have, to one degree or another. She calls them "evasion strategies."

In the writing workshops I teach, I regularly encounter these strategies. The most common is employed by students after workshop. They feel the story now needs to "rest" or "breathe." Then, after a month, it doesn't have that zip of inspiration, and they abandon it. These students, believing writing should be "fun" and "spontaneous," become highly accomplished at writing unpublishable first drafts.

Most often in workshop, craft considerations (plot, characterization, imagery, etc.) receive primary emphasis. This may lead apprentice writers to think their most important problems are craft problems. They aren't. Craft knowledge has nothing to do with tenacity. Students can learn plot, but they can't learn hunger. Desire, like discipline, must be cultivated.

The "treadmill" journal cultivates both. I call my daily writing journal a "treadmill" journal because I like the analogy to exercise. It's hard to romanticize a treadmill. But you can't get in shape if you jog two miles every few weeks, and trying to write a meaningful piece of literature is like training for a marathon.

Each day you make five entries:

## 1. The date and time

Simple. Except many apprentice writers can't do it. They're "intuitive," not record-keepers. Record-keeping matters. I can tell when I'm writing well simply by glancing at all the consecutive dates in my journal. Good writing depends on habit. Poet Mary Oliver says, "Attentiveness cannot be kept casually, or visited only in season, like Venice.... The patterns of our lives reveal us. Our habits measure us."

## 2. How long you will work

This entry organizes your writing day and helps you resist the urge to quit early. If you started at 9, intending to work until noon, and your friend calls and offers to take you to breakfast, you say, "No. I'm writing." If your friend is also a writer, this doubles as an admonishment, for which you can feel smug. But better not to answer the phone at all.

How long should you write each day? I require my graduate students to write 18 hours a week. That's three hours a day, six days a week. My editor at *The Writer* has cautioned me against advising this generally. It's too daunting and unrealistic. He's right. But I must. This is how much I write. I have a full-time job and two little boys, ages 3 and 6. I coach soccer. I grocery-shop. I'm sleep-deprived. I drink too much coffee. But I put in the hours.

Most writers I admire work as much as I do, or more. They have full lives. I wish I could say that talent wins out, and if you have some you'll eventually publish and win awards. But I've met too many talented writers with no discipline and no readers.

If 18 hours a week seems like a lot, start with 10 and work your way up.

## 3. What you plan to work on

Intending to "make the story better" is like intending to explore the meaning of life. The desperation of vague intentions keeps many people from writing regularly. Step 3 minimizes despair. In this step, be as craft-specific as possible. Choose a craft element that clearly needs work. Plot. Characterization. Imagery. Dialogue. Point of view. You're not trying to be profound. *Work on turning point*, which I jotted down while working on my memoir *Mountain City*, simply meant revising the part of my plot that dealt with my grandfather and his macular degeneration and the change in our relationship. If after five minutes on the turning point you get an idea for the characterization of Gramps, fine. Do that. You don't have to be inflexible; you just have to be purposeful and aware.

### 4. How it went

When you're finished, take inventory. This is the place for mild pride or shame or simple relief. In Step 4, I write things like "Good work" or "Too tired, get to bed earlier." My journal helps me choose between conflicting short-term wants—between watching college basketball past midnight and writing productively in the morning.

### 5. When you will work tomorrow and for how long

If you wake up not knowing when you'll write, there's a good chance you won't write at all. If you wake up knowing that at 6 A.M. you're going to work on "turning point" for three hours, chances are it will happen.

Try not to take any days off. Try. Keep your momentum, even if this means writing for only half an hour. Thinking you can't be productive without a big chunk of time is an evasion strategy.

### A sample entry

1. Sept. 15, 1998. 8:30 A.M.
2. Work until noon.
3. Work on turning point (in "macular degeneration" section).
4. Sluggish until coffee kicked in. Worked most on characterization of Gramps, especially physical description.
5. Tomorrow: Six to nine. Work on turning point.

Would you train for a marathon without meticulously tracking your progress? Do you want to limp across the line or sprint? The treadmill journal is a barometer of your ambition.

Most of my students hate the treadmill journal at first. Months later, after they publish their first essay or story, they're treadmill evangelists. They've experienced the kind of momentum that makes sitting down each day almost easy. I can't take credit for their finished products, but I do take satisfaction in making them surrender to a regimen rather than a romance.

Gregory Martin is author of the memoir *Mountain City* (North Point, 2000), a look at a tiny mining town in Nevada, with only 33 residents but a wealth of stories and intriguing characters. It was named a *New York Times* Notable Book and received a Washington State Book Award. He teaches at the University of New Mexico.

This article first appeared in April 2007 (120th Anniversary) issue of *The Writer* under the title, "Want to Be Productive?"

# THE CRAFT OF WRITING

# The Art of The Start

*by Brandi Reissenweber*

Mom, Dad, and the career counselor teach us early that first impressions are important, and this is no less important in fiction. Think of everything that happens at the very beginning of a story: The reader makes decisions about the story. They haven't yet committed to completing it and they are feeling their way around for how much they want to commit.

Your reader is not a penniless and weary traveler who will be happy to take any bed you can offer. They are discerning, with plenty of money for a night's sleep and if you show them something uninspired, they're off to the next inn. You have to work to get them to stay with you. That's the first need for a good beginning: do not take your reader for granted. They've no reason to stick with you if you're not going to tell a story and tell it well.

Many writers feel they have to create a grand and loud splash in the first few lines: "On her first day of high school, Geraldine was run over by the school bus and pinned to the road for hours." While this does get the reader's attention, it can feel too overt and the rest of the story can seem anti-climatic. Don't look for ways to trick your reader into reading on. A burned reader might make it through the story, but they're going to remember your name so they can avoid your work in the future.

The beginning's job is to lure—you want to entice the reader into the story and deliver on that enticement. At the same time you have some logistics to deal with, like characterization, setting and conflict. Here's what a good beginning should offer:

1.  **Establish the main character(s).** The characters you introduce in the beginning will hold emotional weight and readers will expect them to be important since they are the first to appear.

2. **Ground the reader in place and time.** Nothing is more frustrating than a story that starts all floaty, with characters seeming suspended in mid air. Put your character and your reader somewhere in a moment quickly to abate this aimlessness.

3. **Raise a dramatic question.** You want to intrigue the reader and keep them reading, so offer something that will make them curious. Invite the reader to wonder about the character or his or her behavior or situation. Character is the foundation of fiction, so look for how you might get the reader quickly engaged in the character's specific conflict.

4. **Write well.** Ah, you're probably thinking this is a given, but a lot of writers keep their initial beginnings, the one they wrote when they first sat down to write the story, and that's often a lot like the clearing of the throat before a speaking engagement. Show the reader they can trust you to tell a good story and tell it well. Set up expectations in the quality of the images, in the clarity of the language. It will pay off.

Jhumpa Lahiri's "A Temporary Matter" starts like this:

> The notice informed them that it was a temporary matter: for five days their electricity would be cut off for one hour, beginning at eight P.M. A line had gone down in the last snowstorm, and the repairmen were going to take advantage of the milder evenings to set it right. The work would affect only the houses on the quiet tree-lined street, within walking distance of a row of brick-faced stores and a trolley stop, where Shoba and Shukumar had lived for three years.
>
> "It's good of them to warn us," Shoba conceded after reading the notice aloud, more for her own benefit than Shukumar's. She let the strap of her leather satchel, plump with files, slip from her shoulder and left it in the hallway as she walked into the kitchen. She wore a navy blue poplin raincoat over gray sweatpants and white sneakers, looking, at thirty-three, like the type of woman she'd once claimed she would never resemble.

The main characters are introduced and we are grounded in a place— Shoba and Shukumar's house. The story also immediately begins to set up a conflict, with the electricity going out every evening. We are invited to wonder about Shoba in that last line when we learn she has become the woman she didn't want to be. This is just a glimmer of conflict—nothing overt—but it's enough to raise a dramatic question that the reader wants satisfied.

If you prefer an opening that packs more punch in addition to achieving all it needs to, you might add some strong sensations, as Kiana Davenport does in her story "Bones of the Inner Ear:"

> Lightning, and a woman breaks in two. Zigzag of ions, her bone-snap of scream. I remember skies crackling. A roasted peacock falling from a tree. I remember a man's hair turning fright-wig blue. Is what one remembers what really occurred? Uncle Noah said every moment has two truths.
>
> We came from the rough tribes of the Wai'anae, wild west coasts of the island. Here, native clans spawned outcasts and felons, yet our towns had names like lullabies. Makaha, Ma'ili, Nanakuli, Lualualei. In Nanakuli, a valley slung like a hammock between mountain and sea, I was born in a house known for its damaged men.

We still see the basic elements at work here: the writing is strong, the narrator is introduced, and the reader is grounded in a specific sense of place. We also get a dramatic question in the last line about the damaged men: who are these damaged men? how are they damaged? how will they impact our narrator?

In addition, the story starts with strong sensory details: the "bone-snap of scream" the "skies crackling," the "roasted peacock falling from a tree" and the man's hair, which turns "fright-wig blue." We get an immediate and strong impression of this world and the harshness of it, which resonates throughout the entire story. This gives the readers a clear and direct entry into the story, as they don't yet have to start working to fill in any blanks; they just experience the words on the page.

Beginnings exist to lure the readers in and to orient them to this new world. Use openings for what they are—an entrance into something larger than themselves. The beginning should lead somewhere; the threads that start here should continue throughout the story.

Brandi Reissenweber has been published in many journals, including *North Dakota Quarterly*, *Aspects*, and *Rattapallax*, and is an online instructor for Gotham Writers' Workshop (www.writingclasses.com) and assistant editor for *Zoetrope: All Story*. She authored the chapter on Character in *Writing Fiction* (Bloomsbury), part of GWW's series of writing guides. She also writes an online column for *The Writer* magazine. She has taught at NYU, St. John's University, and Il Chiostro in Italy, and holds an MFA in Fiction Writing from NYU.

This article originally appeared in *Letterpress*, her monthly newsletter on fiction writing. To subscribe, send your email address to: letterpress@att.net.

# The 3-Act Structure

*by Ridley Pearson*

THERE ARE conventions, structures, and forms to writing fiction that help you hold all the pieces together and transform an idea into a story. The form called the three-act structure, handed down to us from the ancient Greeks, is one that's proven successful for thousands of years.

The study of the three-act structure has been ongoing since it evolved from the mythic adventures that have long been part of classical education, but Christopher Vogler put it into accessible terms. Each writer defines the three-act structure in his own way. Fiction is a fluid art form. But I highly recommend any writer pick up a copy of Vogler's *The Writer's Journey* before writing another word.

We dream our dreams in a basic structure, and the Ancient Greeks followed this structure in their myths. To write fiction in the structure in which we dream gives the reader a level of familiarity that makes stories meaningful and accessible.

The three acts are known by various titles and their ingredients referred to in various ways: Beginning, Middle, End; Opening, Development, Conclusion; The Decision to Act, The Action, The Consequences of the Action.

Following this form, or at least being aware of its long-proven success, will help you get a handle on what's working and what's not in your stories.

In starting an outline, I like to think up four or five big moments that will occur in the story. These are turning points, or darkest moments. From here, I bridge to connect these scenes, adding several smaller turning points to connect the dots.

My technique is a holdover from scriptwriting. I card these scenes and hang them on the wall. But regardless of how you start the massive job of assembling the character(s) and story lines in your novel, in the end, the story should be structured in three acts.

## Act One: The Challenge

This first act establishes action, characters, and what's at stake. Our protagonist, or lead character, faces something new—something that requires his participation. A journey. A quest. He must decide to accept the challenge. Vogler talks about the Hero leaving the "Ordinary World" and stresses that the early part of the story shows the Ordinary World in order to later distinguish the "Special World."

I think of it in terms of set-up. You want to establish your character(s) in the real world; to set up the world where your character(s) exist. The reader needs a reference point, and somewhere early in the story is your chance to show the protagonist in his everyday life. That way, when we see the challenge that's the central conflict of the story, we'll start at the level ground from which the protagonist must climb the mountain. By seeing the mountain more clearly, this also allows us to identify the antagonist. By inference, we learn not only who our protagonist is, but also what he's made of, or at least the level of threat the antagonist presents.

In the first act, we learn what's at stake for the protagonist—what he has to lose, and therefore we begin to imagine what he might gain.

Vogler refers to the early element of Act One as the "Call to Adventure." The Hero is presented with a problem, challenge, or adventure that he must solve or complete. In a detective mystery, it's the first crime. In a story of revenge, it's a wrong to be righted. In a romance, it's an early encounter with a future love interest.

Story is character. Act One shows the reader the boundaries that the protagonist must operate within. This includes phobias, fears, limitations, and other flaws. They may be physical or mental; real or imagined; age-based or gender-based. Show your character as human. Show his flaws and his vulnerability because this is the character mountain he must climb while he follows his call to adventure. The protagonist is often reluctant to accept the challenge. He's facing his biggest fears and is in no hurry to jump into the fray. The characters face internal conflicts (character issues) just as they face external conflicts (the challenge of the story). Act One is where all of this is brought to the page.

He can still turn back at this point. You see the internal and external conflicts, and the reader is rooting for him to go for it. But before he does, he may need to be pushed.

Vogler writes of the mentor, the sage, the Obi-Wan character who's consulted and is the catalyst for the Hero to make the commitment to the Adventure. The mentor prepares the protagonist for the challenge. Think: The Good Witch explains about the Wizard and the Emerald City and then delivers the Ruby Slippers to Dorothy.

Consulting a mentor also gives the writer a chance to show, not tell, the reader about the protagonist. The mentor verbalizes the fears the protagonist must face; he can tell us or show us something about the protagonist by remembering something from the past. The mentor is therefore a vehicle to the backstory (and as the writer you must know the character's backstory, whether or not you choose to ever share it with the reader). The mentor is a great tool for exposition about the emotional depth of the protagonist and what events may be responsible for his greatest fears.

The end of Act One throws the protagonist into the decision to accept the challenge. This is the first big moment. This could be a first-hand confrontation with the evil—personified or not—and by taking a stand or simply by not running away from the challenge, the decision is made.

Here the protagonist overcomes the concerns, accepts the complications, passes the tests and, with an awareness that it's dangerous, decides to take on this challenge.

The conflict is now fully realized; it's no longer just talk. The protagonist's decision to move forward is seen by the reader as a defining moment; it forms a lasting impression of character in the reader's mind. We get our first really good look at what kind of person this is—and we like him.

Vogler calls it crossing the first threshold. The Hero faces the consequences of accepting the Call to Adventure. The story takes off. The Hero takes action. Think: Dorothy heads out onto the Yellow Brick Road.

## Act Two: Action

Act Two involves development of story and character and the darkest moment. Action heats up. Challenges complicate. Characters expand.

The protagonist has accepted the challenge, and he must come to face that challenge and move forward to survive.

Vogler defines the start of the second act as a series of tests, a time to confirm allies and enemies. The Hero learns the rules of this Special World. Vogler points out that surprisingly often, saloons and bars offer the necessary backdrop (think Star Wars), settings that allow exposition of both the new world and the various characters involved.

Complications make the pursuit (of truth, of love, of a treasure or individual) more difficult than expected. In a detective story or mystery, there might be more murders discovered at this stage. Whatever the case, the level of confusion for the protagonist and the reader increases.

In romance, relationships entangle and nothing is as it seemed. Preparation is needed to face one's fears and one's mortal enemy. This next phase isn't to be taken lightly.

It's during this preparation that there's a reflective moment where lovers or fellow protagonists share backstory and further inform us of who they are. This is the "sitting around the fire" moment—and it precedes entering the dark place.

Vogler talks about the Hero standing at the mouth of the cave. Plans must be made before he enters. When he finally crosses that line and enters the inmost cave, he crosses a second threshold, or another big moment. Very often the ordeal takes place, literally, in a cave or dark underground place. (In my novel *The Art of Deception*, I used a little-known subterranean space under Seattle.) Stories are rich with these locations for the obvious reference to Hell. The Hero faces the ordeal and appears to die. The reader is depressed by the apparent loss of the Hero, only to be overjoyed when he resurfaces. Having survived and beaten the dragon, he grabs the sword (the treasure, truth, knowledge, or relationship) and leaves the inmost cave.

This darkest moment is when everything goes to ruin, and we fear for the protagonist's life (or relationship or whatever's at stake). The airplane is out of fuel, and the parachutes turn out to be 20 years old and made of rotting cloth, for example. But the protagonist prevails, surviving when we thought he was doomed. He puts the challenge behind him. Or so we think. This is the beauty of the end of the second act: What feels like a finale is in fact a set-up to the third and final act.

The second act is a balance of action, story development, and interiorizing the characters. We're not going to have time to resolve everything in the third act without it feeling forced. This is a place first-time novelists make mistakes. Near the end of the second act is a good time to resolve subplots, or at least move them along so you can resolve them quickly in the third act. Red herrings in mysteries need to be exposed and/or new developments need to arise that eliminate many of them as well as many of the earlier complications. We clear the reader's mind to focus on the protagonist getting home safely with the treasure in hand. We're not going to want to stop and explain things in the third act, so now's the time to get stuff out of the way. You can use dialogue to do this, letting one character explain or show something to another character that, in turn, informs the reader that we don't need to think about that (person, place, or thing) any longer.

## Act Three: The Consequences

Now it's time for the unexpected to give rise to a final threat that brings closure. The third act is where the chase hits full stride. It begins with the unexpected and ends with the long anticipated. This is where winning at the end of Act Two turns out to be only a minor victory, and the threat the protagonist overcame turns out to be not the only one he'll have to overcome. This is also the act for the big twist; shock value pays off. The character, having achieved new heights, must remain on or above those heights; there's no return, no lessening of strength in this act—the character has hit his stride and now, if anything, must run even faster. If we spent the first two acts making our protagonist flawed, vulnerable, and human, here's where he overachieves and becomes superhuman. Dorothy will kill the witch. Luke will slay Lord Vader.

The opening of Act Three typically involves a chase. Vogler explains that the Hero is pursued on the road back by the same forces he disturbed by Seizing the Sword. The Hero elects to return to the Ordinary World from which he came; the Special World must be left behind. Challenges, dangers, and more tests still lie ahead.

Act Three provides for the big twist. What we thought was true turns out to be false. The elusive truth finally takes hold, and we realize we've been wrong all along. This propels the protagonist to a final threat.

The final threat is the "dead" guy jumping in from stage left, not dead at all. This is the guy pulling himself out of the river and dragging himself to shore to attack the protagonist one final time. It's the lover coming back to mend the wounds, only to see the protagonist with a new lover.

The protagonist, having learned something (about himself or others) at the conclusion of Act Two can now reap the benefit of that knowledge and prevail one final time. In doing so, he's a changed man. He's made it. It's over. He can return with no desire to be somewhere else or someone else. He's whole again.

Vogler writes that the story is meaningless if the Hero returns without what he calls the elixir. This is a truth, an antidote, a treasure, a lesson. Dorothy realizes there's no place like home. Someone graduates from college, or training camp, or boot camp. There's a truth gained, and it's worth all he's gone through.

This is the payoff. All that's been accomplished, all that's been learned. Not only has he gained the external treasure, but he's also cemented a character change in the protagonist that will affect him in a positive way and allow for healing, or a better relationship, or stability. We celebrate with the protagonist that this has all been worth it.

The end often shows the reuniting with someone from whom the protagonist separated at the start of the story: This could be an idea, a belief system, or a person. The protagonist, and the reader along with him, is made whole. Ordinary life can continue again.

There's no simple formula for fiction. But there's a centuries-proven form to good storytelling that follows this three-act structure. All of these conventions are there to be fooled with—there's no right way. In my novel *Cut and Run*, I started the book in Act Two by weaving the elements of Act One into a story that was already moving at the pace of an Act Two. The result is a fast read, but it was no simple task to construct the story this way.

The three-act form is there because it works. Name a film or book you think rises above others, and chances are, if you go back and study it, the story line will fit into this form. We often think of the start of a story as a blank page—nothing there but our idea. But it's not true. With the three-act structure, we have a massive foundation to support, sustain, and maintain our stories.

Ridley Pearson writes crime thrillers for adults, most recently the suspense novel *Killer Weekend* (Putnam, 2007). He also writes adventure novels for young readers, including the Never Land Adventure series (Disney Books), co-written with humorist Dave Barry.

This article appeared in the April 2007 issue of *Writer's Digest* under the title, "Getting Your Act(s) Together."

His website is www.ridleypearson.com.

# The Invisible Writer

*by William G. Tapply*

AT THE BEGINNING of every writing class and workshop I teach, I ask my students to state their goals. Their responses are usually variations on similar themes:

"I want to develop a distinctive style."

"I want to be a great writer."

"I want to entertain my audience."

They want, in other words, to be noticed and admired.

Readers, I remind them, do not pick up a novel or a short story hoping to applaud the author. They don't think of themselves as your audience; they don't want to watch you perform. Readers, in fact, don't want to be aware of the author at all. They want to be engrossed in a good story.

It's not about you, I tell my students. It's about your readers and your story. Don't think about style. Style is self-conscious and attention-getting. The concept of style has unfortunately become confused with flowery language, elaborate figures of speech, convoluted sentences, fancy vocabulary words. Nobody except an English major opens a book looking for those.

Focus instead on writing clear, crisp sentences that create pictures your readers can see and emotions they can feel. William Strunk, Jr. and E. B. White, the authors of the indispensable handbook *The Elements of Style*, used the word "style" to mean concise, precise, uncluttered writing that is devoted entirely to unambiguous communication between author and reader.

That's the kind of style worth developing.

Forget about becoming a great writer. Work instead on writing great stories. Think about your reader, not yourself. When you write well, your readers suspend their disbelief and immerse themselves in the characters and the conflicts and the worlds you have created in your story. They are unaware of you. You are invisible.

## Back to School

To make yourself invisible, you'll probably have to unlearn many precepts about writing that you were taught in school and that were (and still are) emphasized on the SATS. Here are a few you should forget:

> Good writers flaunt their impressive vocabularies, your teachers preached. So they required you to memorize lists of Vocabulary Words, and they quizzed you on them every Friday, and they rewarded you for using them in your stories and essays.
> Good writers use lots of showy similes, metaphors, and symbols. So you hunted for them in the literature you studied, you copied them into your notebook, and you analyzed them and admired them and envied the writers who created them. Then you were urged to invent your own, the more eye-popping, the better.
> Good writers use alliteration and allusion and other literary maneuvers. So you looked for these writerly tricks in the stories you read, and you were encouraged to weave them abundantly into your own writing.
> Good writers write long, complicated sentences. The 19th-century novelists you studied wrote long, convoluted sentences with plenty of subordinate clauses and participle phrases, so you should, too.
> Good writers fill up lots of pages. You were evaluated according to the length of the story or composition you submitted; long papers were worth more than short ones. So you practiced piling on the adjectives and adverbs. Wordiness, padding, and repetitiveness were rewarded. Long, detailed, descriptive passages earned you that A.

Your teachers, I'm afraid, had it all backwards. Big words, figures of speech, literary devices, and long, dense sentences are never admirable for their own sake. Unless used sparely, and always in the service of the story, they just call attention to themselves—and to the writer.

## The Visible Writer

But wait, you say. There are plenty of contemporary authors who are read and admired for their wordplay, for the richness of their language, for their use of allusions and symbols and metaphors. They send us running for the dictionary, and we love them for it. What about the so-called literary and experimental writers who tell their stories backwards, write in the present tense, or use second-person narrators? Their in-your-face "styles" are praised by reviewers and studied in literature classes.

Well, in the first place, there aren't "plenty" of these writers. There are relatively few. Some of them are genuinely brilliant, and they can carry it off. Few of them are widely read, though, because most modern readers, editors and agents (unlike professors of English literature) want good stories, not show-offy writers.

Most writers who flaunt their brilliance fall flat on their faces.

Strive to be a visible writer, if you insist. "But just remember," warns John Dufresne, author of *The Lie That Tells a Truth: A Guide to Fiction Writing*, "if you do decide to be unconventional, then you are calling attention to yourself and to your cleverness, and you have to then be better than everyone else. You're saying, I don't need to limp along on the crutch of plot the way that Faulkner did or Tolstoy did. Watch me dance, you're saying—and indeed we will. We'll be watching for the slip."


## Fancy Words

"When I was twenty," wrote Wallace Stegner, "I was in love with words, a wordsmith. I didn't know enough to know when people were letting words get in their way. Now I like the words to disappear like a transparent curtain."

Readers should not be stopped by a word, whether it's because they don't know it, or because it's flowery and attention-getting ... or because it's just not quite the right word. Whenever that happens, you've yanked them out of the story and forced them to think about you and your intentions.

"The difference between the right word and the almost right word," said Mark Twain, "is the difference between lightning and the lightning bug." In most cases, the right word is the most straightforward and familiar one. Write "thin," not "pellucid" or "transpicuous."

Go for simple, down-to-earth, active verbs. If you're tempted to make your character "insert" a key into a lock, consider having him "stick" or "shove" it in. Instead of surrounding a bland verb with descriptive adverbs, find a strong, vivid verb. "She went slowly and painfully down the aisle" is dull, vague, and wordy, and those adverbs call the reader's attention to the lazy and/or incompetent writer. "She hobbled [or limped, or shuffled, or shambled] down the aisle" creates a sharp picture.

Precise nouns work better than general nouns that need to be propped up by adjectives. Name things specifically. "Hemlock" communicates more clearly and concisely and is less attention-getting than "towering verdant evergreen tree." Instead of "diminutive grayish songbird," call it a chickadee.

Focus your reader's attention on the story's action with specific nouns and verbs. Don't let your character "eat breakfast" when she can "slurp her oatmeal," "gulp a glass of prune juice," or "crunch a toasted bagel."

Consult your thesaurus or synonym-finder at your own risk. If you're looking for a fancy, show-offy word to replace the plain, serviceable one that first occurred to you ... don't.

The thesaurus can help your find the right word to replace your almost-right word—provided you recognize the difference.

There are very few exact synonyms in English. "Happiness," for example, can mean "joy," "elation," "jubilation," "gusto," complacence," "bliss," "rapture," or "mirth." But none of those words—or conditions—means precisely the same thing as any of the others.

Sometimes the right word *will* be fancier than the almost-right one. You've got to trust your ear. It depends on the context of your story, your characters, your narrative voice. If "speak" doesn't sound right, try "speechify" or "sermonize" or "proclaim." Sadly, you may never find a good opportunity to write "confabulate" or "colloquize."

## Figures of Speech

Similes and metaphors ask readers to compare something in your story to something else. They require your readers to pause and ponder the comparison you're suggesting. Any time readers do this, their attention shifts, however briefly, from the story to the creator of the comparison. It's risky. "[When} a simile or metaphor doesn't work," warns Stephen King in *On Writing*, "the results are funny and sometimes embarrassing."

Constructed carefully and used sparingly, though, figures of speech create vivid images and convey complicated emotions. "The use of simile and other figurative language," says King, "is one of the chief delights of fiction—reading it and writing it, as well. When it's on target, a simile delights us." Raymond Chandler was known and admired for peppering his stories with on-target similes ("I felt like an amputated leg") and original metaphors ("She gave me a smile I could feel in my hip pocket"). Chandler's figures of speech gave his stories life and made them fun to read.

If creative figures of speech risk distracting readers, old hackneyed ones will surely bore them. Clichés ("as clean as a whistle") and trite expressions ("when it rains, it pours") call unwanted attention to the lazy, uncreative writer. Banish them from your writing.

Similes and metaphors, by their nature, can stop readers in their tracks, shift attention to their creator, and spoil an entire story. On the other hand, crisp, clean writing requires no figures of speech at all. Readers won't miss them—won't even notice—if you never use them.

## Verbosity

Long, convoluted sentences, flowery descriptive passages, and meandering dialogue divert the reader's attention away from the story and onto the writer.

Short is good. Sure, for the sake of your story's rhythm you'll need to vary the length and structure of your sentences. But you can't go wrong building your stories on declarative sentences made up of active verbs and specific nouns. The most useful sentence structure is subject-verb-object.

Cut, cut, and then cut some more. Sydney Smith, the 19th-century English essayist advised: "In composing, as a general rule, run your pen through every other word you have written; you have no idea what vigour it will give your style."

Elmore Leonard says: "I try to leave out the parts that people skip." Prune those long descriptive passages that cause your reader's attention to wander.

The sections that need the most drastic cutting are often those you admire the most, because they're the ones you wrote to show off rather than to advance the story. "Read over your compositions," advised Samuel Johnson, "and when you meet a passage which you think is particularly fine, strike it out."

## Hey! Look at This!

Banish that exclamation mark from your keyboard. An exclamation mark is the author jumping up and down and waving his arms. It's a poor substitute for words. When you use one, consider yourself a failure. It shouts to your reader: "This is really important [startling, surprising, scary, loud, dramatic, whatever], but I don't know how to convey it with words ... or I'm too lazy to try."

## Avoid Mistakes

Inaccurate facts, figures, names, and dates yank knowledgeable readers out of your story, remind them that there's an (ignorant) author at work, and destroy the fictional reality you've tried so hard to create.

Get it right. Shotguns don't shoot bullets. Belize is not in South America. Spell real names and places properly. Double-check everything. Assume every one of your readers knows the difference.

Master your tools. Correct punctuation, grammar, and spelling produce clear sentences. Sloppy mechanics make for murky sentences that confuse readers and call attention to the writer.

## Don't Flaunt What You Know

Perhaps you're an expert wine taster, or fly fisherman, or gladiolus breeder. Maybe you've devoted months to researching liver disease or boat building for your story. The urge to share all your fascinating knowledge with your readers, either in long expository passages or by creating a character as expert as you, can be irresistible.

Don't do it. Spewing information for its own sake is another form of showing off that will shift attention from your story to that long-winded bore, the author.

"A fiction writer," says John Dufresne, "should not worry about linguistic brilliance of the showy and obvious kind, but instead worry about telling her story."

Strunk and White put it this way: "Young writers often suppose that style is a garnish for the meat of prose, a sauce by which a dull dish is made palatable. Style has no such separate entity; it is nondetachable, unfilterable. The beginner should approach style warily, realizing that it is himself he is approaching, no other; and he should begin by turning resolutely away from all devices that are popularly believed to indicate style—all mannerisms, tricks, adornments. The approach to style is by way of plainness, simplicity, orderliness, sincerity."

The writer, in other words, should remain invisible.

William G. Tapply is the author of about 40 books, including more than two dozen New England-based mystery novels. *Out Cold,* his 22nd novel featuring Boston lawyer Brady Coyne, appeared in September 2006 (St. Martin's Press). Tapply's handbook, *The Elements of Mystery Fiction: Writing a Modern Whodunit* (Poisoned Pen Press, 2004), is used in writing classes and workshops across the country.

He has also written a dozen books and nearly a thousand magazine articles, mostly about fly fishing and the outdoors. He is a Contributing Editor for *Field & Stream*, a columnist for *American Angler*, and a member of the Editorial Board for *The Writer* magazine. He teaches writing at Clark University and at The Writers Studio at Chickadee Farm in Hancock, New Hampshire, where he lives.

His website is www.williamgtapply.com.

A version of this article appeared in *The Writer*, November 2005, under the title "Don't Be a Show-Off."

# Beyond Showing & Telling

*by J. Mark Bertrand*

THIS MIGHT raise some hackles, but ...

The first bit of advice every novelist receives is this: show, don't tell. As ubiquitous as it is misunderstood. Why misunderstood? Because writing fiction isn't the same as making a film. It's all about words, all about telling.

The way many teachers discuss showing and telling, you'd think that film was the inherently superior medium, and that good writing aspires toward the transcendence of words. As a result, a lot of writers think of their task as forming clean, generic sentences that don't call attention to themselves, sentences a reader can "see through" to get to the Image, which is what really matters.

This is ridiculous. The real antithesis in writing isn't between showing and telling, or even between scenes and exposition. The real antithesis is between living and dead prose.

One way to bring prose to life is by dramatizing action. The writer imagines the scene and finds vivid, concrete ways of bringing the details into focus. When this is done well, the reader "sees" the scene in his mind.

That's what people really mean when they talk about showing. The words conjure images in the mind—but they do even more than that. They conjure sound and smell. They invoke thought and emotion. Writing that merely "sees" makes for a fast, superficial read. The difference between fiction and film is how much more depth the novelist can bring to any moment, by helping the reader to go beyond seeing.

Scenes are easy, though. Bringing a scene to life involves many different things, but they're fairly obvious. The more concrete, the better. Suggestive details are better than meaningless ones. Particulars are better than abstractions. You get the idea.

But exposition is where the real challenge comes in. How do you write "living" exposition? Some writers try to get around the problem by minimizing exposition or cutting it altogether. (After all, exposition in the strictest sense isn't possible in film, and film is seen as storytelling's purest form.) That's fine, but it's also cheating. Books that read like film scripts are never as good as the film; they're incomplete.

Living exposition is one of the reasons some brilliant 19th-century books are almost unfilmable. You'll never see a film of a Henry James novel, for example, that lives up to the experience of reading one. Part of the reason is that, for James, exposition isn't necessary dross. It is as living, as well crafted as anything else in the book.

Some of the tools that bring scenes to life will do the same in exposition: particular, well-chosen details, vivid images and sensory interjections. More than these, I think living exposition requires a "slant," a personality to carry it. Remember, exposition is "pure" storytelling. When you tell your friends a story, you rely as much on set-up as on scenes. Your perceptions are colored by word choice and tone, by gesture.

It's not just the story that counts; it's you telling the story.

That's the trick to living exposition, I think. Instead of dumping blocks of undramatized information or "back story," every sentence must be worked and slanted so that it's not just a story, but you telling a story. In that sense, merely showing won't do.

You have to tell the story and tell it well.

J. Mark Bertrand is a writer who lives in South Dakota. He has an MFA in Creative Writing from the University of Houston. He is on the faculty of Worldview Academy, an academic summer camp for high school students, and is fiction editor for *Relief Journal* (www.reliefjournal.com), a quarterly that seeks to bridge the gap between mainstream fiction and Christian writing. His own fiction and nonfiction has appeared in a number of magazines.

His book *Rethinking Worldview: Learning to Think, Live, and Speak in This World* is forthcoming from Crossway Publishers (Fall 2007).

This essay comes from his blog, Notes on Craft, which can be found at his website, www.jmarkbertrand.com.

# A Checklist for Character & Conflict Revision

*by Gregory Martin*

YOUR CHARACTER wants something badly. Your reader wants your character to get what they want. Your job is to disappoint both of them.

Ironic? Sure. Narratives are driven by desire: (1) the character's desire, (2) the reader's desire that the character succeeds, or at least, the reader's desire to see what happens to all this yearning, and (3) the author's desire to thwart both the character and the reader.

It's this thwarting desire that beginning writers need to cultivate. It doesn't come naturally. Far too often, the writer is unwilling to let their characters make mistakes and get themselves into trouble that has both cost and consequence for which the story holds them accountable. In stories with this kind of trouble, the protagonists are far too passive, too coddled by their author, to make the kind of graceless mistakes born of the yearning and desperation that makes for good fiction. You, the writer, can be as poised as you want, act with aplomb, reserve, tact, polish. But your character's can't.

Your task is to put your characters in true dilemmas, where they make hard choices, and don't always make good decisions. These situations, and these choices, ought to be open to the reader's moral imagination, allowing the reader to participate in the life of the story—so that the reader has to ask: What would I do?

The checklist below is a craft guide to characterization and conflict. It's not a crutch or simple remedy. It's asking a lot of you and your story. It ought to make you feel slightly despairing. It's designed to help your draft become more of a story and less a rough assemblage of unsuspenseful, incoherent narrative-ish moments.

The checklist is also a form of triage. It helps you to focus on necessary elements, without which, your draft is not a story. The movement from an early draft to a middle draft is predicated entirely on focusing on major flaws. Your job is to stop the bleeding where the bleeding is most profuse. Don't worry about hangnails.

Too many beginning writers think that tinkering around with syntax and punctuation constitutes revision. Not at the early stages it doesn't. Steven Koch, in his great book *The Modern Library Writer's Workshop*, says, "Don't polish a mess."

Some students find applying a rubric like this "constraining"; they feel less intuitive and spontaneous. It's supposed to feel constraining. Form is a container, a constrainer; it gives shape to what before was amorphous and lacking. You need the constraints of form because your intuition and spontaneity aren't enough to render meaning to readers.

1.  What is your character's ground situation? The ground situation, according to John Barth, is the unstable, but static (tense but unchanging) situation prior to whatever comes along and kicks the story into gear.
2.  What does your character want?
3.  Why? What's the character's motivation? Why do they want what they want? Often this is related in some meaningful way to the answer to question #4.
4.  What is your character's problem rooted not in the situation, but in character? Another way to say this: what is your character's existential dilemma? Dumbo's problem is not his big ears. His problem is how he feels about his ears.
5.  What's in the way of your character getting what he/she wants?
6.  What happens to make this static situation dynamic? I sometimes call this the story's trigger. Things were like this and this, and then one day ... a wig turned up in the garbage ... a blind man came to spend the night.
7.  How does this trigger change the nature of the ground situation? How does this trigger present new obstacles that weren't there before?
8.  Are these obstacles formidable? How? (Each one needs to be formidable.)
9.  Is there complication or rising action? Are these obstacles of a dif-

ferent kind? (They can't just be, in essence, the same obstacle, but just in a sequence.)

10. How is the story a record of choices? Are these choices true dilemmas, open to the reader's moral imagination?

11. Describe your character's reversal? In order for your story to be a story, your character must, in some way, change. No one grabs your collar and says, "You've got to listen to what happened to me. After this happened, I was the same as I was before." That's not a story.

12. How is this reversal both related to (a) action—to something that happens in the story; (b) a choice the character made; and how is it related to some kind of (c) recognition on their part?

13. Does your character get what they want? They shouldn't, at least not in one way.

Are these questions hard to answer without first having a draft finished—without a beginning, middle, and ending? Yes.

How do you write something that has a beginning, middle, and end, without first knowing all the subtle, profound complexities?

Here's how. Write down the basic sequence of events. This happened. And then this happened. And then this happened. And then this happened. Until you're done.

Then, apply the checklist. Revise accordingly.

Then, go back and make it subtle and profound.

Gregory Martin is author of the memoir *Mountain City* (North Point, 2000), a look at a tiny mining town in Nevada, with only 33 residents but a wealth of stories and intriguing characters. It was named a *New York Times* Notable Book and received a Washington State Book Award. He teaches at the University of New Mexico.

# Lyricism in Sex Scenes

*by Rosina Lippi*

IN A RECENT POST from a friend on the matter of evaluating sex scenes in novels:

> *Two hallmarks of a Generic Sex Scene: (1) You can grab a few such scenes at random from different books, juggle the names and eye colors, and be hard-pressed to tell which scene goes with which story; and, even more damning, (2) you can remove the scene entirely, substitute the sentence, "Then they had sex," and the larger narrative will not suffer.*

Which I think is a good place to start with a list of general guidelines for writing sex scenes.

The excerpt below is from A.S. Byatt's *Possession*, which won the Booker Prize some years ago and is as high-brow as a novel can get. It's a hugely complex story, but at its center is a romance set in the Victorian age. A correspondence between a well-established poet (Randolf Henry Ash) and a lesser-known woman poet (Christabel LaMotte) begins when they meet at a breakfast given by a mutual friend. Ash is married; Christabel lives with a woman artist in a relationship that may go beyond friendship, something that is never made clear. They are intellectual equals; they fall in love, and eventually they travel to Yorkshire together, secretly.

> *She met him with passion, fierce as his own, and knowing too, for she exacted her pleasure from him, opened herself to it, clutched for it, with short animal cries. She stroked his hair and kissed his blind eyes, but made no more specific move to pleasure him, the male—nor did she come to that, all those nights. It was like holding Proteus, he thought at one point, as though she was liquid moving through his grasping fingers, as though she was waves of the sea rising all round him. How many, many men have had that thought, he told himself, in how many, many places, how many*

*climates, how many rooms and cabins and caves, all supposing them-*
*selves swimmers in salt seas, with the waves rising, all supposing them-*
*selves—no, knowing themselves unique. Here, here, here, his head beat,*
*his life had been leading him, it was all tending to this act in this place,*
*to this woman, white in the dark, to this moving and slippery silence, to*
*this breathing end. "Don't fight me," he said once, and "I must," said she,*
*intent, and he thought, "No more speech," and held her down and caressed*
*her till she cried out. Then he did speak again. "You see, I know you," and*
*she answered breathless, "Yes, I concede. You know."*

This passage is observed by Ash, who is a historian and poet. It sounds like him, the places his mind would travel, the associations he would make. His physical observations are given to us again with verbs: opened, clutched, stroked, kissed, pleasured; there are very few directly sexual turns of phrase. Mostly we get imagery and metaphor: fire and sea and rising waves. There are few adjectives, but the ones used are very evocative: moving and slippery silence.

There is a great deal of very exacting, very deep emotion in this short paragraph—which fits, because this is not a casual sexual encounter. This is a life-changing experience for a man who had reconciled himself to a loving but platonic marriage and a life of celibacy, and who has now found—but will not be able to keep—a woman who is his intellectual and sexual equal.

The short bit of dialogue here echoes their whole relationship: he leads past the point of her comfort, she resists and so they move beyond the language which drew them together in the first place. There is change for both characters as individuals, and the relationship has shifted, as it must in this circumstance.

Rosina Lippi was born in Chicago, but has lived in the Austrian alps, on the East coast, where she earned a Ph.D. in linguistics from Princeton, and Michigan. After years as a professor, she now writes full-time from her home on Puget Sound. Under her pen name Sara Donati, she is author of the Wilderness series (Bantam). Recent titles include *Fire Along the Sky* and *Queen of Swords* (2006), with a sixth volume in progress.

Her blog, Storytelling 2 (this August 2004 essay appeared on an earlier version), can be found at her website, www.rosinalippi.com.

# Haiku Techniques

*by Jane Reichhold*

IN MY EARLY years of haiku writing, I accepted the prevalent credo being espoused on how to write haiku: if the author's mind/heart was correctly aligned in the "proper" attitude, while experiencing a so-called "haiku moment," one merely had to report on the experience to have a darn good haiku.

This system of defining a haiku bestowed near-religious honor on the author of a passable haiku. No one knew exactly why a particular haiku was "good" but it was clear that the author had experienced a moment of enlightenment (or *satori* for the Zen inspired). If the moment was holy (and the form fit the group's philosophy publishing the ku), the haiku was said to be an excellent one.

However, many of us shared the frustration of having a truly life-altering moment of insight and then never being able to write a decent haiku that expressed the wonder and majesty of that moment. They would ask, what was wrong with me? Was I not spiritually prepared enough? Was I too common? Too inattentive? Too word-numb?

I felt rescued when I came across *Aware: A Haiku Primer*, written by hand and illustrated by Betty Drevniok, at the time president of the Haiku Society of Canada. Among the many great tips for writing haiku I came away with this: "Write [haiku] in three short lines using the principle of comparison, contrast, or association." She used an expression I had been missing in the discussion of haiku when she wrote: "This technique provides the pivot on which the reader's thought turns and expands."

Technique! So there are tools one can use! I thought joyfully.

And I practiced her methods with glee and relative (to me) success and increased enjoyment. Suddenly I could figure out what was wrong with a haiku that failed to jell. I could ask myself if there was a *compari-*

son, a *contrast*, or an *association* between the images and if this relationship was clear and understandable for the reader.

Slowly, over the years, I found by reading the translations of the old Japanese masters and the haiku of my contemporaries whom I admired, that there were more factors than just these three. Here are some of those techniques which I have used. To avoid my seeming to accuse others of using techniques, the ku quoted are all my own.

**The Technique of Comparison.** In the words of Betty Drevniok: "In haiku the something and the something else are set down together in clearly stated images. Together they complete and fulfill each other as one particular event." The comparison shows how two different things share similar aspects.

> *a spring nap*
> *downstream cherry trees*
> *in bud*

Expressed is the thought that buds on a tree can be compared to flowers taking a nap.

**The Technique of Contrast.** Now the job feels easier. All one has to do is to contrast images.

> *long hard rain*
> *hanging in the willows*
> *tender new leaves*

The delight from this technique is the excitement that opposites creates. You have instant built-in interest in the most common haiku "moment." Most surprises of life are the contrasts, and therefore this technique is a major one for haiku.

**The Technique of Association.** This can be thought of as "how different things relate or come together." The Zen of this technique is called "oneness" or showing how everything is part of everything else.

> *ancestors*
> *the wild plum*
> *blooms again*

If you do not equate your ancestors with plum trees, perhaps it is easier to understand with:

> moving into the sun
> the pony takes with him
> some mountain shadow

I was watching some ponies grazing early in the morning on a meadow that was still partially covered with the shadow of the mountain. As the grazing pony moved slowly into the sunshine, I happened to be focused on the shadow and actually saw some of the mountain's shadow follow the pony—to break off and become his shadow. It can also be thought that the pony eating the grass of the mountain becomes the mountain and vice versa.

When the boundaries disappear between the things that separates them, it is truly a holy moment of insight.

**The Technique of the Riddle.** This is probably one of the very oldest poetical techniques. It is no surprise that riddles still form a serious part of poetry's transmission of ideas.

> spirit bodies
> waving from cacti
> plastic bags

The "trick" is to state the riddle in as puzzling terms as possible. What can one say that the reader cannot figure out the answer? The more intriguing the "set-up" and the bigger surprise the answer is, the better the haiku seems to work.

The old masters favorite trick with riddles was the one of: is that a flower falling or is it a butterfly? or is that snow on the plum or blossoms and the all-time favorite—am I a butterfly dreaming I am a man or a man dreaming I am a butterfly? You can ask yourself the question: if I saw snow on a branch, what else could it be? Or seeing a butterfly going by you ask yourself what else besides a butterfly could that be?

**The Technique of Sense-switching.** This is another favorite of the Japanese haiku masters, but one they have used with a great deal of discretion. It is simply to speak of the sensory aspect of a thing and then change to another sensory organ. Usually it involves hearing something one sees or vice versa or to switch between seeing and tasting.

*home-grown lettuce*
*the taste of well-water*
*green*

**The Technique of Narrowing Focus.** This is something Buson used a lot because he, being an artist, was a very visual person. Basically you start with a wide-angle lens on the world in the first line, switch to a normal lens for the second line and zoom in for a close-up in the end. It sounds simple, but is very effective.

*the whole sky*
*in a wide field of flowers*
*one tulip*

**The Technique of Metaphor.** I can hear those who have had some training in haiku sucking in your breath in horror. There is that iron-clad rule that one does not use metaphor in haiku. Posh. Basho used it in his most famous "crow ku." What he was saying was that an autumn evening comes down the way it feels when a crow lands on a bare branch.

I never understood this hokku until one day I was in my tiny studio with the door open. I was standing so still I excited the resident crow's curiosity, causing him to fly down suddenly to land about two feet from my cheek on the tiny nearly bare pine branch. I felt the rush of darkness coming close, as close as an autumn evening and as close as a big black crow. The thud of his big feet hitting the bare branch caused the tiny ripple of anxiety one has when it gets dark so early in the autumn. In that moment I felt I knew what Basho had experienced.

It is extremely hard to find a haiku good enough to place up against Basho's rightly famous one, so I'll pass giving you an example of my ku. But this is a technique that can bring you many lovely and interesting haiku.

**The Technique of Simile.** Usually in English you know a simile is coming when you spot the words "as" and "like." But the Japanese have proved to us that this is totally unnecessary. It is enough to put two images in juxtaposition to let the reader figure out the "as" and "like" for him/herself. Besides, by doing this you give the reader some active

part that makes him or her feel very smart when they discover the simile for him/herself.

> *a long journey*
> *some cherry petals*
> *begin to fall*

**The Technique of the Sketch or Shiki's Shasei.** Though this technique
is often given Shiki's term shasei (sketch from life) or shajitsu (reality), it had been in use since the beginning of poetry in the Orient.
The poetic principle is "to depict as is." The reason he took it up as a
"cause" and thus, made it famous, was his own rebellion against the
many other techniques used in haiku. Shiki was, by nature it seemed,
against whatever was the status quo. If poets had over-used any idea
or method, his goal was to point this out and suggest something else.
(This seems to be the way poetry styles go in and out of fashion.)

Shiki favored the quiet simplicity of just stating what he saw. He
found the greatest beauty in the common sight, simply said. And
many people still feel he was right; there are some moments which
are perhaps best said as simply as it is possible. Yet, he himself realized that used too much, even his new idea can become boring. So the
method is an answer, but never the complete answer of how to write
a haiku.

> *evening*
> *waves come into the cove*
> *one at a time*

**The Technique of Double Entendre (or double meanings).** Anyone
who has read translations of Japanese poetry has seen how much
poets delighted in saying one thing and meaning something else. In
some cases the pun was to cover up a sexual reference by seeming to
speaking of something commonplace. There are whole lists of words
with double meanings, such as spring rain = sexual emissions and jade
mountain = the Mound of Venus. But we have them in English also,
and haiku can use them in the same way.

> *eyes in secret places*
> *deep in the purple middle*
> *of an iris*

**The Technique of Using Puns.** Again we can learn from the master punsters—the Japanese. We haiku writers in English may not be so well-versed in using these because there have been periods of Western literary history where this skill has been looked down upon. And even though the hai of haiku means "joke, or fun, or unusual" there are still writers whose faces freeze into a frown when encountering a pun in three lines.

> *a sign*
> *at the fork in the road*
> *"fine dining"*

**The Technique of Close Linkage.** This could come as a sub-topic to association, but it also works with contrast and comparison, so I like to give it its own rubric. In making any connection between the two parts of a haiku, the leap can be a small one. Usually beginners experiment first with this form. They feel comfortable using the technique.

> *winter cold*
> *finding on a beach*
> *an open knife*

**The Technique of Leap Linkage.** As a writer's skills increase, such "easy" leaps quickly fade in excitement. So the writer begins to attempt leaps that some readers may not follow and therefore find the ku nonsense. Sometimes it is days later when I will go, "Ah-ha!" and in that instant understand what the ku was truly about.

> *wildflowers*
> *the early spring sunshine*
> *in my hand*

**The Technique of Sabi.** I almost hesitate to bring up this idea as a technique because the word sabi has so many meanings. As fascinated as Westerners have become with the word, the Japanese have maintained for centuries that no one can really, truly comprehend what sabi really is. Bill Higginson in *The Haiku Handbook* calls sabi: "(patina/loneliness) Beauty with a sense of loneliness in time, akin to, but deeper than, nostalgia." Donald Keene sees sabi as "an understatement hinting at great depths."

*rocky spring*
*lips taking a sip*
*from a stone mouth*

or

*coming home*
*flower*
*by flower*

**The Technique of Wabi.** The twin brother to sabi can be defined as "poverty; beauty judged to be the result of living simply. Frayed and faded Levis have the wabi that bleached designer jeans can never achieve."

One can argue that the above haiku samples are really more *wabi* than *sabi*—the big debate. I offer a ku that I think is more *wabi* than *sabi* because it offers a scene of austere beauty and poignancy.

*parting fog*
*on wind barren meadows*
*birth of a lamb*

**The Technique of Yûgen.** Another Japanese state of poetry, usually defined as "mystery" and "unknowable depth." Haiku writers use the atmosphere of *yûgen* to force their readers to think and to delve into the everyday sacredness of common things.

(In a letter from Jeanne Emrich, she suggests one can obtain *yûgen* by having something disappear, or something appear suddenly out of nowhere, or by the use of night, fog, mist, empty streets, alleys, and houses.)

*tied to the pier*
*the fishy smells*
*of empty boats*

**The Technique of The Improbable World.** This is an old Japanese tool which is often used to make the poet sound simple and child-like. Often it demonstrates a distorted view of science—one we "know" is not true, but always has the possibility of being true (as in quantum physics).

*evening wind*
*colors of the day*
*blown away*

or

*waiting room*
*a patch of sunlight*
*wears out the chairs*

**The Technique of Humor.** This is the dangerous stuff. Because one has no way of judging another person's tolerance for wisecracks, jokes, slurs, bathroom and bedroom references, one should enter the territory of humor as if it is strewn with land-mines. And yet, if one is reading before a live audience, nothing draws in the admiration and applause like some humorous haiku. Often the humor of a haiku comes from the honest reactions of humankind.

*dried prune faces*
*guests when they hear*
*we have only a privy*

**The Above as Below Technique.** Simply said: the first line and the third line exhibit a connectedness or a completeness. Some say the first line and the third line make a complete thought.

When the images in the first and third lines have the strongest relationship, the haiku usually feels "complete." For exercise, take any haiku and switch the lines around to see how this factor works or try reading the haiku without the second line.

*holding the day*
*between my hands*
*a clay pot*

In searching for these examples, I found many of my haiku did not fit into any of these categories, which tells me there are surely many more techniques in use. I hope I have given you enough to pique your interest in the quest and new ways of exploring the miracles of haiku.

Blessed be!

Jane Reichhold has long been involved in the international community of haiku writers. She founded Aha! Books in 1987 and the website Aha! Poetry in 1995. She is a member of the Haiku Society of America and similar societies in Canada, Germany, and Japan. She is twice a winner of the Museum of Haiku Literature Award (Tokyo), three-time winner of an Haiku Society of America award, and has won awards for several of her books, including *Tigers In A Tea Cup*, *Silence*, and *A Dictionary of Haiku* (1992). This piece is excerpted from a longer article first published *Frogpond*, journal of the Haiku Society of America, Autumn 2000.

# What Dr. Seuss Can Teach Us

*by Laura Backes*

In 1954, in an article in *Life* magazine, Pulitzer Prize-winning author John Hersey challenged Dr. Seuss and other authors to write reading primers for America's first graders that were more interesting than the Dick and Jane books currently being used in schools. Dr. Seuss took up the task, and 50 years ago *The Cat in the Hat* was published. The book was remarkable for several reasons: the text was completely comprised of 236 different words from Houghton Mifflin's reading list, most of which have only one syllable (Houghton published the school edition of the book, though Random House published the trade edition); it made Seuss an instant household name and became the foundation for Random's Beginner Books imprint; the story continues to hold its appeal after several generations; and it changed the way children learned to read.

It also changed how children's book authors learned to write. Instead of telling a thin story based on a simple, everyday incident, Seuss packed the plot with action that escalated on every page. Rather than relying on one-note characters, he populated his book with quirky, complex and surprising personalities that didn't always cooperate with one another, thus creating tension and conflict. When I used the Dick and Jane books in first grade, I was very aware that I was being Taught To Read. Every word stood out on the page as something to be sounded out. When children read *The Cat in the Hat*, they're swept into the story and entertained.

Seuss raised the bar for easy readers, requiring authors who came after him to tell a good story with simple words. But his special gift was making these words rhyme (which helps beginning readers with word recognition and sounding out similar words). However, the story and characters always came first; the rhyme was simply the format he chose to present the plot. If *The Cat in the Hat* were written in lyrical prose, it would still be a timeless book. The lesson here for authors: the rhyme is the last thing you should think about. If you have the knack for it, great. If not, don't even try. When kids list what they love about this book, they never mention that it rhymes.

Other lessons authors can learn from Seuss include:

Young children need page-turners. Picture books and easy readers from the 1940s and 1950s—in which pages often broke in the middle of a scene or even a line of dialogue—had very different pacing than their modern counterparts. We owe a lot of this change to *The Cat in the Hat*. Every two-page spread contained a complete idea; another beat in the action of the plot. The spreads often ended with a line of text that raised the stakes and promised more trouble on the next page. Kids couldn't help but want to see what happened next.

Subtext is important. Seuss understood that young children can comprehend subtleties that they can't read. In other words, their understanding of a story is more advanced than the actual words they're able to read on their own. He never wrote down to his audience. His stories were often metaphors for moral dilemmas children face everyday. The *Cat in the Hat*'s unnamed narrator and his sister Sally were alone in the house when the Cat shows up, and the narrator wrestled with knowing that his mother wouldn't approve of the visitor. The fish gave voice to these concerns in no uncertain terms, and the children wavered between listening to the fish and getting caught up in the fun. At the book's end, the narrator didn't know whether to tell his mother about their day when she returned, and then posed that question directly to the reader: Well ... What would *you* do if your mother asked *you*? Seuss never told his audience what to think, leaving it up to the reader to make his own choices.

Children have lives separate from adults. Seuss understood that many of the best stories inhabit that world where children navigate through situations without direct adult intervention. While this caused *The Cat in the Hat* to get banned from many schools (and still does), it also paved the way for everything from picture books like Maurice Sendak's *Where the Wild Things Are* and Ian Falconer's *Olivia* to Scott Westerfeld's chilling young adult novels (such as *Peeps* and the *Uglies* trilogy) in which teens must save society in a not-so-distant future.

Books can be fun. They can be silly and nonsensical, they can be exciting and absurd. They don't have to have a clear-cut lesson attached. The Cat was a mischievous, self-centered, destructive troublemaker, and yet he's become such a part of the fabric of our culture that everyone knows who you're impersonating if you don a tall red-and-white striped hat. When Linda White and I registered our Children's Authors' Bootcamp workshop several years ago, the clerk at the county office asked what title we each held in the company. I said, "Thing One and Thing Two." She replied, "Sounds like this Bootcamp will be a hoot."

Here's hoping *The Cat in the Hat* will last another 50 years, making even government employees laugh.

Laura Backes is the publisher of *Children's Book Insider*, a newsletter for children's writers. For more information about writing children's books, including free articles, market tips, insider secrets, and much more, visit www.write4kids.com. To learn about Laura's writing workshop, Children's Author's Bootcamp, visit www.WeMakeWriters.com.

This article appeared in the March 2007 of *Children's Writing Update*, a free e-zine from *Children's Book Insider*.

# Glamour & Grammar

*by Evan Morris*

"GLAMOUR" AND "GRAMMAR" are essentially the same word. In classical Greek and Latin, "grammar" (from the Greek "grammatikos," meaning "of letters") covered the whole of arts and letters, i.e., higher knowledge in general. In the Middle Ages, "grammar" was generally used to mean "learning," which at that time included, at least in the popular imagination, a knowledge of magic.

The narrowing of "grammar" to mean the rules of language was a much later development, first focusing on Latin and only in the 17th century extended to the study of English and other languages.

Meanwhile, "grammar" had percolated into Scottish English (as "gramarye"), where an "l" was substituted for an "r" and the word eventually became "glamour," used to mean specifically knowledge of magic and spells.

"Glamour" was then introduced to English (by, among others, Sir Walter Scott), and took on the meaning of "enchantment," and later "alluring charm" and our current "exotic and fashionable attractiveness."

Evan Morris is editor and publisher of *The Word Detective*, a print and online column (www.word-detective.com) in a humorous vein, answering readers' questions about words and language. It is the essential destination for those "puzzled by posh" or "flummoxed by flabbergast," with an index of hundred of word and phrases in an online archive. This item is from the May 22, 2006, issue.

# M-Factors: Qualities that Help You Break into Major Magazines

*by Marcia Yudkin*

What differences mark the divide between so-so writers who never make it beyond 50-cent-a-word markets and those who consistently get top dollar and bylines in famous-name magazines? To answer this question, I spent several days in the periodical room of my public library, examining and analyzing articles in top magazines. I took plenty of notes while searching for the virtues that enable writers to entice and satisfy publishing's most selective editors.

Of course every magazine has a distinctive voice and particular story and style preferences, but the following five characteristics appeared to be widely valued. Increase your ability to deliver these qualities and you'll boost your success rates, prestige and pay at major magazines.

## M-Factor #1: "High-concept" stories

These involve story angles destined to create a buzz or make issues fly off the newsstand because the story surprises or tantalizes. People in the target market can't help wanting to read the article after hearing or reading the idea. "High-concept" appeal might derive from:

> Catchy concept. *Men's Journal* had a cover story attempting to sum up the spirit of our era: "He who has the best time wins," illustrated by three guys pitching through white water on a raft. Similarly, *Fast Company* had a cover story a while back called "Free Agent Nation," proposing a name for the growth in numbers of independent contractors in the U.S. Likewise, lots of magazines describe how to live longer, but *Modern Maturity* labelled it "The Methuselah Factor."

> Controversy. "Bottom-of-the-barrel public schools" for a city magazine, "Eliminate most hunting laws" for an environmental magazine or "The hidden virtues of HMO's" for a political magazine all

have the power to startle their respective readerships and generate talk.

> Cutting-edge research. "Want to buy Internet stocks? Your teenager probably knows more about the Internet than your broker": This was a media-release headline that led to coverage on CNBC, CNN, and other national broadcast stations, but it could just as well have been a cover line for *Money* magazine. Compare "Stockbroker survey reveals Internet ignorance," which also fits the content of the story, but lacks that imaginative twist of bringing in the teenager.

To master this factor, study the teasers on magazine covers and for each article come-on that seems especially appealing, imagine a more pedestrian and less inventive version of the concept. Then reverse the process, imagining a straightforward topic and putting a creative spin on it. In addition, practice generating "high concepts" by copying a list of titles from covers of a particular magazine and then adding to the list yourself.

## M-Factor #2: Depth of content

In contrast to one-dimensional, factual reporting, many of the major-magazine stories I examined offered some additional element that made the article more absorbing or admirable. This way, readers would come away from the piece not merely informed, but also educated, persuaded, spiritually enlightened or emotionally moved. Examples of the extra dimension:

> Education: In *Martha Stewart Living*, an article on capers treats readers to the cultural, historical, botanical, Biblical, culinary, and medical aspects of this condiment. A *Sierra* article called "Living with Floods" went deeply into the ecology of flood plains, complete with schematic diagrams. Typical readers of each of these pieces would emerge having learned quite a bit.

> Persuasion: I once heard an *Atlantic Monthly* editor state that they always prefer their writers to take a stand. That priority was evident in an article on the controversy over coffee-growing's impact on the environment, which came down on the side of "sustainable coffee." Likewise an *Atlantic* article on Waldorf schools, where imagination gets as much attention as knowledge, was reverential even while

mentioning criticisms. In *Parents*, an article announced on the cover with the question, "Should your children watch the news?" landed squarely on the "No" side of the issue.

> Enlightenment: This wouldn't work for every magazine, but in an article on creativity for *New Age Journal* a number of years ago, I made a special effort to relate the piece to eternal themes, as in this conclusion: "For every human being always has the capacity to fashion something out of nothing. That's the God in us, as real as sky and blood. And perhaps that's why creativity gives us such a unique, unearthly buzz. When each visitation brings with it a taste of the infinite, no wonder that we yearn for more, and more, and more."

> Emotional involvement: An article in *New Choices* called "You Can Go Home Again" intensified visceral reader identification with the theme by lacing other people's stories with the author's high-pitched personal vignettes. Similarly, a portrait of Las Vegas in *National Geographic Traveler* demonstrated what the destination still means to visitors today through the author's reminiscences of going there with his gambler dad in the early sixties.

> Literary echoes: A *New Republic* article on the marketing of "social phobia" as a disease offered as garnish evocative quotes from Aldous Huxley's *Brave New World*. In *Field & Stream*, an article on hypothermia began with reminiscences about the author having read Jack London's "To Build a Fire" at age ten. You may not be a novelist yourself, but with such allusions you borrow some literary impact.

Sometimes the major-magazine depth does not involve a single added element but the kind of value one normally finds in a book, compressed into a piece the length of a chapter. For instance, you can find tons of articles on Internet dot.coms, but a cover story in Worth magazine called "Rich.com: How to Build Your Own Web Business Before It's Too Late" distilled a profusion of success stories into twenty principles taking up just eight authoritative, anecdote-strewn pages.

## M-Factor #3: Resonance with readers

A former writing student of mine broke into *Ladies Home Journal* with a personal-experience piece about how she'd lost one hundred pounds and kept it off by coming to terms with having been sexually assaulted in her teens. The magazine told her the article generated more reader mail than any article they ran that year, and possibly ever. From her initial query the editors probably recognized the power of this story to hit home with women in their thirties and forties. But reader resonance doesn't occur only with personal-experience articles.

How-to articles, traditional reporting and think pieces can also produce intense emotional identification and response when they tune in perfectly to what readers deeply care about or most want to know. Readers respond because they get the feeling that the magazine knows and understands them. This leads to a sense of intimacy with the magazine, which in turn boosts subscription renewal rates. Sometimes the resonance comes from an often-overlooked subset of readers feeling recognized and acknowledged for the first time.

> *Parenting*: An article announced on the cover as "Discipline: How to Keep Your Cool" began this way: "Here's a confession: I have hit my children. I was angry when I did it—out of control, even. It scared my kids, and scared me too. It also filled me with shame." What conscientious parent wouldn't identify with this revelation? This article by Joyce Maynard included anecdotes from other parents and from parenting experts.

> *New York*: Seventy-something Ed Koch appears on the cover with the blurb, "Single and fabulous? You may be alone, but you're in good company; 3 million people, including a certain former mayor—are looking for love in the city. Here's how to find it." The article talks about how prominent, rich New Yorkers reasonably paranoid about gold diggers have trouble finding romance. Its likely response from readers: heck, if they have a hard time, I'm probably not doing so badly.

> *Discover*: "The Secret Life of Sharks: And why they may not like the way you taste," reads the cover line, making this article connect with the fear and curiosity many of us feel about killer sharks. It turns out most humans attacked by great white sharks survive. Why? Framed that way, readers can't help wanting to learn what scientists do and don't know about these legendary creatures.

> *Skiing*: "Urban Ski Bum." This article claimed you could really have it all—a big-city job that still gave you the freedom to ski, moun-

tain-bike and wind-surf 50 days a year. For every top magazine, there's probably a certain fantasy shared by many of its readers.

## M-Factor #4: Dramatization of the non-dramatic

I was impressed by many of the top-notch business and science stories I looked at, which took normally dry subjects and created a compelling and illuminating article instead of boring readers. Techniques they used included:

> Making the people involved come alive on the page. Writers describe the main characters' physical appearance, manner, working environment, hobbies, personal history, idiosyncrasies, and motives, which helps readers care about what these entrepreneurs, executives or scientists care about.

> Relating the esoteric to the familiar. An article in *Worth* tamed the abstract concept of medical savings accounts by, among other tactics, connecting the idea to a historical icon: "The basic notion was advocated by Ben Franklin (though, in his day, for fire insurance): Insure only the part of your risk you couldn't possibly pay for, self-insure the rest, and bank the premium savings in an interest-earning account."

> Making the most of irony. An article called "Faster than a Speeding Photon" in *Discover* opened and closed with a man trying by night to find success as a country music songwriter and by day to disprove Einstein's theory of relativity. A profile in *Boston* magazine of a bank CEO highlighted the fact that the man once lived in an ashram in India.

> Using organizing metaphors. In *Popular Science*, a writer discussed antibiotic bacteria in terms of the metaphor of counterintelligence warfare, using just enough original verbal twists to keep it out of the realm of cliché. In *Bloomberg Personal Finance*, an article called "Anatomy of a Startup" exploited the anatomical metaphor (muscles, bones, blood, lung capacity) from beginning to end to discuss business processes, using it for the illustrations as well.

## M-Factor #5: A distinctive voice

Think of Dave Barry's overgrown-adolescent persona; Annie Dillard's lush descriptiveness; Tom Peters' scolding enthusiasm; Miss Manners' stuffy edicts; Tom Wolfe's garrulous fervor. Certain top magazines become more interested in your work when you evolve a personality in print so characteristic that an isolated paragraph by you becomes recognizable as yours.

Voice encompasses not only writing style but also attitudes. When you write with a distinctive voice, readers feel they haven't merely absorbed information but have been in contact with you. Readers also get a clear picture of your likes and dislikes, your personal habits, your age and background, even your physical appearance. Note, for example, how impossible it would be to confuse any of the following writers I found in top magazines with one another.

> "In the southern Rwandan hill town of Gikongoro, the electricity had failed for the night; the Guest House bar was lit by half a dozen candles, and the eyes of the three soldiers who invited me to drink glowed the color of blood oranges. A single glass of beer was passed, from which I was the last to sip—a ritual signifying that I was not to be poisoned." [Philip Gourevitch in *The New Yorker*]

> "Everything was textbook: the wind in my face, tall grass to conceal my stalk, a bear rolling on his back in the yellow grass, oblivious to my presence. At 30 yards I nocked an arrow. Why he looked directly at me when he got up, I still don't know. Swinging his huge head side to side, 1,200 pounds of Alaskan brown bear took a step my way." [Bob Robb in *Field & Stream*]

> "My friend Indi and her fiance David (this month they'll be sentenced to life—oops, getting married) live about two floors down from Him. Apparently you can hear His voice fairly well at that height (4,000 feet about sea level) because these two live as close to godliness as you possibly can without actually abstaining from sex and being declared saints. The Goat Couple, as I now call them, are vegetarian. They have orgasms talking about tofu and soya milk—both of which they make themselves." [Nazma Muller in *Panache*]

> "Already a certain nervousness hangs in the air. People at 40 forget a phone number and say 'early Alzheimer's.' People at 50 realize this may not be such a good joke and so have invented the jaunty euphemism, 'a senior moment.' We are obsessed with age—our own, of course, primarily—but increasingly with that of the whole

society, which so recently (and for most of its history) was the very embodiment of youth." [Richard Todd in *Worth*]

How do you develop your voice? Usually it develops on its own if you get out of your own way and stop trying to sound like some other writer you admire. But you can also stretch and experiment by introducing new or unaccustomed elements into your prose, such as occasional one-word sentences or a sentence running breathlessly on for seven lines; vocabulary, either slang or esoteric, you don't ordinarily use; a different rhythm within sentences; attitudes you've never felt free to express; an alternative kind of imagery; a certain volume and emotional pitch, such as quiet and elegant or loud and insistent.

You needn't get trapped in it when you find a voice you like, that feels like you and that editors and readers respond to. I have one friendly voice for how-to writing, a more intimate one for personal essays and a philosophical/informative one for journalistic reporting. To keep my love affair with writing alive, every once in a while I deliberately inject a new element into my work, such as shorter sentences, more humor or spiritual overtones.

Although I've been writing for highly visible publications since 1981, I found my foray into the periodical room illuminating and motivating. If you don't have a wide reading diet of magazines, I highly recommend such study. Regardless of your writing experience, deciding to improve your skill with these five aspects of writing will help you break into the big time.

Marcia Yudkin, author of *Freelance Writing for Magazines & Newspapers* (HarperCollins), a Book of the Month Club selection in print continuously since 1988, is a magazine writing coach whose publication credits range from the *New York Times Magazine* and *Psychology Today* to *Cosmopolitan* and *Yoga Journal*.

She teaches a home-study course on advanced magazine writing through her web site, www.yudkin.com/majormagazines.htm.

# Recreating Nonfiction Scenes

*by Larry Getlen*

JULIAN RUBINSTEIN's *The Ballad of the Whiskey Robber* is the true tale of, among others, the Robin Hood of Eastern Europe; a cop whose knowledge of police work came from Hungarian episodes of *Columbo*; and his deputy, a man so stupid he was known as "the Mound of Ass-head." To fully capture these and the other outrageous characters in his story, Rubinstein knew that his reporting needed to be thorough and meticulous. He did his job so well that in writing the book that Borders named its Nonfiction Book of the Year for 2004, he used less than one percent of the material he uncovered during his research.

Narrative nonfiction writers—excluding memoirists—are faced with the daunting task of comprehensively recreating history they did not witness. They cannot use memory and invention the same way memoir and fiction writers can, and they have an unassailable obligation to both their subjects and their readers to be completely accurate and honest in their writing.

If you're embarking on a narrative nonfiction project, therefore, the key to writing a compelling, detailed, and truthful narrative is extensive reporting.

"Oftentimes, weakness of writing is a reflection of not having done the job as a reporter," says Robert Vare, an editor for over twenty years for publications such as *The New Yorker*, *The New York Times Magazine*, and *Rolling Stone*, and currently Editor at Large with *The Atlantic Monthly*. "You want to create the experience of being there by giving the reader physical detail, character, description, dialogue, all the things that help put them in the moment." He emphasizes that learning as many details as possible during the reporting process allows you to fully convey the essence of your subject, adding, "it's a sure sign of bad writing when people write in generalities."

"When you're writing nonfiction, if you don't have the reporting, it's like painting with only primary colors," says Julian Rubinstein, author of *The Ballad of the Whiskey Robber*. "If you want to tell your story novelistically or have it read like fiction, you have to know as close to everything as you can."

## The Power of the Interview

One of the most powerful tools for uncovering as many details as possible is extensive and detailed interviewing. When speaking with sources, you should seek to uncover the interviewee's thoughts, feelings, perspectives, memories, and complete background knowledge on the subject in question.

"In interviews, I'm trying for three things," says Sebastian Junger, author of *The Perfect Storm*. "One is to figure out the emotional reality for this person. If it's a woman who lost her boyfriend at sea, what's that feel like? You want to get into that person's heart, and get a sense of how a person reacts to a tragedy like that. Second, I try to nail down, in a very reportorial way, the facts of the matter. That sometimes means very mundane details—where were you living at the time, was it mid-afternoon when you drove to the harbor, etc. But you need that to create an armature for the emotional issues. And finally, there are the visual issues."

There are many creative tactics you can use to unearth descriptive details. In *Black Hawk Down*, Mark Bowden wrote that one character felt like "someone had taken a knife to his knee and driven it in with a sledgehammer." While the man in question volunteered this quote, he did so only after Bowden masterfully steered him toward a detailed description. "I urged him to describe exactly what it felt like," says Bowden. "I'm looking for a picturesque or powerful description, so if a guy says 'I got shot in the knee and it hurt like hell,' I'm gonna say, 'well, exactly how did it hurt? Did it burn? Did it feel like somebody dropped a cinder block on your knee?' He thought about it, and said what he described."

According to Junger, making the subject feel like their contribution is important can help you open them up, and get them to paint a complete picture. "I'll say to a subject, 'that's really interesting. Very moving. Help me close my eyes and picture the scene here. Are you sitting on the left hand side of the room?' If people think you're interested in understanding their life as deeply and honestly as possible, they'll tell you almost any detail."

When interviewing, it's important to remember that the information you obtain will be used to set the scene for the reader, so at this point in the process, no detail is too minor. "I'll often send a manuscript back to a writer with very specific questions where I think it'll enhance the narrative," says Vare. "I'll ask for a physical setting, or, how did a character talk when that character is quoted? These things fill out the storytelling." As an example, Vare cited an article he edited about Chief Justice William Rehnquist. The writer noted that Rehnquist smoked, and Vare sent the writer back to his sources to find out how many packs a day Rehnquist went through. "If a man is smoking, and then he gets thyroid cancer, you want to make the connection."

In order to obtain as much information as possible, you should expect to interview people more than once. "Interviewing subjects multiple times is the key to entering that other world we're trying to all get to," says Rubinstein. "You have to talk to someone long enough that you can fall into their life."

## Use Every Resource

Documents, newspaper articles and old clips are also valuable sources of information that can uncover not only facts, but character details and perspectives as well.

Rubinstein spent five weeks in the Hungarian Supreme Court House combing through every police and court file even remotely related to his subject. When a police chief told him repeatedly how unimportant the Whiskey Robber case was, Rubinstein knew from old newspaper clips that more than fifty people in the department had been rewarded for their efforts in the case, so he knew that the man wasn't telling the truth.

Old video or TV news clips are also a useful tool for not just determining the facts, but for setting the stage as well. For his book *Killing Pablo*, about cocaine kingpin Pablo Escobar, Bowden was able to describe how Escobar's mother arrived at the scene of his death by carefully viewing TV footage of the event.

You can use video clips to provide detailed descriptions, including what people or places looked like, someone's mood, or even the weather, as Rubinstein did when describing how "the blue sky yawned" on a certain day.

Of course, for descriptive details, there is no substitute for personally viewing where your story took place. When Rubinstein spoke with the police officer referenced above, as the man described the Whiskey Robber's unimportance to his police force, Rubinstein noticed that the man had nothing on his wall but two framed photos—pictures of the department's first and second arrests of the Whiskey Robber.

## Filling in the Blanks

Describing what a subject was thinking or feeling at a given moment is a common nonfiction technique that is often tricky, and sometimes mishandled.

"You just can't say, 'Joe was thinking this and then Joe died,'" says Junger. "Unconsciously, the reader thinks, the writer's telling me something he can't possibly know, so how much of this book is true? It casts into doubt everything you've discovered through your hard work and your research."

There are creative ways, however, for you to convey your subject's inner life.

Bowden profiled Saddam Hussein for *The Atlantic Monthly*. Needless to say, he did not have direct access to Iraq's then-leader, and he understood his responsibility for truthfulness to his reader. "One of the things I learned was that he was an avid swimmer, and that he would do dozens of laps in the pool every morning. Of course, I had no idea what went through Saddam's head as he swam in a swimming pool, so what I did is I just wrote what he *might* be thinking, and I wrote it that way. What that says to the reader is, I'm speculating here."

You should only use this tactic, however, when there's reason to believe you actually know what that person might have been thinking. "If you say, 'so and so thought this,' you have to have a very good reason for knowing that," says Junger. "Otherwise, you have to say, 'so and so *probably* thought this, so and so *undoubtedly* was scared.' There are so many graceful ways of doing that. There's no reason to betray the readers trust by claiming to know something you can't know. There are too many good alternatives."

If your subjects are unavailable, you can also interview people in similar situations and use them to set a scene, as Junger did to illustrate the sinking of the *Andrea Gale* in *The Perfect Storm*. "When the *Andrea Gale* sank, six guys died. I had to describe it, and I had no idea how it happened. Had I imagined what it was like and penned a 'realistic' account, 'then the bow went down, and then blah blah blah' and lots of bad writing of that sort, it would have been very obvious to the reader I was just making this up."

Instead, Junger located men who had been in similar situations and survived, and interviewed them about what it would have been like to be stuck in those conditions. "I put the question very directly to them. I described the storm conditions, said, 'the boat was this many feet long doing this kind of fishing in this part of the ocean, she went down seventy-foot breaking seas. Okay. You're a fisherman, you've survived similar things, paint me a picture. What do you think it was like? Roll.' Almost like I'm a director filming something, and the guy's acting it out for me. And that worked."

Of course, in this case, you must make it clear to the reader what you've done. "As long as you say to the reader, 'this is a guy named Ernie off of another boat, this is not the *Andrea Gale*, but he's got a pretty good idea of what those guys went through,' it's fine," adds Junger.

Ultimately, there will be times when, for whatever reason, you just don't have as much information as you would like. In these cases, you need to make the best of what you have.

"Maybe you don't get the living room scene because the grandmother just didn't remember anything, but the scene ten pages later on the boat, that person was a great interview," says Junger. "So you give the reader his descriptive fix on the boat, and you skip through the living room scene very quickly. It's inevitable. You use what you have, and what you don't have, you don't call attention to the fact that you don't have it."

There will be times, however, when despite your best efforts, the information about an event or topic feels too scant for a convincing or informative narrative. In cases like these, sometimes you have to make the hard choice and leave something out. Bowden recalls a dramatic incident he heard about while researching *Black Hawk Down*, a story of a soldier taken hostage. In the end, his information was too sketchy to verify the incident, and even though it would have added substantial drama, he left it out of the narrative.

## Defining the Line

In the end, you'll have to make numerous judgment calls about what information to include and what to omit. Always remember that for a narrative nonfiction writer, absolute truth must be the standard, no matter how minor a detail may seem.

Bowden once wrote an article about Hall of Fame baseball player Mike Schmidt. "During one at-bat, he stepped out for a moment and took two very deep breaths," recalls Bowden. "And I wrote that he took these deep breaths trying to calm himself. After I wrote the article, Schmidt said to me, 'How did you know I was trying to calm myself?' It turned out he was doing it for another reason altogether. I shouldn't have said that."

While it seems a minor detail, Bowden was called on it, illustrating that no detail is too minor to make sure you have it right. In the end, it's clear that for narrative nonfiction writers, the better your reporting and the more facts you have, the stronger your story will be.

Asked if he had any final comments on the subject, "reporting, reporting, reporting" was Rubinstein's mantra. "You can't write narrative nonfiction unless you have the material. You have to know everything. Then, and only then, can you decide what is best to illustrate your story."

Larry Getlen is a veteran journalist and author. He has written for the *New York Post*, *Radar*, *Esquire*, and *Maxim*. This piece appeared in *Writer's Digest* in January/February 2007 as "The Way It Was."

# Getting the Tough Interview

*by Linda Formichelli*

YOUR EDITOR at the *East Nowhere Business Journal* assigned you an article that involves interviewing Fortune 500 CEOs. You're psyched! But soon your excitement turns to fear as, one by one, your calls to the execs go unanswered. Their assistants keep promising to pass on your message, yet the CEOs never deign to call you back. You wonder if the assistants have actually been filing your messages in the shredder.

Or try this one on for size: A famous author is touring in your area, and the local arts rag has agreed to run an interview—providing you can get Ms. Popularity to sit down and talk with you. You call the author's PR rep—repeatedly—but it's as if your messages are falling into a black hole.

Assistants, agents, and PR reps are the gatekeepers who keep their clients and bosses from going nuts trying to talk to every yahoo with a phone and an index finger. But what if that yahoo is—you? And what if your making a living depends on getting through to ever-busy execs, doctors, government officials, and celebrities?

You'd think that anyone with something to sell would be happy for any publicity he can get, but that's not always the case. Cathy Lewis, president of the book publicity firm C.S. Lewis & Company Publicists, offers three reasons a PR person or other gatekeeper might not set an interview for you:

> Your publication's demographics are not in sync with the personal brand a client is trying to build. "For example, an alternative medicine practitioner trying to win over mainstream audiences might want to steer away from 'new age' publications in favor of more conventional health magazines," says Lewis.

> The client is looking for prominent features only. "Some clients believe less is more," Lewis says. "They're willing to forgo being

quoted or mentioned in an article, in favor of being the sole subject or expert source for a piece."

> The snob factor is at work. "Although we love to work with clients who will talk to anyone, no matter how small or specialized the publication, some busy clients will simply not find the time to talk to the little guy, preferring instead to wait for more prestigious placements," says Lewis. How true! When I say I'm writing for *USA Weekend*, the gatekeepers are thrilled to line up an interview with their clients or bosses. But when I'm writing for a small pub like, say, *Graduating Engineer*—or, even worse, I'm working on a query and don't have an assignment in hand—sometimes all I hear is the scary sound of silence.

Put down that phone and listen up. No matter who you're writing for, these tips will up your chances of landing that juicy interview.

## Play Nice

It probably goes without saying, but I'm going to say it anyway: Being courteous and professional and doing your homework will take you a long way towards landing that coveted interview. "This includes, when appropriate, using results of research or just asking good questions to let them know you're aware of the [source's] interests beyond the immediate project they may be promoting," says Kerry Dexter, who writes about musicians and other music professionals. "It's also a technique which writers from small publications could use effectively."

So if you want to interview a busy exec, do a little research into the executive and her company. Then, when you speak to the gatekeeper or leave a voicemail message, you can say, "I know that Ms. Bigshot is interested in promoting the company's new line of rock climbing gear. I'd love to ask her some questions about this for my magazine's audience of avid sports people."

## Bait the Line

If you're writing for a small magazine or you don't have an assignment in hand, name-dropping a few well-known pubs can get the gatekeeper to take notice. "If the publication is really small or unknown, and that's proving to be a problem, I'll mention that I'm a freelancer and name-drop a couple of the bigger publications for which I write," says Gwen Moran, a freelance magazine writer and co-author of *Build Your Own Home on a Shoestring* and *The Complete Idiot's Guide to Business Plans*. "Often, I find different angles in an interview, especially if the source is high-profile, and this not only opens the door, but it clears the way for me to shop those other angles around with my bigger-name clients." If you don't have any bigger credits yet, mention the magazine that you plan to send the query to; for example, "I'm working on a query for *Family Circle* about X, and I'd love to have a few minutes with Mr. Bigwig to speak about the topic."

## Play Phone Tag

Call any business after-hours and it's likely you'll reach a voice-mail system that allows you to enter an extension or dial by name. "Leave a message directly in that voice mailbox—no intermediary assistant to screen your message," says Julie Sturgeon, who writes mostly for business and trade magazines.

Another of Sturgeon's techniques is to dial a different extension or change the last number of the contact information in an attempt to get someone else from the company on the line. "Tell them your situation—many times they'll grease the skids for you by walking the message to that person directly," she says.

## Think Like a PR Person

"Frame the topic and sweep of your piece in PR terms," suggests Lewis. "While you can't compromise your journalistic objectivity, it is perfectly valid to tell the PR person that this piece will reach X number of readers in a specific demographic, and that it has relevance to several hot topical news trends that maximize her client's expertise."

## Go to the Right Guy

Sometimes the obvious person—the PR rep or the source's assistant— isn't the one you want to go to. "I once had an assignment to interview Michael W. Smith, who is a very big name in Christian music," says Pat Curry, a freelance writer who specializes in personal finance and business operations. "He was coming to our area and I was doing an advance on the show. I had to get a phone interview with him and it just wasn't happening." She asked herself, "Who needs this article the most?" and ended up contacting the show's promoter, a local man who stood to lose ticket sales without an article in the paper. "He made it happen in a heartbeat," she says.

The PR person later called Curry to apologize that she couldn't make the interview happen and to offer her some free tickets to the show. "I told her I'd already done the interview," says Curry. "She was stunned."

This lesson extends to all types of sources. For example, if you're looking to interview an author, try going to his agent—the person who makes money when the author makes money. Or, if he's on tour, try calling one of the venues he'll be speaking at. If it's a CEO you're trying to corral, skip the assistant and go to the company's marketing or PR department; they know the value of good press. For a celebrity, find out the cause she represents—for example, many celebs put their famous faces to use promoting disease awareness—and contact that organization, which stands to gain publicity from the interview.

## Name Drop

Say you've landed interviews with all your sources except one. Sturgeon suggests leaving the hold-out a message that mentions who else you've spoken with about the article (preferably the big-shot's competitors or enemies) and tell them they have until X time to call you and get their viewpoint included in the article.

In another vein, sometimes it's helpful to cite other prominent sources you'll be using in your article so that the PR rep can relay this information to a client who might feel as though he's downgrading his "brand," according to Lewis. For example, Dr. Topdog might think twice about declining an interview with your small publication if she knows that Dr. Bigkahuna agreed to an interview.

## Call in the Big Guns

If you're not making any headway on your own, it may be time to ask your editor to step in and make the call. "For a book I'm working on I wanted to get a blurb from a well-known novelist," says Brette McWhorter Sember, author of 15 books including the soon-to-be-released *Your Plus-Size Pregnancy*. "My editor suggested I e-mail her on her Web site—no response. My editor then followed up with her and got a response in five minutes."

Linda Formichelli is the co-author of *The Renegade Writer: A Totally Unconventional Guide to Freelance Writing Success* and *The Renegade Writer's Query Letters that Rock!* This article appeared in the January/February 2007 issue of *Writer's Digest.*

Her website is www.lindaformichelli.com.

# The Line between Fact & Fiction

*by Roy Peter Clark*

JOURNALISTS should report the truth. Who would deny it? But such a statement does not get us far enough, for it fails to distinguish nonfiction from other forms of expression. Novelists can reveal great truths about the human condition, and so can poets, film makers, and painters. Artists, after all, build things that imitate the world. So do nonfiction writers.

To make things more complicated, writers of fiction use fact to make their work believable. They do research to create authentic settings into which we enter. They return us to historical periods and places that can be accurately chronicled and described: the battlefield at Gettysburg, the Museum of Natural History in New York City, a jazz club in Detroit. They use detail to make us see, to suspend our disbelief, to persuade us it was "really like that."

For centuries writers of nonfiction have borrowed the tools of novelists to reveal truths that could be exposed and rendered in no better way. They place characters in scenes and settings, have them speak to each other in dialogue, reveal limited points of view, and move through time over conflicts and toward resolutions.

To make things more complicated, scholars have demonstrated the essential fictive nature of all memory. The way we remember things is not necessarily the way they were. This makes memoir, by definition, a problematic form in which reality and imagination blur. The problems of memory also infect journalism when reporters—in describing the memories of sources and witnesses—wind up lending authority to a kind of fiction.

The post-modernist might think all this irrelevant, arguing that there are no facts, only points of view, only "takes" on reality, influenced by our personal histories, our cultures, our race and gender, our social class. The best journalists can do in such a world is to offer multiple frames through which events and issues can be seen. Report the truth? they ask. Whose truth?

Caught in the web of such complexity, one is tempted to find some simple escape routes before the spider bites. If there were only a set of basic principles to help journalists navigate the waters between fact and fiction, especially those areas between the rocks. Such principles exist. They can be drawn from the collective experience of many journalists, from our conversations, debates and forums, from the work of writers such as John Hersey and Anna Quindlen, from stylebooks and codes of ethics, standards, and practices.

Hersey made an unambiguous case for drawing a bold line between fiction and nonfiction, that the legend on the journalist's license should read "None of this was made up." The author of "Hiroshima," Hersey used a composite character in at least one early work, but by 1980 he expressed polite indignation that his work had become a model for the so-called New Journalists. His essay in the *Yale Review* questioned the writing strategies of Truman Capote, Norman Mailer, and Tom Wolfe.

Hersey draws an important distinction, a crucial one for our purposes. He admits that subjectivity and selectivity are necessary and inevitable in journalism. If you gather ten facts but wind up using nine, subjectivity sets in. Context can drop out, or history, or nuance, or qualification or alternative perspectives.

While subtraction may distort the reality the journalist is trying to represent, the result is still nonfiction, is still journalism. The addition of invented material, however, changes the nature of the beast. When we add a scene that did not occur or a quote that was never uttered, we cross the line into fiction. And we deceive the reader.

This distinction leads us to two cornerstone principles:

Do not add.

Do not deceive.

Let's elaborate on each:

## Do not add.

This means that writers of nonfiction should not add to a report things that did not happen. To make news clear and comprehensible, it is often necessary to subtract or condense. Done without care or responsibility, even such subtraction can distort. We cross a more definite line into fiction, however, when we invent or add facts or images or sounds that were not there.

**Do not deceive.**
This means that journalists should never mislead the public in reproducing events. The implied contract of all nonfiction is binding: The way it is represented here is, to the best of our knowledge, the way it happened. Anything that intentionally or unintentionally fools the audience violates that contract and the core purpose of journalism—to get at the truth. Thus, any exception to the implied contract—even a work of humor or satire—should be transparent or disclosed.

Because these two principles are stated negatively, we decided not to nag journalists with an endless list of "Thou shalt nots." So we've expressed four supporting strategies in a positive manner.

1. Be unobtrusive. This guideline invites writers to work hard to gain access to people and events, to spend time, to hang around, to become such a part of the scenery that they can observe conditions in an unaltered state. This helps avoid the "Heisenberg effect," a principle drawn from science, in which observing an event changes it. Even watchdogs can be alert without being obtrusive.

We realize that some circumstances require journalists to call attention to themselves and their processes. So we have nothing against Sam Donaldson for yelling questions at a president who turns a deaf ear to reporters. Go ahead and confront the greedy, the corrupt, the secret mongers; but the more reporters obtrude and intrude, especially when they are also obnoxious, the more they risk changing the behavior of those they are investigating.

2. Stories should not only be true, they should ring true. Reporters know by experience that truth can be stranger than fiction, that a man can walk into a convenience store in St. Petersburg, Fla., and shoot the clerk in the head and that the bullet can bounce off his head, ricochet off a ceiling beam, and puncture a box of cookies.

If we ruled the world of journalism—as if it could be ruled—we would ban the use of anonymous sources, except in cases where the source is especially vulnerable and the news is of great import. Some whistleblowers who expose great wrongdoing fall into this category. A person who has migrated illegally into America may want to share his or her experience without fear of deportation. But the journalist must make every effort to make this character real. An AIDS patient may want and deserve anonymity, but making public the name of his doctor and his clinic can help dispel any cloud of fiction.

Fired *Boston Globe* columnist Mike Barnicle writes:

> *I used my memory to tell true tales of the city, things that happened to real people who shared their own lives with me. They represented the music and flavor of the time. They were stories that sat on the shelf of my institutional memory and spoke to a larger point. The use of parables was not a technique I invented. It was established ages ago by other newspaper columnists, many more gifted than I, some long since dead.*

A parable is defined as a "simple story with a moral lesson." The problem is that we know them from religious literature or ancient beast fables. They were fictional forms, filled with hyperbole. Mike Barnicle was passing them off as truth, without doing the reporting that would give them the ring of truth.

In the Middle Ages, perhaps, it could be argued that the literal truth of a story was not important. More important were the higher levels of meaning: how stories reflected salvation history, moral truth or the New Jerusalem. Some contemporary nonfiction authors defend invention in the name of reaching for some higher truth. We deem such claims unjustifiable.

3. The next guideline is to make sure things check out. Stated with more muscle: Never put something in print or on the air that hasn't checked out. The new media climate makes this exceedingly difficult. News cycles that once changed by the day, or maybe by the hour, now change by the minute or second. Cable news programs run 24 hours, greedy for content. And more and more stories have been broken on the Internet, in the middle of the night, when newspaper reporters and editors are tucked dreamily in their beds. The imperative to go live and to look live is stronger and stronger, creating the appearance that news is "up to the minute" or "up to the second."

Time frenzy, however, is the enemy of clear judgment. Taking time allows for checking, for coverage that is proportional, for consultation, and for sound decision-making that, in the long run, will avoid embarrassing mistakes and clumsy retractions.

4. In a culture of media bravado, there is plenty of room for a little strategic humility. This virtue teaches us that Truth—with a capital T—is unattainable, that even though you can never get it, that with hard work you can get at it—you can gain on it. Humility leads to respect for points of view that differ from our own, attention to which enriches our reporting. It requires us to recognize the unhealthy influences of careerism and profiteering, forces that may tempt us to tweak a quote or bend a rule or snatch a phrase or even invent a source.

So let's restate these, using slightly different language. First the cornerstone principles: The journalist should not add to a story things that didn't happen. And the journalist should not fool the public.

Then the supporting strategies: The journalist should try to get at stories without altering them. The reporting should dispel any sense of phoniness in the story. Journalists should check things out or leave them out. And, most important, a little humility about your ability to truly know something will make you work harder at getting it right.

These principles have meaning only in the light of a large idea, crucial to democratic life: that there is a world out there that is knowable. That the stories we create correspond to what exists in the world. That if we describe a velvet painting of John Wayne hanging in a barber shop, it was not really one of Elvis in a barbecue joint. That the words between quotation marks correspond to what was spoken. That the shoes in the photo were the ones worn by the man when the photo was taken and not added later. That what we are watching on television is real and not a staged re-enactment.

If you try something unconventional, let the public in on it. Gain on the truth. Be creative. Do your duty. Have some fun. Be humble. Spend your life thinking and talking about how to do all these well.

Roy Peter Clark is senior scholar at the Poynter Institute (www.poynter.org), a school for journalists in St. Petersburg, Fla., and author of a number of books, including *Writing Tools: 50 Essential Strategies for Every Writer* (Little, Brown & Co., 2006). This is an excerpt from a longer article with the same name that originally appeared in the journal *Creative Nonfiction*, and can be found in its entirety at that site or online at the Poynter Institute's website.

# Psychological Action in Nonfiction

*by Lynn Franklin*

FICTION WRITERS have known for centuries that some of the most powerful action in a story occurs in the mind of the protagonist. When we read a novel we expect the writer to show us what the character is thinking. Bringing the reader close to the psychological action helps readers empathize with the character and, thus, enhances emotional impact.

Nonfiction writers can also use psychological action to increase the power of their stories. The writing techniques are the same, with one critical difference: journalists actually *report* on their protagonist's thoughts by using inferences. Nothing is made up.

"Narrative journalists report on people's thoughts all the time," said Jon Franklin, two-time Pulitzer prize winner. "And they do it objectively, safely, honestly, and effectively. They just don't say 'he thought.'"

Franklin, author of *Writing for Story* and a pioneer in narrative non-fiction, urges reporters to look at some of the masters and follow their lead. The best of these writers show the subjective experience rather than falling back on "he thought."

"Awareness, consciousness of our own lives, is essentially experiential," Franklin said. "It's how our minds react to something that happens that affects us. It is also peculiar to the individual, in that each of us responds to the world in a way determined to varying degrees by genetics and also the environment. When we have an experience, from a handshake and a greeting to a professional struggle, we respond to it in accord with our past experiences and prejudices. People don't think in words. They think in the experience of the moment. So to quote thought is usually absurd.

"What we so sloppily call 'thought,' in other words, can be best described as a collision between a character and his world."

One of Franklin's favorite examples is a scene in Ernest Hemingway's *A Death in the Afternoon* in which a novice bullfighter walks into the ring to face his 2000-pound opponent. As the man waits for the bull to appear, he stands perfectly still—except for his feet. Hemingway describes the way the man's feet keep twitching. While the rest of his body held the classic confident pose, his feet did a sort of tap dance. Hemingway never says the boy is scared. But the detail he chooses to show conveys the young man's fear as clearly—even more effectively—than if he'd written "he was afraid" or "he thought the bull was terrifying."

The best fiction writers do the same thing. One of my own favorite examples is from fiction. In William Faulkner's short story "Barn Burning" he shows a teenage boy struggling to understand the world controlled by his passive aggressive father. Even though "Barn Burning" is fiction, Faulkner never shows his character *thinking* his father is passive aggressive or how embarrassing it is to live with a man who oozes anger. Nor does he bring us into the father's mind. Instead, he uses carefully selected detail so that it's the *reader* who feels the anger and ascribes it to the character.

In one scene, the boy is following his father to the new employer's house, where they've been summoned to report for duty. On the way there, the boy watches his father suddenly veer to one side of the road so that his boot clomps down into a pile of horse poop. He then tracks the horse poop all over the employer's white carpet, making the wife shriek in horror and throw him out. Outside, he calmly scrapes off his boots and comments about the whiteness of the house's interior. The action gave a stronger sense of the man—and the boy's own shame—than any explicit thoughts Faulkner could have planted in either character's mind.

In both of these examples, the characters' states of mind were all revealed by reportable observations.

Reporters can also interview people about their emotions, and most good reporters do this all of the time. While this is a good, going-in method, Franklin cautions that there are limits and dangers.

"It's an old truism that writers must be good psychologists," Franklin said. "In the last twenty or thirty years, the neurosciences have learned a great deal of value to writers. Most obviously, it is quite clear to neuroscientists that people don't think in quotes. That is, we don't articulate most of our interior workings. We simply have them, usually in nonverbal form, act on them and if we articulate them we do it later in response to a question or a situation as justification after the fact. This means that there is absolutely no basis for putting thoughts in quotes even if we knew what those thoughts were. They do not exist as such.

"Consider, for openers, how many of us write (at least in the beginning of our careers). We have thoughts and feelings and intuitions and we put them down on paper. *Then* we study them and see if they mean anything and, if so, they might have value. In other words, the words are not a product of clear thought, but rather clear thought is arrived at by studying what we said. A more straight forward way to put it is that most often we don't know what we are saying until it comes out.

"*Thought*, whatever it is, is simply not conducted in language," Franklin said. "Rather language is the conscious explainer of thought (sometimes too good an explainer, as in the classic Freudian slip). That's why, when someone asks us what we're thinking, we're often nonplussed. We were definitely thinking. Our minds were at work. But we weren't finished. The inner workings were still nonverbal and the very question chases them out of our minds. That doesn't stop us from saying something social, like, 'What a nice day it is.'"

So what does a narrative nonfiction writer do? Report on your character's thoughts, and then show them through experiences—experiences that you can see or document.

For example, in the opening to Franklin's "The Fastest Man on Earth" (in the book *Guinea Pig Doctors*), Franklin uses only reportable details to establish the story's psychological tension. The first short three grafs established the five orienting threads—subject, time, place, character and mood. Franklin uses what I call the "camera sweep" technique, just like a movie might open with a long shot of a scene, then slowly bring the camera in to a close-up of an individual in that scene. In this case, the camera zooms in to focus on Dr. John Stapp, standing in the desert in his flight suit.

As you read this, notice how when Franklin first enters Stapp's mind—the psychological action—he qualifies it with "he knew" (as opposed to "he thought"), but that as he continues (effectively inside of Stapp's mind) he drops the qualifiers:

*December, 1954.*

*The ugly blue-gray overcast stretched all the way from the Sacramento mountains in the east to the San Andres range, on the opposite horizon. The clouds had remained unbroken since dawn.*

*Dr. John Paul Stapp stood, in his flight suit, on the desert floor, just a few miles from where the atomic age had been born in wind and fire. He stared at the bright spot in the clouds that hung halfway between the peaks of the Sacramentos and the zenith.*

*Occasionally the brightness wavered as the boiling clouds moved across it. That meant, he knew, that parts of the overcast were thin. That meant that there might be a break.*

*Five minutes of sunshine. That's all he needed, five minutes.*

*Dr. Stapp looked around him. Even with the muted sun, there was almost enough light. There was enough, for instance, that the red and white rocket sled to cast a fuzzy shadow. The two small hills to the south, toward Mexico, had swelled to the size of a mountain, so there was enough light for a mirage. There was more than sufficient light to satisfy the news photographers, who were sitting in and on the parked Jeeps.*

*It was almost bright enough for the high-speed scientific cameras in the sled and chase plane.*

*Almost, but not quite.*

*Maybe there would be a break, and they could get on with it.*

*Sure, there would be a break. That's what he told the crew, anyway. Even in science, you've got to have faith.*

*"Testing," said the blockhouse speaker, booming out over the desert. "Testing, one, two ..."*

*Perhaps he should go get strapped in and wait for a bright spot. If the sun came out, and the restraints weren't fastened, it'd cloud over again before they could get ready.*

*Of all the bad luck. How can you plan to expect clouds over White Sands?...*

Before I go on, remember that none of this is made up. Franklin reported on every single fact; he interviewed the principals and viewed film taken at the event.

The psychological action begins with "That meant, he knew, that parts of the overcast were thin." How did Franklin know Stapp knew this? He asked. And Stapp told him about his tension, about worrying about whether or not the weather would clear.

Once we're in Stapp's mind, Franklin dropped the qualifier. So the next sentence is: "That meant there might be a break." No need for the "he thought" or "he told this reporter." Those phrases would yank the reader out of the story.

Here's where the magic happens: After Franklin has established his orienting threads, his character, and his character's concerns *he no longer needs to convey the character's thoughts.*

Franklin calls it "stepping through the looking glass." The reader is there, in the scene. The rest of the scene *appears* to be in Stapp's mind and does reflect what's going on psychologically. But in reality, it is straight reporting.

Take, for example, the next graf:

*Five minutes of sunshine. That's all he needed, five minutes.*

Did Stapp think this? How could we know? Stapp later *said* he needed only five minutes. So I suppose we could assume he knew it. Either way, it was objective fact.

But the way Franklin set this up, we don't *need* to assume. All we need to do is be reporters.

*Five minutes of sunshine. That's all he needed, five minutes.*

Those are both statements of fact. Something that can be reported. They're not in quotes, they're not qualified with "he thought." We don't need to know if Stapp thought this. It was enough that it was burning knowledge. It's true, it's factual. We write the facts *but* because of the set-up, the reader sees the world through Stapp's eyes and knows that Stapp is thinking this.

In the next two grafs, Franklin pulls the camera back and shows the scene. But this is different from the opening, camera-sweep scene. In this graf, we see the scene through Stapp's eyes:

*Dr. Stapp looked around him. Even with the muted sun, there was almost enough light. There was enough, for instance, that the red and white rocket sled to cast a fuzzy shadow. The two small hills to the south, toward Mexico, had swelled to the size of a mountain, so there was enough light for a mirage. There was more than sufficient light to satisfy the news photographers, who were sitting in and on the parked Jeeps.*

*It was almost bright enough for the high-speed scientific cameras in the sled and chase plane.*

By pulling back and showing the scene through Stapp's eyes, Franklin keeps the reader close to Stapp. So when he zooms back in to Stapp's interior experience, the reader goes willingly with him; again, no need for qualifiers:

*Almost, but not quite.*

*Maybe there would be a break, and they could get on with it.*

*Sure, there would be a break. That's what he told the crew, anyway. Even in science, you've got to have faith.*

Are the three grafs above Stapp's thoughts? Of course not. Who said they were? The writer is stating facts. But the set-up prepares the reader so that these facts become part of the psychological action.

To put the reader into a nonfiction character's mind, the first thing the writer must do is build a context. This involves more than just showing the character's interior psychology through his or her actions. The writer also needs to foreshadow the close-in scene and to pull the reader into the world the character inhabits.

That's what Franklin did with the preparatory copy that came before each moment of close-in psychological action. All of that in and out builds until, when the reader gets to the final graf of this scene, she's prepared for the final close-up:

*Of all the bad luck. How can you plan to expect clouds over White Sands?*

As you do your own reporting, remember that each person reacts to a situation as an individual. So for the experiences to mean anything to the reader, we have to show who this character is.

"To get inside a person's head," Franklin said, "we have to first show how that head developed. Then we show the critical scene ... and lo, we don't have to say what the character 'thought.' The reader knows instantly and exactly what he 'thought.' We don't know it in words, and don't really want to know it in words, since words are not really applicable to such descriptions."

Though we need to establish the individual character before their actions have psychological meaning, this does not mean we need to spend pages and pages showing the character develop. Instead, we just need to reveal enough of the individual quirks to make the action meaningful.

Here's how Franklin handled it in "Bringing Judy Home," an article published in the *Raleigh News & Observer*. Unlike the Stapp story, which started with a fairly distant camera sweep, this story begins close in, focused on a car chasing an ambulance through the night. Like the Stapp story, much of this story had to be reconstructed; Franklin was not present for the crazy car ride.

However ... not only did he have the main character as a source, he also had the character's daughter, the wife (the patient), the emergency techs, the doctors ... enough people were present for this story that he could obtain the necessary detail—and check it—to recreate the action.

As you read this example, notice how the first two and a half paragraphs not only orient the reader, but also establish a foundation for the long-standing, loving relationship. So by the time the reader comes to "Trying to follow the wailing ambulance, his daughters muffled sobs in the background ..." the reader is prepared to travel closer into the world as seen through Jim's eyes at this critical moment in his life:

> Jim Vertucci drove fast, bent over the wheel, peering through the streaks of the wiper blades, trying to stay tucked in behind the ambulance as it whipped in and out of traffic, racing north from Sanford. Beside him, his daughter cried softly. He struggled to keep his thoughts in line, his head clear, face the facts, even these facts that threatened to numb his mind and rob him of ... everything.
>
> For more than two thirds of his life Judith had shared his days and his mind. She had borne his children, prepared his meals, cleaned his house, washed his clothes, arranged the birthday parties and bought the Christmas presents and generally provided the warmth and civilization without which life is only existence. She had been the entire family's anchor during

*those long years in Queens and Long Island when he was a New York City cop and often had to be away during nights and holidays.*

*He had reciprocated, of course—played the role of devoted provider, almost in the old country sense. Family had come first, for both of them, and it had all worked out, produced strong blood bonds and a productive life for them all. Along the way they'd had their problems, but they were not remembered at this moment. Trying to follow the wailing ambulance, his daughter's muffled sobs in the background, it was the joy that mattered. And joy had been theirs. The reunions they'd gone to, the parties, the movies. They'd loved the movies, he and Judy alike—especially the John Wayne movies, and they'd seen them all. They had laughed a lot. One of the things Judy said was that he could always made her laugh.*

*Said. Had said.*

*Now, just a few days short of their 40th anniversary ...*

Did you notice that the part of the story that seems to be Jim's thoughts were actually statements of fact—facts a journalist can document? It was simply told from Jim's point of view.

Look at it again:

*Trying to follow the wailing ambulance, his daughter's muffled sobs in the background, it was the joy that mattered. And joy had been theirs. The reunions they'd gone to, the parties, the movies. They'd loved the movies, he and Judy alike—especially the John Wayne movies, and they'd seen them all. They had laughed a lot. One of the things Judy said was that he could always made her laugh...*

Fact: The ambulance wailed as it headed towards the hospital.

Fact: Jim's daughter sobbed.

Fact: Jim and his wife had gone to John Wayne movies, reunions, parties.

Fact: They laughed a lot (can check this with outside sources).

Fact: One of the things Judy said was that he could always make her laugh (Judy says this).

The only fact you might question is the statement "it was the joy that mattered." But both characters told Franklin this in an interview. And conversations with others supported this statement.

So all of the information is reported fact. But it was set up and presented in such a way as to be evocative both psychologically and emotionally. This is psychological action—action that can be documented, but that gives us a view of the human interior. And all of it is true.

Lynn Franklin is a freelance writer, teacher, writing coach, and editor of WriterL, an online discussion group for people who write narrative. She can be reached at www. writerl.com.

# Join a Critique Group

*by W. Terry Whalin*

A CRITIQUE GROUP is a small group of writers who encourage each other and provide regular help to each other. Joining a group is not something to be taken lightly. It means a commitment to write something each month, polish the writing and then share it with the group. Also it's a commitment to carefully critique the other members' manuscripts and come prepared to help others.

"Sounds wonderful," you think. "Where do I find one?"

First, see if your local writers group has critique groups. For example, the Society of Children's Book Writers has critique groups scattered across the country.

You need to determine where will you meet and at what time. Decide on the maximum number of participants and how often the group will meet. The larger the group, the more time will be needed for each person and his manuscript. So a small number like four persons in a group is better.

One essential requirement is that people be committed to writing as well as willing to critique other writer's materials. If people do not write and bring materials, the group degenerates into a chatting session rather than a work session.

Some groups bring the manuscripts to the meeting, read them aloud, and then critique them. Other groups send the manuscripts out ahead of time and do not read the manuscripts during the meeting. Instead, they talk about the content. I prefer the latter method since I find it difficult to catch the content from reading aloud. In my opinion, the manuscript receives a better critique when read in advance.

During the meeting, agree on the amount of time for each manuscript so that no one person or manuscript dominates the critique session. For example, a group of four may meet for one hour each month and spend 15 minutes on each manuscript.

## Tips for Critiquing Another Writer's Work

First, begin with praise. Find something that you like about the manuscript, possibly the format or the main character or the general theme or plot. In this way, we build up one another and give encouragement.

Critiques vary according to the type of material. Here are some basic questions to consider for nonfiction, then fiction.

## Critiquing Nonfiction

1. Examine the overall structure. Is it logical? What kind of article is it and does it fulfill the proper requirements? Can you restate the premise in a single sentence? Does the article clearly point out the problem, then offer a sensible conclusion? Is there adequate information for the reader to draw his own conclusions and learn what he needs to learn? Is it easy to read? Entertaining? Does the writing show rather than tell ideas? Are there illustrations and anecdotes and are they effective?

2. Detailed examination. Are the facts accurate? References correct? Transitions smooth? Point out any awkward phrases, incorrect grammar, misspellings, and trite phrases. Is the title eye-catching and appropriate? Do you want to keep reading after the first paragraph?

## Critiquing Fiction

1. Overall examination. Did you like the story? Why or why not? Did it work as a whole? Who was the main character? Did the beginning set up an immediate, important (to the character) problem? Was the fictional dream maintained? Were there rough spots? Was the main character's behavior consistent? Were the other characters consistent? Did the story have a beginning, middle and an end? If in a particular genre, did it work? Is it appropriate for the chosen audience? Were the plot and the character's motive in sync? Was the tone appropriate? Was the pacing appropriate? What was the theme? Did it work? Can you restate the theme in a single sentence?

2. Detailed examination. Did the author tell rather than show the story? Point out any awkward phrases, incorrect grammar, misspellings, trite phrases and poor transitions. Was there any metaphors or analogies? Did they work? Was the dialogue realistic? Did it forward the plot? Did the first paragraph grab your attention? Did the title grab

you? Was there a balance of narrative and action? Was the sentence pattern varied?

## Advantages of a Critique Group

First, it provides you a writing deadline. Each month the group needs to keep writing and that means constantly producing new material. This deadline will push you to schedule time for writing and polishing your work.

As other writers examine your work before you send it to a publication, it gives you an edge over other freelancers. Other writers can give you fresh insight, marketing ideas and help on the manuscript before an editor sees it. This extra polish makes your manuscript stand out from the others on the editor's desk.

Showing your manuscript to another person involves risk. What if they don't like it? Better to hear that from a fellow writer and polish it some more, than send the article all over the country, receive rejections slips, and never know why. Take the plunge and either begin a group or get in one.

## After the Critique

After I collect the input from my group. I don't always take their comments but I do follow most of them. The process works for me and has helped give my writing an edge over others who don't take advantage of help from other writers.

W. Terry Whalin is a literary agent at Whalin Literary Agency, LLC. For the last five years, he has been a book acquisitions editor for Howard Books, an imprint of Simon & Schuster, and Cook Communications. A prolific writer and editor, his articles have appeared in more than 50 magazines including *Christianity Today* and *Writer's Digest*. Whalin is currently on the board of directors of the American Society of Journalists and Authors (ASJA), the leading organization for nonfiction writers in the U.S. He has written more than 60 nonfiction books including *Book Proposals That $ell: 21 Secrets To Speed Your Success*. To encourage writers of nonfiction and fiction, he is the creator of www.Right-Writing.com, which offers a free newsletter, *Right Writing News*.

# Running a Critique Group

*by Linda Adams*

FELLOW WRITER Emory Hackman and I started our critique group three years ago and have learned a lot about how to run them since then. I think a lot of people start one because they want their own work critiqued—and the reality sets in as the personalities of each member clashes. These are some things that we learned in the course of our meetings:

## Things to Do

Be willing to lead the group. That means doing some things that you may not like to do: Deciding who gets critiqued each meeting; interrupting the meeting when it goes off topic for too long; dealing with a member who is being defensive or abusive; or encouraging someone to leave the group.

Set rules and follow them. This gives guidance and direction and helps everyone get along. Some of the rules we used include:

> Have a minimum of 100 pages completed before submitting for critique. We had several members receive a critique on projects where they'd written a chapter or two—and both gave up the project after receiving the critique. After writing 100 pages, a writer is not as likely to drop a project because of a critique as he will be for 15 pages.
> Submit 50 pages to the group. We came up with this number because it's enough to start to see how the story is taking shape. More than that is too much for most people to deal with easily.
> Email material two weeks before the meeting. This particular rule was created because we had two writers during our first year who would routinely email chapters out a day before the meeting. It just simply wasn't enough time to read and critique the material. Two weeks allows everyone to fit it into their schedules.

> Writers being critiqued cannot explain or defend their work. The writer's not going to be there to look over the reader's shoulder and explain it, so the manuscript has to stand up for itself.

Stick to your guns. There's always going to be some member who doesn't like the way things are done and will try to convince you to change, even if you don't think it's good for the group. Do be willing to listen to ideas, but don't let the members tell you what to do.

## Things to Avoid

No booze during critiquing. It's just a bad combination, especially if the person being critiqued is also drinking. Alcohol will only make his reactions worse.

Reading the stories aloud at the meetings. This is apparently pretty common in many meetings. The problem with this is twofold: First, the book is not being read the way an agent will be reading it, and second, the writer can add subtle details with their voice that may mask problems that would be visible in text.

Not sharing the critiques aloud at the meeting. At another critique group, the members wrote down their comments and passed it to the writer (after the writer read the story aloud). No one else heard or saw any of the critiques. One of the huge benefits of critiques is for everyone to hear what everyone has to say. There is always something to be learned from hearing everyone do critiques.

Critiquing can be fun and a good learning experience, but it does start with good leadership.

Linda Adams served nine years in the U.S. Army, with service in the first war in the Persian Gulf. She now lives in Northern Virginia. With co-writer Emory Hackman, she is working on a Civil War thriller set in the Shenandoah Valley. She is a member of International Thriller Writers and Washington Independent Writers.

This piece appeared October 2006 as a guest entry on the blog of Backspace website coordinator Karen Dionne.

# Snappy Introductions

*by Judy Bridges*

THE PERFECT WAY to introduce your work to a critique group is simply. No set up. No apology: "This is the first half of chapter one."

This way, the group is welcomed to the page and can respond the same as the final reader or editor.

But even the most confident, competent writers can get nervous now and then and turn simple introductions into blinkers. In Redbird Studio workshops, we save the intros that don't tell us quite as much as the writers hoped they would.

*This is the beginning of something longer.*

*This is a possible first draft.*

*This is a little experiment. It's like an idea, okay?*

*I was so sure no one would be here.*

*Let's just get this over with.*

*My thing is really stupid.*

*This is too long.*

*I didn't write for crap this week.*

*This is the start of something.*

*I hope this measures up to my usual standard of mediocrity.*

*This is something I wrote so I might as well read it.*

*This is just a continuation of something I started.*

*I can't seem to write, so this is just something.*

*I had to bring something 'cuz I wanted to come.*

*A word of caution about this ...*

*I'm going to read this anyway, because I wrote it.*

*This is half of a short story I just started writing.*

*This is the first draft of the possible start, or it could appear in the middle....*

Judy Bridges is the founder and director of Redbird Studio in Milwaukee, where she and other writers and teachers lead workshops and enjoy the challenge of helping writers find their voice. She says she makes less money teaching than when she was writing, but teaching is a whole lot easier. She holds degrees in writing and adult education and has also taught at Alverno College, University of Wisconsin–Milwaukee, and The Clearing.

Her website is: www.redbirdstudio.com.

# My First Rule of Information

*by Marylaine Block*

MY RULES of information developed from watching students flounder and misfire in their quests. Often the reason they don't find what they want is that they are looking in the wrong place—trying to find articles about Bosnia in Medline, for example.

That's why my first rule of information is *go where it is*. We librarians know, as our users sometimes do not, that information comes in different forms, and each form has different advantages and drawbacks.

**Books** are where we go for extensive background, history, and analysis. Books generalize. If you think of original research as the pieces of the puzzle, the authors of books are putting the pieces together and figuring out what the pattern is.

**Journal articles** are small, very specific pieces of the puzzle that report on original experiments and surveys, or analyze extremely narrow aspects of a topic. Where a book might generalize about the decline of frog populations, a journal article would speak only about what the researcher could observe and test: the decline of one specific population in one specific location, or the results of an experiment testing one possible cause.

**The internet** has a little of everything. Its greatest strength is that it is always available. It is also an unparalleled source for pictures and demonstrations. Any time your question is "what does it look like?" or "how does it work?" the internet should be our source of choice. The federal government is totally online, and the states are well on their way, so if you want laws, tax forms, statistics, information about NIH drug trials, think internet first.

The net is your best source for late-breaking news (but stick to reputable news sources like CNN or Reuters). Frequently Asked Questions Files and online encyclopedias provide great introductions to topics at an elementary level.

Check the Librarians' Internet Index (http://search.lii.org/index.jsp?more=SubTopic10) for a set of sites that answer our most common questions. Because internet sites are keyword searchable, you have a decent chance of finding the lyrics to a rock song, the name of a book you only remember the plot to, your cousin's zip code, which DVD player to buy, which movies Kevin Bacon appeared in—you name it.

Is there scholarly research available on the net? Yes, just as there are, in fact, zebras in the U.S. But when you want zebras in bulk, you go to Africa, and when you want scholarly studies in bulk, you go to your library's website and use the full-text online journal indexes it purchased with your tax dollars. You see, the net is more than just a collection of web sites. It's also a delivery medium for high-quality, full-text magazine, newspaper, and journal articles.

You want the quality assurance librarians provide because the greatest flaw in the internet is that there are no IQ requirements for admission—all anyone needs is a computer and a service provider.

### Ask a Librarian

Knowing how to play nifty tricks with search engines is one reason librarians are good at finding answers on the net. But I think the real reason we succeed so often is because we know where to go in the first place; we understand how information works, who produces it, and where is the most likely place to search for anything.

When people ask us a question, we automatically start by figuring out who would produce that piece of information. If somebody wants to know what cities have the biggest roach problem, I head immediately to a full-text database of business magazines, figuring that the people who might have an answer are the people who will make money by knowing it: the pesticide manufacturers and their advertisers. They lay out lots of money for market surveys, and the results of these are often reported on in business and marketing magazines.

Not long ago, I did a couple of workshops for the Delaware Instructional Technology Conference, and one of the questions that came up was a standard research project their students are asked to do on Delaware watersheds. I immediately began itemizing the agencies that logically might collect information about those watersheds: the U.S. Geological Survey, the Army Corps of Engineers, the Delaware Department of the Environment, the U.S. Environmental Protection Agency, the U.S. Fish and Wildlife Service.

I sensed a theme emerging here, so I immediately went to Google Government Search (www.google.com/ig/usgov), which searches sites from federal, state, regional, and local governments, fed in the term "Delaware watershed," and got an immense collection of documents from all levels of government.

But I also figured this was not just a policy question but a science question as well, so I also went to SciSeek (www.sciseek.com) and asked the question there. There was overlap with the Google Government Search results, but there were also a lot of unique results from scientific and engineering sites here.

Since this topic would be written about by researchers in science journals, the next step was going to full-text article databases. In EbscoHost, I searched simultaneously through MasterFile Premier, Newspaper Source, and Academic Search Elite, and found hundreds of articles, not only from science journals, but from regional newspapers and magazines like *Fly Fisherman*.

Librarians are good at internet searching because we know where we need to go and the quickest routes for getting there; we are equipped not just with compasses but with mental maps of the information landscape.

> Because we know our collections cold.
> Because sometimes people give up when the answers weren't in the places they expected to find them. (How often is the real question concealed behind the question, "Where's the *Readers' Guide?*")
> Because we try to figure out the actual information need and fit it to the way our systems are organized.
> Because we are better at thinking up and down a continuum—if we don't have books on Siamese cats, we do have books on cat breeds and cat care; we also have magazine indexes and databases that will find us articles on Siamese cats; we may even have the right sort of books in the children's collection where the patron didn't think to look.
> Because we know how to make the databases sit up, roll over, and lick our faces. The fact that our users did not find an answer doesn't mean it doesn't exist. (The fact that *we* didn't might, however.)

> Because, unlike our users, we start out with the gut-deep convic-
tion that the answer *exists*, and by God, on our honor as librarians,
we *are* going to find it.

We also know that, for many questions, search engines won't help at
all, because the information needed is not *on* the Internet. Perhaps it's
hiding in a 1935 issue of *Harper's*, or an 1865 issue of the *New York Times*,
or a book that compares and contrasts the administration of health
insurance in various European nations, or an unpublished disserta-
tion, or a proprietary market survey conducted by Proctor & Gamble,
or a Senate committee hearing from 1965.

Whether consciously aware of it or not, when anybody asks us a
question, the first thing we do is sort through our mental maps of the
information territory. By the time we say, "Let's try running a search on
Medline," we've already assessed the user's need (information about
a specific therapy for a medical condition) and knowledge-level (medical professional or student) and decided where the relevant and useful
information can most likely be found (articles in the medical literature).

No matter what the question, we go through that same mapping
and sorting process: asked for reproductions of art works, we go to our
art encyclopedias or to the Internet; asked what a dollar would buy
in 1966, we go to *Historical Statistics* or *Statistical Abstracts* or to ads in
local newspapers from 1966. Different tools retrieve different kinds of
information, and part of the art of librarianship is knowing which tool
works best for each job.

We also know better than to trust the authority and accuracy of the
Internet. You will almost certainly find a quote you seek on the Internet—often multiple versions of it. Don't count on being able to tell
which one is correct, because their source is rarely specified. Our attitude toward Net sources is as suspicious as a Cold War warrior: Trust,
but only after you verify.

We know that sometimes the best sources are ordinary people,
individually or in groups, who are passionate about a subject—and the
third thing the net does is let you find and talk to each other. When
our users want solid, authoritative information about diabetes, for
example, we lead them to the Web page for the American Diabetes
Association. When users want to talk to fellow sufferers about their

experiences and what it's like to live with the disease, we lead them to support groups.

When we want to know whether a brand-new technology or game works, we listen in on discussion groups on the Net. And when a topic is utterly obscure, we go online, because the Net is the perfect place for eccentrics to share their passion for bagpipes, or medieval maps, or bad Scrabble hands.

Think of us searchers as travel agents in the world of information: we help our travelers get there faster because we know the best routes and whether to go by plane, train, or automobile.

Marylaine Block was an English teacher, then a librarian for 22 years, eventually associate director for public services at St. Ambrose University in Davenport, Iowa, where she established the website Best Information on the Net. She now edits a weekly e-zine, *ExLibris*, for librarians and speaks and writes on the topic of the Internet and information. She has authored two books for the library profession, *Net Effects: How Librarians Can Manage the Unintended Consequences of the Internet*, and *The Quintessential Searcher*.

Her website is: www.marylaine.com.

# PITCHING & PROPOSALS

# How to Pitch your Stories to an Editor

*by Paula Neal Mooney*

"HELP A YOUNG WRITER," read the subject line of an e-mail I received from a newspaper copy editor friend. He'd landed a gig moonlighting as a journalism professor, and one of his female students was itching to break into the glossies.

So I showed her three of my pitches, along with their laminated published counterparts in my portfolio. But equally as beneficial to the newbie writer (and upon reflection, to me) were the stories not on the pages—the real deals behind what it took to get each byline, and the education gained with each clip:

## 1. Get in where you fit in.

Simultaneous submission freak that I am, I pitched an article titled "Ten Ways to Beat the Stay-at-Home Blues" to several parenting publications, but no one bit. Then one night many months later I saw the article's headline printed in a magazine's index in my dream. Moving on divine impulse, I dug up my old query, rewrote the boring thing into a lively and punchy pitch, and shot it off to *ePregnancy*.

A senior editor at the magazine named Julia Rosien was interested, but said her editorial calendar was chock full of features. She gave me three choices: to wait it out and try to squeeze in the following year, cut it down and sell it to them as a filler, or pitch it somewhere else.

Letting go of my center-spread fantasy, I cut out huge chunks of tips and so did Julia, leaving a scant 350 words and $50 fee. Why did I choose this drastic route? With its current readership of 1.6 million, *ePregnancy* was a clip worth "slaying all my darlings" to get—ASAP.

## 2. Give editors tons of space and grace.

Soon after I sent the pitch that became "Dutch Twins: How to Manage Two Kids Under age Two" to *MetroBaby* magazine, I received a handwritten note from an editor saying she'd look at it on spec. I completed the manuscript, shipped it off with excitement, then heard nothing but silence. I slumped into my writer funk, assuming she hated it.

A whole year later, I received a package containing the latest issue of the magazine with my 4-page spread and a $100 check. At first I berated my neophyte self for not following up sooner, but in retrospect, this wait-and-see tactic was a lot more successful than the antagonizing "tell-me-yay-or-nay-now-Busy-Editor-so-I-can-pitch-this-gem-to-a-more-worthy-monthly" approach I adopted later.

Unexpected manna in the mailbox taught me that editors need time to respond—a lot more than eager scribes afford them. Proposed ideas may flourish when allowed to germinate and resonate, to nag at guts till folks can't help but call you. Forget about that latest pitch for the time being and get busy planting lots more good seed in other markets. Besides, magazines shift focus. Scheduled articles fall through. Planets shift. Don't be a bugaboo.

## 3. But move like lightening when they call.

I was lounging around in bed when *Woman's Life* called and asked me to write "Guests Coming? Six Fast and Fun Ways to Clean," a letter I'd snail-mailed them the previous year.

Instead of seething over the fact that my genius took forever to climb Mt. Slush, I dug up what I promised them to begin with (some pitches were languishing on my old computer in the basement) and got busy writing. After a while I had another much-needed mag to add to my bio and 250 more bucks in my bank account.

All in all, what rang true for one pitch rang true for the trio. I learned that the trip from initial query to tear sheet can be a matter of patience and proper timing. And that peddlers of words need to be flexible, forgiving and fast—lessons well-worth the journey it took to learn them.

## Real-life Pitch #1

Ms. Julia Rosien
Senior "Steps" Editor
*ePregnancy*
5742 West Harold Gatty Drive, Suite 113
Salt Lake City, UT 84116

Dear Ms. Rosien:

Cabin fever in a house with kids can drive anybody to the brink of *The Shining*-like madness.

"Ten Ways to Beat the Stay-at-Home Blues" is a 750-word article that helps caregivers overcome some of the major downfalls of raising children full-time.

The piece describes how to convert the house into a haven for both adults and kids, plus lays out a plan to develop some of the fun activities which children in formal day-care settings experience. Quotes from successful full-time mothers are included.

Accompanying photographs are available by request.

I am a freelance writer and stay-at-home mom of two who specializes in parenting topics. Enclosed please find my recent clip from *Pregnancy* magazine that appeared as a cover article.

Please reply to cpmooney@aol.com or return the enclosed SASE to request a copy of the article or to discuss other assignments.

Sincerely,
Paula Mooney

## Real-life Pitch #2

Ms. Susan DeMaggio
MetroParent Publishing Group
22041 Woodward Ave.
Ferndale, MI 48220

Dear Ms. DeMaggio:

"Wow! You had them close together," most people exclaim upon seeing my 3-month-old daughter and 21-month-old son. "How do you manage?"

"Manage 2 Kids Under 2" is a 750-word article which helps parents raising a baby and a toddler together keep their sanity.

The piece details how to synchronize sleep schedules, make everyday tasks such as grocery shopping easier and keep an infant safe from their rambunctious older sibling. Quotes from parents of two children under two years of age and experts in the child-rearing field will also appear in the article.

Accompanying photographs are available upon request.

I am a freelance writer who specializes in parenting topics. Enclosed please find a copy of my cover article that appeared in a recent issue of *Pregnancy* magazine.

Please return the included SASE or email cpmooney@aol.com for a copy of the article.

Sincerely,
Paula Mooney

### Real-life Pitch #3

Ms. Jennifer L. Knaack
Articles Editor
*Woman's Life*
500 N. Commercial St.
Neenah, WI 54956

Dear Ms. Knaack:

It's Saturday; you're relaxing. Suddenly your husband's parents call from their cell phone to say they'll be over in ten minutes. Your mind's eye darts from the line of grime that circles the tub to the shards of Doritos enmeshed in the carpet. What do you do?

To the rescue comes "Six Fast and Fun Ways to Clean," a 750-word article that explains how to spruce up quickly and have a blast doing so. Included are tips to help readers:

Tidy Up Fast ...
> via disposable cleaning products (and how to create inexpensive home versions)
> through doubling up on appliances like vacuum cleaners and clothes dryers

> by practicing daily tasks that cut time spent cleaning huge week-end messes

Make Chores Fun ...
> when you turn straightening up into a game and involve the kids
> by employing music to distract from the most distasteful duties
> with the latest storage gear designed to make organizing enjoyable

As for me, I'm known as "Burn 'Em Up, Jr.," offspring of "Old Burn 'Em Up," as my dad fondly dubbed my mother. Neither of us are gifted to cook—our forte is cleaning.

I am a freelance writer who specializes in parenting and marital topics. Enclosed please find a copy of my cover article that was featured in the November issue of *Pregnancy* magazine. Accompanying photographs are available upon request.

Please return the enclosed SASE or email cpmooney@aol.com for a copy of the article.

Sincerely,
Paula Mooney

Paula Mooney is editor-in-chief of *Real Moms* magazine and lives in Akron, Ohio.

# The Blind Pitch

*by Whitney Joiner*

So, YOU HAVE an idea for a freelance feature that's absolutely perfect for *Glamour*, but everyone you know works at *Money* or *Fortune*. And no one they know works at *Glamour*, either. Time for one of the most terrifying aspects of freelancing: the blind pitch.

Emailing an editor blindly to propose your amazing idea can be incredibly daunting. But just because you don't have any connections to a magazine doesn't mean you'll become a media Sisyphus, destined to write for the same five titles forever. Here are some tips on how to get your pitch noticed.

### 1. No phone calls, please.

Never, ever, cold-call an editor. She's super busy, or she's late for a meeting, or she's thinking about that night's drinks date—whatever. She'll feel like she's been put on the spot (well, she has) and she won't have time to actually listen to your idea. Email your pitch instead.

"If I have something in writing, I'm going to follow up on it," says *Outside* dispatches editor Jason Daley. "If you just call me and I'm doing something while we're talking, you're probably not going to hear back from me."

Email is faster and easier, and it gives editors the chance to mull over your ideas. "I can read email on my timetable," says *Yoga Journal* senior editor Matthew Solan. "I can print it out."

And email allows the editor to forward your pitch. "If a query jumps that first hurdle of being interesting and plausible, you're going to send it around to a couple of people on staff," says *Reason* editor-in-chief Nick Gillespie. "Emailing really facilitates sharing."

### 2. Get in and get out.

Brevity is essential to a good blind pitch. A short concise pitch shows an editor that you're a tight writer and you respect her time.

"Ideally, you should outline the story in a format that's as short as the space allocated for the Table of Contents page," says *Gear* senior editor Luke Dawson. "You should be able to express your idea in three or four lines." Your emailed blind pitch should be about three paragraphs, says Gillespie.

In the first graf, introduce yourself: who you are, where you've published, what you know about the publication, and the idea itself.

Then add a graf detailing why you're qualified to write the story and why it would be of interest to the audience.

Finish with a graf that thanks the editor and points her to your clips. (If you have amazing clips that you can't email, send them simultaneously via snail mail.)

### 3. Know the magazine.

Why do editors toss most of the blind pitches they receive? Because the writer doesn't have a firm grasp of the magazine's content. It's the number-one editorial complaint about blind pitches.

"Believe it or not, I think 90% of the people who email me have never even picked up *Latina*," says *Latina* senior lifestyle editor Anamary Pellayo. "They'll pitch things and I'm like, 'If you've ever read us, [you'd know] we've never covered that type of topic.'"

Don't pitch a piece on prostate cancer to women's health and fitness magazine *Self*, for instance. "That's happened," says Elizabeth Anne Shaw, *Self*'s senior health editor. "Or little kids, or elder care— issues we've never covered and never would. I ignore pitches if they completely miss the boat and clearly have no idea what *Self* is about."

Obviously, you're not at the weekly editorial meetings; you don't know what the staff has planned for upcoming issues. Editors realize this. (In fact, if you've pitched something that's similar to a feature in the next issue, it works in your favor—it shows that your thinking jibes with the magazine's.) But make sure that you're extremely familiar with the most recent newsstand issue, at least.

### 4. Focus, focus, focus.

"The more focused a story can be, the stronger the pitch is going to be. If it's too big you're relying on me to whittle it down, and I don't want to do that," says Solan.

Tailor your idea for a specific section in the magazine, and pitch that editor. He'll appreciate your effort, and if he can't use it, he might send it to another editor.

### 5. Do the research.

A blind pitch is a long shot, sure, but that doesn't mean you should skimp on the background for your pitch. Make a few calls: one or two for a small item; a few more for a feature pitch, suggests *Self*'s Shaw.

Yeah, it's a lot of work for something that might not pay off—but from your editor's point of view, it's worth it.

"I get a lot of pitches that say, 'I want to do five ways to beat a cold and flu, and I'm going to talk to this expert,'" she says. "But they haven't talked to them yet, and they haven't given me any hint as to what the advice will be like. I can't bring that to my editors. Save yourself the aggravation and the delay and do a little bit of research."

### 6. Offer alternatives.

Make sure an editor knows you're flexible: suggest a few different ways to use your idea. It shows her that you're creative and committed to your idea, and it increases your chances to get in the magazine.

"Sometimes we may be working on a story that a pitch falls into," says Pellayo. "You want to make sure that if that happens you can get in there and be part of that story—even if it's just a small sidebar."

Scoring a blind pitch isn't impossible; in fact, most editors say they want to find new writers and new ideas. It's just more challenging than using your connections.

"Blind pitching is very hard," says Pellayo. "But it also feels like quite a coup when you do grab an assignment and you can say to yourself, wow, I got that without knowing anybody. It's the greatest feeling. You think, okay, maybe I am in the right profession."

Whitney Joiner is a former features editor at *Seventeen* magazine. Her work also appears in the *New York Times*, *Salon*, and *Spin*. She lives in Marfa, Texas.

# Pitching your Book to an Agent

*by Katharine Sands*

DO YOU REALLY need an agent? Why would you want a complete stranger to take 15% of the monies you might generate as an author?

If you need convincing, try this test: call a major publishing house yourself and see what happens. Chances are you'd spend a frustrating time and never get out of voice mail. If you do manage to get a live person on the phone, it will probably be an editorial assistant, who will tell you to get an agent. Agents are, in effect, a screening service for their publishers. Editors want agents to do the representing and to bring to them writers whose works fit their publisher program.

How could you possibly know which editor at each imprint might want to acquire and publish your book? Only agents know this, learning—lunch by lunch, call by call—which editor is looking for which kind of book, who does not want to acquire certain categories, and how much each editor's personal taste and house "personality" affects who gets published.

## Making the Pitch to an Agent

It's the pitch and nothing but the pitch that gets a writer selected from the leaning tower of queries in a literary agent's office. Are you writing a novel that will keep readers turning pages, instead of turning in for a good night's sleep? Will your book show readers how to talk to the dead, trim their thighs, manage their money, make better love—or all at the same time? Then get ready to distill the most dynamic, exciting, and energized points about your work: your pitch.

Your pitch is the passport that you carry into the literary marketplace. Why is pitching your work so important? Because whether for fiction, faction, nonfiction, thriller, chiller, cozy, category romance, or chick lit, it's the pitch and nothing but the pitch that gets an agent's attention.

The writing you do about your writing is as important as the writing itself. To effectively introduce a novel or book idea to a literary agent, you must persuade him/her that there is a readership for your book. The writing about your writing is part "hello," part cover letter, part interview for the coveted job of book author. It's the best of the best of the best of your writing. If you were an Olympic figure skater, it would be your triple axel on the ice.

Yes, agents do deeply care about the craft of writing. But understand that now you are taking your work into the literary marketplace. Like any other industry, the book business has certain quirks and processes and challenges. For you, the writer, these are separate from the act of creativity itself.

"Publishing must tread the tightrope between art and commerce," says agent Michael Larsen of San Francisco. "Publishers want books that they can publish with pride and with passion, but to survive, they must publish books that sell."

An agent needs to know from the get-go why you will appeal to readers. You must put aside your deep connection to your work and even the amount of work you have put into it. Your work is literary wares that you are now selling in the literary marketplace.

Although many agents became agents because they love literature, venerate books, and wrote papers on the novels of Jane Austen in school, this alone does not spell success for an agent in the business. One succeeds by having what P.T. Barnum described as "the ability to see what is all around you just waiting to be seen." We see raw material, raw ideas, and the gleam in authors' eyes. Then, we envision how these could be grown into a book. We ask ourselves how your writing will be considered inside a publishing house, how your writing—as a literary property—would succeed in its bid for publication. This is paramount in our minds from first write to last rights.

The way you query an agent—the way you introduce your work—must be influenced by these things. They are more than trends. If you want to understand and speak the language of bookselling, answer the question posed by editor Max Perkins (who discovered Hemingway and Fitzgerald), still being used by editors today: "Why does the world need this book?"

Make sure the reasons readers would like it are clear. The way publishing professionals look at your work is the difference between how a loved one looks at you and how your doctor looks at you. To your loved one, you are a sight for sore eyes, loved, chosen. But to your doctor, you're a bunch of symptoms and a gaggle of body parts. You're still you; but you are regarded differently. Literary agents read writers' works to diagnose the page, to make a prognosis—a professional assessment of how that work will fare.

## Your Query Letter

Imagine you are Atticus Finch arguing for the life of an innocent. Because you are. Your query letter is a plea for life.

> A good query answers the three questions I will have: why [nonfiction writers] are uniquely qualified, who the audience is for the book, and what the competing books are.... For fiction, I'm just really looking for good writing; I think the letter should really pique my interest in some way. If the letter isn't well-written, it is unlikely that I'll believe that the novel will hold my interest. The letter is the first indication for me of their ability to communicate.
> —Anna Ghosh (literary agent)

Go ahead, give these a try: Start writing long descriptions of your book, your market, yourself. Then shrink them down to query size. What is your strongest area? Your credentials? Your book idea? The potential market?

> One page, that's how brief your query letter should be. Never, ever, go longer than one page. You need to distill your brilliance, your wisdom, and your expertise into one potent page-long brew that will leave a reader reeling from its power.
> —Sheree Bykofsky (literary agent)

## Some Tips

1. Interview yourself.

Pretend you are about to be interviewed on your favorite talk show. What would you say if you were on *Oprah*? What would you want your listeners, your readers to know about your work?

Think of and write out five questions. Answer them. Your answers can now be crafted into your pitch in 25–50 words. Practice your pitch in front of the mirror or the cat. Think of your pitch as a show—produced, written, and directed by you. Your query is a kind of performance; think of it as theater of the page.

2.  Practice your pitchcraft in the form of a sound bite.
What are the best words and phrases to use? Remember to pick a set of complementary descriptive words that work well together.

3.  Have you identified your hooks?
Hooks are the most exciting elements to compel your reader and propel your story. Think of a way of building in a cliffhanger, a question in the reader's mind to be answered by more reading.

 "The best query letters have a strong hook in the first two lines. What is a strong hook? Something that grabs the reader's attention and keeps them reading," says Sheree Bykofsky.

4.  Think of your pitch as a movie trailer.
Imagine your setting, your world, your universe for someone who has not lived in it before. You, the writer, are a camera. Put the camera on one character, the setting, the aliens ...

 Have you set up the reader and communicated quickly your concept and the overview, the impact? Have you identified what is provocative and compelling in your overview, your argument for the book's life, your insights, what's fresh and unique, your ability and authority?

 Have you told a story arc? "It starts here, ends there ... boy meets girl, boy loses girl, boy gets girl." It is the old Hollywood chestnut, but it works.

 "Study ads, movie trailers, junk mail," says Jeff Herman. "Junk mail is a free mail-order course in how to write excellent copy. Junk mail is a billion-dollar industry that test-markets how to write copy that will have an impact."

 Are you leading with the most important points?

 Do you have evidence, statistics, articles, zeitgeist? Point out why readers want this book. Argue your case. Pretend your book is on trial. Indeed, an acquisitions editorial meeting is a trial for life for your work.

Do the descriptive words, tone, and intention match? If you are writing a dark and disturbing thriller, the pitch should reflect that. For chick lit, you want a cute, punchy title and voice.

5.  Communicate the excitement!

Writing is solitary; publishing is collaborative. The key point: you want to get others excited about what is exciting to you. If you don't get them to read your work, you are not going to get anything else. An assistant or editorial reader's job is to review and pass the promising queries to the agent. Each query gets a cursory glance from the reader. She looks at the work for a minute and makes the decision to read more or to reject it. This is why it's so important to give a reader a reason to read more, and why you have to do it fast.

"Now is the most exciting time ever to be alive, and it's the best time ever to be a writer," says Michael Larsen of the Larsen-Pomada agency. "[T]he age of information is also the age of the writer."

It is indeed an exciting time to be writing. Machines cannot produce content. We need hearts and minds for that.

We need writers!

## Resources

Association of Authors Representatives (AAR)
www.aar-online.org

National Writers Union (NWU)
www.nwu.org
Trade union for writers of all genres; members have access to databases, including one for agents, and materials on understanding the agent-author relationship.

Genre Associations
Professional associations for writers of mystery, science fiction and fantasy, romance, western, and other genres maintain and share lists of agents most active in that genre.

Agent Query
www.agentquery.com
A searchable database of agents, with tips on how to submit your work.

Publisher's Marketplace
www.publishersmarketplace.com
Includes a searchable database of agents.

## Books

*Literary Market Place*
This large reference book, available at your local library, includes agents, submission guidelines, and interests.

*Jeff Herman's Guide to Book Publishers, Editors, and Literary Agents*
Features hundreds of agents, and details their likes and dislikes.

*How to Get a Literary Agent,* by Michael Larsen (Sourcebooks, 2006)

*The Complete Idiot's Guide to Getting Published,* by Sheree Bykofsky and Jennifer Basye Sander (Alpha, 2006)

Katharine Sand is a literary agent with the Sarah Jane Freymann Literary Agency, located in New York City, where she represents a range of authors in diverse categories. She is also a frequent speaker for writers' conferences around the country and the editor of the book *Making the Perfect Pitch: How To Catch a Literary Agent's Eye* (The Writer Books, 2004). Portions of this piece appear in that work in an article titled "Practicing Pitch-craft."

# How to Write a Query Letter

*by Brenda Coulter*

So you've written—or are in the middle of writing—a romance novel. Sooner or later, you'll work up the nerve to query an editor. But where do you start? How do you write an effective query letter?

Maybe the best way to explain this is to show you the query letter that worked for me. Give it a quick read-through. If you like it, ask yourself why. If you think I did something wrong, try to put your finger on it. Then we'll break it into parts and discuss those.

## A Successful Query Letter

[On my letterhead, with my name, address, and e-mail address.]

August 31, 2001
Ms. [Editor's Name, Editor's Title]
Steeple Hill Books
Address

Dear Ms. [Editor's Name]:

Steeple Hill's "Love Inspired" series is a breath of fresh air in the romance genre. I'd love to partner with you in offering these wholesome choices to romance readers. I hope you'll agree that the story I've written is perfect for your line.

In *A Regular Sweetheart*, Dr. Charles Hartman is a gifted trauma surgeon with all the people skills of a wounded grizzly bear. Although he maintains that he cares nothing for people or for God, he begins to believe differently after Hope Evans, a softhearted graduate student, slams into his Mercedes—and his life—putting a completely different spin on his carefully-ordered world.

Charles has never believed in anything, but he learns to trust Hope's rock-steady friendship. When she falls for him and he is unable to return her love, the only honorable course is for him to walk away. But how can he turn his back on the only true friend he has ever known? Can he bear to give up Hope?

*A Regular Sweetheart* is long on the romantic tension your readers clamor for. And with its twin themes of trust and loyalty, the story is spiritually uplifting as well as emotionally satisfying.

The manuscript is complete, waiting only for me to lick a few stamps and send it to you. It weighs in at 75,000 words.

I'm enclosing a synopsis. Thank you for your consideration.

Sincerely,
[My signature]
Enclosures

After this story was sold, the title was changed to *Finding Hope*.

## A Closer Look

I knew nothing about how to query an editor, so I just wrote this up like a normal business letter. In retrospect, I think it worked pretty well. I had a product to sell, so I began with a compliment, told her exactly what I had to offer, explained how it would meet the needs of her customers, and finished by thanking her for her consideration of my sales pitch. Pretty simple, huh?

*Dear Ms. [Editor's Name]:*

First off, I knew which editor I was targeting. "Dear Editor" or "To whom it may concern" would have marked me as someone who hadn't bothered to do her homework. I'm glad I didn't shoot myself in the foot.

*Steeple Hill's "Love Inspired" series is a breath of fresh air in the romance genre. I'd love to partner with you in offering these wholesome choices to romance readers. I hope you'll agree that the story I've written is perfect for your line.*

This wasn't meant as a smarmy compliment. I wanted the editor to know that I was very familiar with Love Inspired and had specifically targeted that line.

*In* A Regular Sweetheart, *Dr. Charles Hartman is a gifted trauma sur-*
*geon with all the people skills of a wounded grizzly bear. Although he*
*maintains that he cares nothing for people or for God, he begins to believe*
*differently after Hope Evans, a softhearted graduate student, slams into*
*his Mercedes—and his life—putting a completely different spin on his*
*carefully-ordered world.*

    *Charles has never believed in anything, but he learns to trust Hope's*
*rock-steady friendship. When she falls for him and he is unable to return*
*her love, the only honorable course is for him to walk away. But how can*
*he turn his back on the only true friend he has ever known? Can he bear*
*to give up Hope?*

This is the most important part of the letter, but there was nothing
scary about writing it. I simply set up my story, explained the conflict,
and then added a little teaser. (This is similar to the "blurbs" we see
on the back covers of books. Think along those lines and you'll be on
the right track.)

The purpose of these two paragraphs was to get the editor interested in reading my synopsis. That's it. That's why I didn't go into any
detail, and that's why I didn't give away the story's ending. If she's
intrigued, all she has to do is turn the page and start reading the synopsis.

There is absolutely no reason to make your query letter more than
one page long.

A Regular Sweetheart *is long on the romantic tension your readers*
*clamor for. And with its twin themes of trust and loyalty, the story is spir-*
*itually uplifting as well as emotionally satisfying.*

Again, I was telling her that I know her line very well. I know why readers buy Love Inspired books, and I believed my story would appeal to
them.

*The manuscript is complete, waiting only for me to lick a few stamps and*
*send it to you. It weighs in at 75,000 words.*

Okay, that sounds a little flippant, but that's me. I write the way I talk.
The salient fact was that the manuscript was complete. This told the

editor two things: that I'm capable of finishing what I start, and that she could have the full manuscript right away, should she request it.

Mentioning the length told her that, again, I had done my homework. (Love Inspired wants 70–75,000.) Also, there was no need for me to say "about" 75,000 words. Of course it's a ballpark figure.

*I'm enclosing a synopsis. Thank you for your consideration.*

Short and sweet: Here it is, thanks for your time. No flowery phrases, no "Should you have any questions, please do not hesitate to ... blah, blah, blah."

*Sincerely,*
*[My signature]*
*Enclosures*

The enclosures were, of course, my synopsis and my self-addressed, stamped envelope. And by the way, I saw no point in telling her that I was enclosing the SASE. That's an immutable standard in this business, so it would have been a little amateurish to point out that I was conforming to it.

Okay, what was missing from my letter?

Many people would have advised me to list my writing credentials. Well, I didn't have any. I had been writing for less than a year and this was the first manuscript I had ever completed. Maybe you can say more than that, but I think in most cases it comes off sounding a little pathetic. Can't you just imagine an editor rolling her eyes over this:

> *I've been an enthusiastic member of Romance Writers of America for 3 and ¼ years. I'm assistant secretary to the second vice president of my local writer's club. In high school I won an award for writing the best short story in Mrs. Bartlett's class. I have been writing since I could hold a pencil and it has been my lifelong dream to be published. This is the second manuscript I have completed and I have ideas for many, many more.*

Call me a cynic, but I just don't think busy editors give a hoot about our dreams and our little accomplishments. So unless you can say you're a Golden Heart finalist or that you've sold a magazine article, just let your well-written letter stand on its own.

I sent the above letter with a five-page (double-spaced) synopsis. A couple of weeks later, my full manuscript was requested. Several months after that, I was offered a contract.

I hope this real-life example of a "winning" query letter has helped you understand the process.

Brenda Coulter writes "inspirational" romance novels, which are love stories celebrating traditional Christian values. Her award-winning novels include *Finding Hope*, *A Family Forever*, and, forthcoming in Fall 2007, *A Season of Forgiveness*, all published by Steeple Hill.

Her website is: www.brendacoulter.com.

# Perfecting your Live Pitch

*by Paula Roe*

FOR THE AUTHOR, an editor pitch means bypassing the dreaded slush pile and elevating their unsolicited query letter and synopsis to a "requested material" manuscript in 10 minutes. For the editor, it's the possibility of acquiring gold: a new author for their list.

## What a pitch isn't

A pitch isn't you handing over your manuscript in person, nor is it reading your synopsis verbatim. It's a meeting of two professional people, with a view to starting a business relationship.

## How do I prepare?

First, write down the "overview" of the story and characters—their goals, motivations, conflict. Then grab a couple of index cards and sum up your story in a couple of catchy sentences. For example:

> *Is There Love on Mars? is an alternate-historical fantasy set in the year 3100, and targeted at Silhouette's* LUNA *imprint. At approximately 100,000 words, it's a sensual, save-the-world story involving Kane, a geeky time traveler hero and Juno, queen of Mars, who captures him as her sex slave.*

This is known as the "*TV Guide* grab." Back-cover blurbs are perfect for this.

In the above example we've incorporated the marketing and story hooks because the editor will want to know where she can place the novel on the shelves. If your manuscript incorporates a popular story-line or hot premise, use it: marriage of convenience, secret baby, amnesia, in love with the boss, sex for hire, school reunion, bad boy meets good girl. For example, "I have a small-town, second-chance-at-love-story aimed at Silhouette Special Edition."

Make a comparison with films, TV shows or popular themes. This will give the editor a clearer picture of your book (i.e.: *Survivor* in the Antarctic, Lara Croft meets GI Joe, *Charmed* set on Venus). If your story doesn't encompass anything on the screen, use other analogies: "in the tradition of Georgette Heyer," "a modern-day *Wuthering Heights* set in New York city," "Beauty lifting a 100-year-old curse from the beast," or "Cinderfella meets Miss Universe."

## Before your pitch

> Remember to prepare your notes on cards. It's not an exam, so don't struggle with a mental blank!
> Research your editor and his/her publisher. Find out what she's acquiring, what themes, plots or stories that hold her interest. Try a search on Google, check out the *Romantic Times* magazine, back copies of your chapter newsletter, publisher blogs or boards, and by asking questions of other authors and writers;
> Jot down a brief list of your writing achievements;
> Practice your pitch in front of the mirror, with a family member or critique partner. Polish your pitch until you can get the gist of your story across with as little verbiage as possible.

## At the pitch

Generally, pitches run in this order:
> Introduction and exchange of pleasantries;
> You launch into pitch: intro hero/heroine, their basic traits and their inciting incident (how they come together);
> You answer any questions about the novel that the editor may have;
> You talk about your other work, contest successes, other publishing credits, and your background;
> You ask any questions of the editor ("what is your line focusing on now?" "How do you feel about related books in a series?");
> Exchange of business cards and goodbyes.

## Important things to remember

> Be punctual. Lateness doesn't look good, cuts into your pitch time, and tells an editor your writing career isn't that important;

> Wear business clothes to project professionalism: business pants/skirt, shirt and jacket. You can always take the jacket off later;

> Smile and shake the editor's hand when you introduce yourself;

> If applicable, briefly mention meeting her at another conference or online boards (e.g., "I've really been enjoying your 'Editor No-Nos' column at the Ivy authors website.");

> Be prepared to answer questions about other details of your story but resist the urge to keep talking about the plot and overexplaining the details;

> Be modest. Editors are extremely skeptical when writers gush about how fabulous their writing is or claim to be the next Nora Roberts. Let your writing achievements, knowledge of your story and publisher's requirements be proof of your skill;

> Have any other ideas ready if that manuscript isn't what she is looking for (e.g., "I'm also working on a cops-turned-lovers story, aimed at Silhouette Intimate Moments.")

> Be honest. Editor pitches are for complete full manuscripts only but if she wants to see something else, make sure you tell her if it's complete or not (e.g., "The partial on this book is ready to go. Could I send that to you?")

> If there's time, ask her about what she's acquiring: any themes she doesn't want to see, anything she loves;

> Address all requested material to that editor and mark the envelope "Requested Material." Also, in your covering letter, mention when and where you met (editors won't remember every pitch of every book by every writer!).

## Some important don'ts

> Don't pitch an incomplete novel (editors will only buy full manuscripts from first time authors), or one which is inappropriate to the publisher/line (otherwise you're wasting both your time and hers);

> Don't give the editor *anything* other than your business card, which

should have your ms title and "*TV Guide* teaser" on the back. If she wants to see your work, she will request you mail it;

> Don't corner the editor in the toilet/hallway/elevator later and grill her on why she didn't request your manuscript;

> Don't publicly badmouth an editor if she doesn't want to see your work;

> Don't be nervous! Editors are people too, so be yourself and know your story. Enjoy this time to discuss your work because it might just be what the editor is looking for.

Paula Roe is an author of romance novels and a contest judge, web designer, and full-time mom. She is also editor for *Hearts Talk*, a monthly magazine of the Romance Writers of Australia. Her novel *The Forgotten Marriage* is forthcoming from Silhouette Desire (Fall 2007), with a second book to be released in 2008.

Her website is www.paularoe.com.

# Nonfiction Proposals

*by Jeff Kleinman*

WHEN SELLING nonfiction, you don't have to write the entire book: in fact, it's often preferable not to, since that way the editor and publisher can put their own "spin" on the project, provide their own input to make it as marketable as possible to the audience that they (and you) intend to target. Instead of the book, then, you write a "proposal"—a business plan that tells the publisher how you propose to write the book. We're not talking about a long document—anywhere from 10 to 60 pages—but it's a crucial one.

Keep the following issues in mind when you're actually sitting down to write:

**Sales Tool.** A proposal is a sales tool that the agent uses to sell the book to the editor—and that the editor uses to sell the book to the publisher and other editors, to the marketing people, possibly to booksellers and other publishers (for foreign sales), and so forth. You can't be subtle and can't be modest: if you are, at least half the people reading your proposal just won't get it.

**Accessibility.** In most cases, editors and publishers (the publisher is the business person who runs the publishing house—s/he's the editor's boss) are often very young, often in their 20s or 30s. So you need to try to make the proposal as accessible as possible. This means that you should consider using charts, side bars, graphics, tests, and so forth to make the proposal as interactive as possible, as well as to make it look interesting on the page: remember that you're giving this to somebody who was raised on TV, so s/he may have a very short attention span. Of course, the extent of the "look" of your proposal really depends on the subject matter—so if you're dealing with very serious subject matter, and we'll be targeting an academic or very serious house, you need less of the "look"; but a more commercial house may require more bells and whistles.

**Complete & Concrete.** Although the proposal is not supposed to be complete, you should also keep in mind that some editors are not that great at "connecting the dots"—meaning that you should try to make the proposal as complete, and concrete, as possible. Even if your vision of the book changes over time, you still want the editor to feel comfortable and confident that you know what you're doing, that you can write the book, and you know how you're going to do it. This comfort level is very important, and the more ways you're able to demonstrate it, the better.

For example, in your Chapter Outline (see below), you could estimate the number of pages per chapter—even if you really don't have a clue how long the chapter will be, since you haven't written it yet.

Okay, now you hopefully have some general idea on what the proposal will do; here are the issues that every proposal should cover (you can use the sections as we've outlined them here, or modify them as you see fit):

## The Hook
Length: 1 Page. Optional. Depending on the material, it often helps to have something to immediately make the proposal accessible.

For example, if you're writing a book on who needs health insurance, maybe start with a test for the reader, on whether s/he needs health insurance; a proposal for disturbed kids may begin, "Does Your Child Need Help?" Similarly, if the book relies heavily on your writing style, perhaps a brief single page excerpt might do it. Whatever you choose, you want something to immediately grab the reader and pull her in. Some editors say that they like to learn three or four things in the first couple of pages (especially in prescriptive nonfiction), so that's another way of approaching this.

## Overview
Length: 1–3 Pages. Sidebars often helpful here.

This is exactly like the "Executive Summary" of a business plan, if you've ever written one. Here, as clearly and briefly as possible, set out the highlights of the book: what it's about, why it's an important subject, who will be reading it, who the author is, what will set it apart on the bookshelf. Editors, when they're interested in a book, fill out a so-called "Tip Sheet" that they pass around in Editorial Meetings. The Tip Sheet will include the following information:

> Title and subtitle;
> "Sales handle" or "log line"—a single-sentence description describing the proposal in a clever nutshell;
> Production specs including estimated word count, approximate delivery date, and the need/availability for photographs, graphics, or illustrations;
> A paragraph-length positioning "memo," describing where the book will fit in the publishing world;
> The most relevant comparative titles;
> Other relevant marketing information;
> A brief description of the author and the author's credentials, including the author's previous book sale history.

I like the editor to be able to find all the information right in the Overview.

## Author

Length: 1–5 Pages. Your C.V. and previous publications can go in an Appendix.

Who are you, and why are you the best person in the whole world to write this book? That's the biggest question that a publisher will ask. These credentials can quite easily make or break a book sale.

This is no time to be modest: include other books you've written on the subject, your advanced degrees, your media interviews, your lecture schedule (regionally, nationally, and/or internationally), your great personal marketing contacts (e.g., "I was Oprah's Love Slave for years"), whatever—include them here. Your credentials may be nothing more than a passionate interest in the subject, which is also fine—but tell us.

## Annotated Chapter Outline

Length: Varies on the proposal. Plan on spending ½ to ¾ of a page per chapter, assuming that an "average" book chapter will be 20 pages long, when complete.

As clearly and concisely as you can, set out what each chapter will do, and how the book will be organized. Write it as interestingly as possible (so try to avoid "this chapter will discuss …," which adds extra verbiage), in a style that mirrors the book itself (using the same tense, perspective, and so forth). At the same time make clear to the editor that this is only a summary—that there's a lot more material that you haven't been able to cover.

## Sample Chapter

Length: 15–30 pages. May include several sample chapters, but that may not be necessary.

Other than the Author's Credentials, this is the most important part of the proposal. Show that you can write well, communicate effectively, organize your material efficiently, and keep the reader's interest. Obviously what chapter you choose to use will depend on what material you already have available, but you want this chapter to be a representative (i.e., "sample") chapter of the book—not an introduction, or summary. For narrative nonfiction (by way of example), you should show the editor how you address the following types of issues:

> How characters are introduced and developed;
> How facts and medical/expert jargon are dealt with;
> How a scene is set;
> The kind of momentum/pacing the book will have;
> How dialogue and other "novelistic" elements are handled.

You've now dealt with the "personal," most important aspects of the proposal; now you need to concentrate on the supplemental information to really sell this. In order to do this effectively, the basic premise to keep in mind is that you need to fit your book in with the rest of the publishing world. My break-down into three sections here is fairly arbitrary, but all the issues need to be addressed somehow.

## Positioning

Length: 1–2 pages, maybe less.

Fit your book into the greater world of publishing. Find several wildly successful books on whatever subject—it doesn't have to be at all similar to yours—with authors who have credentials similar to yours, with marketing contacts similar to yours, and explain how your book "will be the next" wildly successful book because it has a lot of "package" similarities. Be reasonable and realistic: find books by authors whose credentials really are similar to yours, with a writing style or world view or angle that is somehow similar to yours. "This is *Longitude* for dog lovers," and so forth.

## Market

Length: 2–8 pages. May include letters of support from celebrities, sponsoring organizations, etc.

Who are your readers, and how will you reach them? Do you give lectures and seminars? Have a great web site? Any great publicity tools already in your pocket? (E.g., *Dateline* wants to do a special on you.) This tends to be a hard section to write, but it really helps if you've gone out and gotten information to give the publisher on how many, and what kind, of people will be interested in purchasing your book. It shows you're a "go-getter" and will be effective at selling your book even without the publisher's support.

FYI, never rely on a publisher's plans for publicity. Authors always complain that publishers don't do enough to get the book into the public eye, so you need to be your own best advocate. Show it here.

## Competing Works

Length: 1–4 pages.

Go to your local bookstore and determine where you book will fit on the shelves—and then find the titles that are your book's closest competitors. Show that the book has a niche—that the bookseller will know where to put it, so it doesn't get lost and remain unsold. On the other hand, the book can't get lost among dozens of other similar titles—so explain what sets your book apart from the others, why the reader will buy yours and not theirs.

How you do this depends on the books, but you should never disparage another book (after all, it may have the same publisher/editor who will be looking at your proposal). You should just explain why yours is different (meaning "better"). Complete the following sentence: "My book is the first book that ..."

So that's it. We know it seems like a lot, but when everything's said and done, you're writing one chapter, putting together an outline, and then putting on a lot of ribbons and bows to make this into an effective sales tool. Good luck!

Jeff Kleinman is a literary agent and a founder of Folio Literary Management (www. foliolit.com). He holds advanced degree in Italian Language & Literature from the University of Chicago, and a J.D. from Case Western Reserve University School of Law. He lives in Washington, D.C.

# Working with a Small Press

*by Philip Martin*

LARGE PUBLISHERS increasingly reflect a bestseller mentality, focusing on a strategy of name-brand authors, national ad campaigns, and author tours. But as the big get bigger, small independent press are moving in to fill the gap.

Small presses offer opportunities for new or different authors. As we said in the '60s: small is beautiful. Literary, adventurous, or tightly focused, small presses routinely take chances on new authors. Well-run small presses may have a decent shot at financial success, major awards, and media attention for select titles.

It can be just the right thing for you. But how do you know?

There are thousands of indie presses, as different as cats and dogs and armadillos. They may reflect the personality of a single person working out of a home office. Others have grown into a corporate entities with real offices with potted plants. Some have been around for decades, others for just a few years. Each year a good number disappear, but many new ones rise to take their place.

A tiny micro-press might publish only one or two books a year; others might release a dozen titles a season. First printings tend to be modest, from a digital Print-on-Demand (POD) approach that only prints books as needed to runs of 3,000–5,000 copies.

Their editorial goals range from presenting "new voices" to publishing worthwhile books overlooked by big publishers because they didn't fit somebody's business plan. Small presses create titles from avocado cookbooks to zoo activity guides, and everything in between. The name of the game is: "find the niche."

In total, these myriad presses are responsible for publishing many of the astounding number of well over 100,000 new titles released each year into the American marketplace.

Most prefer the term "independent press" to emphasize their

uniqueness; they don't like to think of their ambitions or talents being diminutive in any sense. However, small press is the term I will use here to focus on the realities of working with most of these publishers: limited resources.

Given this tremendous diversity, what should you expect when dealing with a small press?

## Good Things

**Risk-Taking.** They might consider offbeat submissions or take risks on new writers, something larger presses seldom do.

**Creative & Grassroots Marketing.** The better ones do creative publicity, using grassroots or guerilla tactics. They seek reviews, send catalogs to regional or specialty shops, attend professional conferences. They get books adopted for university courses. They try harder to reach specialized audiences, whether organic gardeners or Hispanic women, and often develop long-term relationships with those communities.

**Editorial Involvement.** A good small press may provide lots of hands-on editorial support to help develop a worthwhile project. Large presses can reject promising but unpolished work, waiting for the ready-to-go, easy-to-sell manuscript. But small presses are generally known for their editorial accessibility and enthusiasm.

**Open to Your Diversity.** Small presses might publish work by an established author who wishes to branch out into a new field. Well-known authors such as Ursula Le Guin, Jane Yolen, Walter Mosley, and Kurt Vonnegut have chosen to publish an occasional book with a smaller press to get important work out into the light of day.

**Patience.** Small presses may shepherd a slow-developing title longer until it reaches its grassroots readership. This is in contrast to large presses, famous for Darwinian tactics of publishing lots of titles, throwing them out to the wolves of trade, then waiting to see which books do well quickly, turning their backs on slow-to-develop titles.

**Loyalty.** Small presses are loyal to their authors. They look favorably on subsequent work, once they have invested their slim resources to develop an author and market interest.

## Negatives

**Minimal Advances.** Small often means just that when it comes to advances. The up-front money handed over to an author can be micro-scopic, from nil to a few thousand dollars. Small presses may point out they prefer to put what money they have into promotions. However, this creates more risk for the author, who must wait for elusive future royalties, without a guaranteed return.

**Small Marketing Budgets.** Smaller presses rely heavily on low-cost efforts: review copies, seeking word-of-mouth support from niche audiences, and such. In the bookstore world, less money for store co-op efforts or big media campaigns results in smaller orders. Small-press books are less likely to get prime placement—if stocked at all. Often a small-press book needs to be special-ordered if a customer takes the trouble to request it.

**Lack of Prestige.** A small-press label may offer little in the way of name recognition. Unfortunately, many people assume that a book published by a small press wasn't good enough to be published by a larger press. You tell people you have been published, but when you tell them by whom, they get a funny look, different than if you had said Random House.

**Meager Reserves.** Small can mean slow to publish or slow to pay. With fewer titles in a hopper, any setback can affect the whole line, if the press doesn't have cash reserves. Of course, authors published by big presses also have horror stories of questionable accounting, mys-terious deductions, editors leaving abruptly, or projects getting can-celled. Still, the slimmer resources of a small press are a concern.

## Helpful Attitudes & Activities

Set realistic goals. Know why you want to be published. To see your work in print? To have more control or involvement? To become rich or famous? To break in? To reach certain audiences? Realistic goals help you decide if a particular small press is right for you. Set achievable goals and discuss them with the publisher in advance.

Be prepared to be a partner in marketing. Can you deliver contacts with specialty magazines, newsletters, conferences, bookstores, inter-est groups, professional associations? Can you contact some of them yourself? Get on an area radio show or arrange signings locally or on vacation? Be prepared to help with grassroots marketing, from join-ing key associations to developing a website to paying for your own travel to book signings.

Develop your niche presence. Be prepared to write well and frequently in your subject area, whether it is zen gardens or feminist literature. If your first book sees good reviews and decent sales, readers might want related books by you in the near future. Is there a follow-up project or a series in you? If so, mention this to your publisher.

## How To Find the Right Match

Finding just the right match in the specialized world of the small press is perhaps even more important than with larger presses.

**Publisher Websites & Compiled Databases.** Many publishers have their own websites with up-to-date guidelines. Or you can subscribe to online compiled databases of market information (at *Writer's Digest*, *The Writer*, etc.) that list publishers and what they publish, by category, and describe in detail how to contact them. Resources at your library include *Literary Market Place*, a directory of publishers that release at least 3 books a year, and the small-press bible, *International Directory of Little Magazines and Small Presses* (Dustbooks).

**Regional Search.** Consider a web search for book publishers in your region. A regional publisher might be more open to your proposal, since they have existing contacts with area stores, newspapers, and reviewers who might show extra interest in you.

**Trade Organizations.** Publishers Marketing Association (www.pma-online.org) lists many small publishers; they join to get access to marketing programs, a good sign of their efforts. Other organizations include the Council of Literary Magazines and Publishers (CLMP), the Small Press Center, Small Publishers Association of North America (SPAN), and other excellent and active regional groups.

**Bookstore Shelves.** For nonfiction publishers, a good approach is to scan bookstore shelves for the names of publishers who have published books to your project. Examine those volumes closely. Do they include illustrations? Charts? Extensive appendices? Make sure your own book proposal includes similar resources.

## What to Look for in a Small Press

**Quality Catalog.** Request their most recent catalog. How do they distribute their books? How much catalog space do they devote to new books and to backlist (which your book becomes after it is released)? Be sure this a group of authors and titles you want to be associated with. Will being part of this program reflect well on you and your work?

**Quality Distributor.** Do they have a good distributor? A distributor with a national sales-rep force has the punch to get a book out to more stores if demand warrants it. And good distributors are picky; they don't want to work with fly-by-night presses or ones that publish occasionally or unevenly.

**Advertising.** Look for ads in key specialty publications. If you have written a science-fiction novel, check *Locus*, *Asimov's*, and other such magazines to see who is actively advertising. Would you rather be with a publisher that runs lots of large ads, occasional small ads, a classified listing in the back … or no ads at all? The answer should be clear.

**Details on Similar Projects.** As you enter discussions with a small press, ask for specific details on the most similar project. How many did they sell? Over what time period? What kind of marketing activities did they undertake? You want to ferret out more than just: "We've sold 20,000 copies of our best title." Why, when, and how?

**References.** If they speak highly of a similar book or feature it on their website or in a catalog, you might try to locate and contact that author yourself. You may hear an earful of praise or complaints, from someone in a position to know.

**Chemistry.** Watch for genuine interest and enthusiasm. It's hard to quantify, but you'll know it when you see it: a publisher that is truly excited by your work and wants to do their best to make it a success.

**Commitment.** What exactly will they commit to a project? A decent advance? What marketing efforts? Ads in key publications? Get as much specified, verbally if not in the contract, as possible.

**Fair Contract.** Negotiate a better contract. Better can mean many things. In particular, consider what happens if a small press folds or does not maintain their contractual commitments. A book contract is a partnership. Like all relationships, while hoping for the best, it's prudent to be prepared for the worst. You may wish to limit the rights (e.g., hardcover but not softcover) or to subsequent works. If things go well, you can then extend the relationship.

What happens if the publishers doesn't meet its obligations? What if it never publishes your work? What if it releases your book but doesn't pay royalties promptly? A fair contract allows provides remedies so that, after a chance to correct the problem, rights revert to you, without extraordinary measures. What's good for the goose is good for the gander.

**Communication.** Don't be a pest, but keep in touch. Ask what's happening throughout the review process. Ask for feedback if you get rejected. If accepted, find out what's next for editorial input and author approvals. And from the beginning, what to expect for advance promotions and sales support. Ask how you can help and who to contact with your ideas!

As many authors know, starting small can be the path to success. Remember, your first book isn't the only step, just the first. Be prepared to establish your credentials and work your way up. A quality small press can be just the ticket.

Philip Martin is director of Great Lakes Literary (www.greatlakeslit.com), which offers development services for writers and their best projects. He is editor of this anthology, *The New Writer's Handbook*, and previously was acquisitions editor for The Writer Books, where he edited guides for fiction and nonfiction writers. He is also author of a book about fantasy fiction, *A Guide to Fantasy Literature* (Crickhollow, 2007), and also runs a small press, Blue Horse Books (www.bluehorsebooks.org), for young readers.

He lives in Milwaukee, Wisconsin, and speaks at writing conferences around the country.

# Understanding Editorese

*by Linda Sue Park*

WE ALL want to know *why* our work is rejected. Some writers include a checklist and ask editors to check off a reason, but even then, what we most often receive is a photocopied form that includes the phrase "not right for our list."

"Not right for our list" can mean a lot of things. Here, in descending degree of desirability, are the possible translations:

## 1. "Not right for our list" (personalized).

(Written by an editor on a personally signed letter.)

Translations:

a) Something about your work—the idea or the writing itself—was good to make the first cut.

**Suggested actions:** Send that editor another manuscript. In your cover letter, include a phrase like, "Thank you for your personal reply regarding my manuscript *Gone with the Breeze*. Enclosed is another piece I hope you will find of interest...." (This is how I sold my first book. The editor rejected a picture book manuscript with a personal note; I sent her a query for my novel manuscript within the week.)

*And*, send the first manuscript out again. If one editor liked it enough to write you a personal note, it just might find a home at another house.

b) We just accepted another book on exactly the same topic ... and I don't even have time to add one sentence to this letter to tell you so.

**Suggested action:** Again, if your manuscript has gotten far enough to merit a personal letter, follow action a) above.

## 2. "Not right for our list" (on a form rejection).

Many possible meanings:

a) I (the publishing house's first reader) didn't get any sleep the night before reading your manuscript because of my sick child/irate spouse/ flooded basement. I therefore failed utterly to recognize the quality of your work. Boy, will I kick myself when it wins a Newbery Medal/ King /Printz /National Book Award. (This is the kinder interpretation; variations impugn the first reader's mental health, moral fiber, and/ or intelligence.)

**Suggested action:** Print a new copy of manuscript, write a new cover letter, and submit to another house.

b) The idea is good, but your writing isn't.

c) Bad idea.

d) Bad idea poorly written.

e) We don't do folk tales/nonfiction/poetry.

Alarm bells: This translation means that you have not done your homework. If you obtain publishers' guidelines *before* submitting, this shouldn't happen.

**Suggested action:** Take the trouble to get those guidelines—if only to eliminate one possible reason for rejection. More and more publishers have their guidelines online. Not knowing what a house publishes is inexcusable.

f) We only glanced at your manuscript because it was unprofessionally presented. It was single-spaced/handwritten/crayoned. You used a fancy font that is difficult to read. You sent it on hot-pink paper hoping to catch our attention; instead, you blinded us. We don't really care how good your manuscript is because we don't want to deal with someone who does not approach his/her work professionally.

**Suggested action:** Get a book on manuscript submission. There are several dozen available; they all say pretty much the same thing. Follow the guidelines. Simple. The easiest part of submission—getting your work to look right. You'd be surprised how many people ignore this part.

Okay, now we get to the nitty-gritty. With form rejections, how do we know whether it's translation 2a)—offering a slender thread of hope for your manuscript—or one of the other, less desirable translations?

Well, we never really know for sure, but here's a general rule of thumb. If a first reader's lack of judgment is truly the reason for a rejection, and a manuscript shows merit in and of itself, eventually you will receive a personal letter from an editor. How many times you submit the (unchanged) manuscript out depends on the individual. But for the truly resilient among you, I would say that between ten and fifteen form rejections means either an awful lot of sleep-deprived first readers—or a manuscript that isn't yet publishable.

It may well be that translation 2b), c), or d) is involved ... in which case, it's back to the keyboard and your critique buddies.

(Of course we've all heard stories about the manuscript that was rejected umpteen times and went on to win the Newbery, like Madeleine L'Engle's *A Wrinkle in Time*. But take a good hard look at your manuscript. Are you saying, "This is so sweet! I don't know why it keeps getting rejected!" or even, "This is at least as good as most of the books my kid is reading now." Sorry, no dice. It's got to be better—a lot better—than most of the books you're seeing now because you're a first-time non-celebrity author with no track record.)

And if you recognize yourself in translation e) or f), it's time to back up a bit. You're not ready to be submitting yet.

Keep writing. Keep reading in the genre in which you wish to write. With a little talent, a great deal of work, a lot of time, and a stroke of luck, someday you'll write something that will be "just right for our list."

Linda Sue Park was born in Illinois to Korean immigrant parents. A graduate of Stanford University, she has written six children's novels, most dealing with Korean and Korean American themes, including *The Kite Fighters* and *A Single Shard*, which won the 2002 Newbery Medal. She also writes picture books for younger readers, and lives now in upstate New York. This article was first published in *Keystrokes* online magazine, 1999, and comes from her website: www.lspark.com.

# MARKETING YOUR WORK

# Your Press Kit

*by Theresa Meyers*

WHAT GOES into a press kit?

**Cover Letter.** Remind them that they requested it and why you are sending it, and keep it to one page. Let them know you'll be contacting them to see about their interest in setting up an interview. And *please* include how they can contact you! This is vital and often missed.

**Photo.** Prefer 5" × 7" or 8" × 10" with an inset caption at the base that gives your name and website, email, and phone number.

**Biography.** Keep it to one page, insert your photo, and write just the highlights of how you got where you are and why you write, also where you live, generally speaking (this is important when pulling the hometown-kid angle with an editor/producer).

**FAQ.** Also called frequently asked questions, this is in a question/answer format that gives them some of the details that you get asked all the time by people who don't write: What's your typical work schedule? Where do you get your ideas? Have you ever put someone you know in your books? Do you make a lot of money writing books? How did you get started?

**Title Sheet.** If you only have one book, then this will feature the back-cover blurb of your book and a photo of the front cover. Also include relevant information a journalist would need, such as publisher, publication date, type of book (genre and format: hardcover, trade, mass market, disk) ISBN, and cover price. Give complete information on all works published, in lesser detail, for as many pages as necessary.

**Statistics.** Journalists *love* statistics. It doesn't matter where you pull them from as long as you can attribute the source for them. They can be about anything related to your topic or industry. These go a long way in making the journalist feel like you've helped them out, which in turn makes them more interested in you.

**Other.** You may also include things like quotes from other people on a page, a page listing your awards if you have them, or an excerpt from the book.

All of these items need a uniform look with the same color scheme and accents throughout. Don't switch to different fonts on each piece or print on colored paper. Clean black and white, with small accents of color if necessary, are always best. The only exception to this is when you are mailing pitch letters to radio or TV for a guest appearance and want to grab their attention as soon as they open the envelope. Then colored papers are appropriate.

How do you incorporate your message points? Think about what you are writing in your cover letter, pitch letter, bio, and FAQ page: How does it link back to your message points? How are *you* connected to them? How is *your work* connected to them?

Theresa Meyers is president of Blue Moon Communications. Located in the Seattle area, Blue Moon specializes in brand development, media training, book promotion, book tours, and marketing communications for fiction authors. This piece is excerpted from a longer article, "Beginning your Publicity Plan," found on Blue Moon's website in a section of advice for authors.

The website is: www.bluemooncommunications.com.

# How Authors Can Help their Publishers with Marketing

*by Linda Carlson*

IF YOU'RE an author who thinks writing is your most important job, think again. Whether you're seeking a publisher or have already landed a contract, it is vital that you consider how you can help market your book.

Today, more than ever, publishers look for authors with platforms. That's shorthand for anything that can help sell a book: celebrity status, promotional tools such as talk show gigs, newspaper or magazine columns, regular speaking engagements and popular web sites.

You're not a star? Nobody invites you to keynote regional conferences, much less state or national events? You're not even a columnist for your neighborhood's free weekly paper? You can still be the crown jewel of the marketing campaign for your book, a valuable and cost-effective extension of the publisher's publicity efforts. This is especially true when your book is backlist, when it's past its introductory season and the publisher is concentrating its efforts on newer titles.

Both you and your publisher probably expect author appearances to be part of the promotional campaign. Your publisher may also have factored back-of-the-room sales arranged by you into anticipated sales. But there is so much more you can do, especially if you can rely on your publisher for appropriate support and reassurance. Everything you do can have a significant effect on book sales (and thus your royalties), as well as your stature within your professional or literary community. This may mean recognition, speaking opportunities (sometimes paid), consulting assignments and a glitzier resume.

Where should you start? Based on my experience since 1981 as an author of nonfiction, a self-publisher and as a marketing consultant to publishers, here are some easy projects with short- and long-term benefits.

## Compile mailing lists.

If you have conducted interviews for your book, you are likely to have the names of dozens of people who should be contacted—either by your publisher or by you, because people who have developed personal relationships with the author may prefer to buy directly, especially if the books are inscribed.

When I attended company-town reunions for my *Company Towns of the Pacific Northwest* (University of Washington Press, 2003), I circulated a sign-up sheet asking for attendees' contact information. When the book was published, I wrote each person on the list, offering the book at a slight discount along with the inscription of their choice. Some people ordered copies for their children, siblings, or former neighbors. As favorable reviews were published, I emailed excerpts to those on the list. A few months after publication, I accompanied a new excerpt with a reminder that this book would make a wonderful gift for grandchildren; that email generated additional sales at no cost except my time.

## Identify specialty media and retailers.

Especially when books have a geographic, industry, or professional focus, you may know more than your publisher does about the publications that serve target markets. You can also tell your publisher's publicist how press releases should be tailored to each publication. You might even consider drafting the press release leads (initial paragraphs) for your publisher.

For *Company Town*, which describes more than 100 communities, I provided the UW Press publicist with a list of dozens of media, museums, and organizations that were likely to be responsive to the book. I also tailored different leads for the press release for each one. For example: "Irondale is one of the Jefferson County communities discussed in ..." Results ranged from two-sentence notices in community newspapers, to a full-page verbatim reprint of the press release in my parents' church newsletter (which reached hundreds of families in a region the book covered), to a review in the *Harvard University Business History Review*.

In addition, I wrote and emailed brief press releases to the home-town papers of the people I had interviewed for the book with hooks like: "Former Woodinville resident Andy Solberg is among the one-time company-town employees quoted in ..."

## Solicit speaking engagements.

Or ask your publisher to help. I'm no shrinking violet, but it can be intimidating to cold-call organizations and say, "I'm available to speak to your group." This is something the publisher can easily do, with a simple form letter that outlines a few talk topics and provides your contact information. You might draft the letter yourself and work with your publicist to compile a list of associations, libraries, bookstores, and festivals to contact.

## Prepare for public appearances.

This has at least three parts.

First, you need to ensure that you satisfy your audiences. This is especially important if you are a first-time author or someone whose previous work was in a different genre. Even though I am an experi-enced speaker, I discovered that doing readings from a history was very different from giving talks promoting my earlier marketing and job-search books. Venues also often differ dramatically: chit-chatting with a book club in a meeting room requires different skills than read-ing to 200 people in a library auditorium or speaking outdoors at an arts festival with a band blaring nearby. If you haven't spoken since that high school speech class, ask your publisher for help. Coaching can easily be done by telephone. Other resources: your local chapters of the National Speakers Association and Toastmasters. At a mini-mum, attend a few author appearances at local bookstores and men-tally critique the presentations.

Second, when you're lining up an appearance, find out specifi-cally what the host wants so you can outline a presentation that will work regardless of the setting and number attending. Make sure there will be an adequate sound system, a stool, a lectern, water, and, if you need them, an easel, slide projector, or computer hookup. It is helpful to create a checklist that you complete for each appearance: include directions and emergency numbers you can use en route to the presentation should disaster strike. If the publisher is setting up your events, insist that they use the same checklist.

Third, do some homework about typical attendance figures so that you are not surprised. Author appearances in some communities are poorly attended simply because there are so many competing activities. However, most appearances result in publicity even when few attend. And publicity, in most cases, equals sales. There may be other benefits. When my most recent book was new, I arrived at one of Seattle's most popular bookstores to find only a handful of people present for my well-publicized reading. It was a fair-weather Saturday and no one wanted to come inside. But one person who did show up was a cameraman for the state cable television network. His video ran a few days later, and within the month I was invited to appear on Author's Hour, another state cable program, which aired several times during the Christmas holiday season.

### Contact booksellers.

You can walk into bookstores, museum gift stores, cookware shops and other retail outlets suitable for your book, ask for the manager or public relations coordinator, and say, "I'm the author of X, and I hope that's a book you're stocking." I've been doing this since 1990 for my books, almost always with positive responses. Booksellers usually are delighted to meet authors and have existing inventory autographed. This process is even easier if you prepare cards with the book cover, title, ISBN, and price. These should be the same size as business cards; they cost just pennies each when ordered them from discount printers.(Ask your publisher to foot this bill; sometimes the cards can be printed with the book covers.)

Authors can also contact booksellers effectively by phone and e-mail. When I began to publish city-specific job-search guides in 1990, I called every independent bookstore in my area every month or so to ensure the book was in stock. "I've got a speech coming up," I'd say, "and I want to know which stores I can refer people to." Now that we're in the 21st century and my geographic region is much larger, I use e-mail to share excerpts from reviews and notices of awards. My list includes bookstores I've read about in *Publishers Weekly*, the online newsletter *Shelf Awareness,* members of the Pacific Northwest Booksellers Association, and stores I've found in telephone directories. You can start with the American Booksellers Association member directories at www.bookweb.org and with the names of retailers with whom your publisher has relationships.

### Create a personal web site.

Many Internet service providers offer free space and easy-to-use web-authoring software so you can create simple sites. These can show the cover of the book and a picture of you, provide author contact information and a bio, and list awards, excerpts from reviews, reader testimonials, and upcoming appearances. If you list contact information for your publisher's publicist, requests for review copies will go to that person, not you. My personal web site also has links to booksellers who responded to my offer to list them. In addition, an author's web site provides a quick way for you to respond to requests from reporters and event coordinators for background information. If you belong to a professional group such as a writers' association that offers brief web pages for members, make sure you keep your information updated.

### Create and use blogs.

Blogs are free and they are even easier to create and maintain than web sites. As a recent crop of books proves, many blogs can be turned into books—which the blog then continues to promote. If you have a new book being sold on Amazon.com, you can set up an AmazonConnect blog. It's free, and it'll add to the information on your book's page.

### Play cheerleader for yourself.

Even the most enthusiastic author will get the blues occasionally—and for good reason. There's nothing worse than spending hours on icy highways to reach a bookstore where only a handful of people show up. Remind yourself that everything you do is a springboard for publicity—and that this publicity results in the book's name appearing both in print and in search engines, when online editions of the magazines and newspapers that mentioned you are indexed on the Internet. This builds awareness of the book for months to come. At Parenting Press, where I handle marketing, we recently had an author drive hours for an appearance that attracted fewer than five. But the store display and publicity in advance of her appearance put the book on the store's bestseller list for the week—and, as a result, it got mentioned in the local newspaper.

### Play PR agent for yourself, too.

When booksellers compliment you on an appearance or a reporter thanks you for an interview, pass the kudos along to your publisher. This increases the chance that you'll be recommended when the publicist gets other store or media inquiries—or when you have a second book to pitch. Keep at least a mental list of your favorite hosts, too, so that you can refer to these well-received appearances when you're pitching yourself to other retailers and to the organizers of book fairs and professional and literary conferences.

Use all your crucial assets. If you or your publisher have been letting your books market themselves, these suggestions may seem intimidating. But today, with book sales stagnating overall and dozens of new competitors every month in every genre, no author or publisher can afford to overlook what an author can contribute. The passion authors have for their topics and their knowledge of specialized audiences are valuable assets that need to be channeled into marketing. It is these assets that may determine whether a book is successful—in both critical and financial terms.

Linda Carlson is a Seattle marketing consultant and the author of eleven books, including *Company Towns of the Pacific Northwest*, which was a finalist for the 2004 Washington State Book Awards.

More about her books and her consulting services can be found at her website, www.lindacarlson.com.

A version of this article appeared in the *PMA Independent*, the newsletter of the Publishers Marketing Association.

# How to Get Great Testimonials

*by Jay Lipe*

TESTIMONIALS are one of the most powerful, yet affordable marketing tools around. Good ones grab a book buyer's attention and encourage them to crack open the book. Great ones take the buyer even deeper by making them think to themselves "Yes, this is the kind of book I've been looking for."

Think back to a time when you were book browsing. Didn't reading a testimonial by a well-known author make you think "Well, if so-and-so liked it, then it must be good"?

Plus, testimonials for your book will also be ready by book reviewers, bookstore owners, distributors, agents, foreign rights contacts and columnists. When you stop to think about it, a powerful book testimonial establishes just as much credibility as a solid website or book flyer (and at a fraction of the cost). Here are some tips on writing great book testimonials:

## Keep them focused

The most convincing book testimonials I read are focused on one central idea. Because book browsers will give you their attention for 30 seconds or less, each testimonial should be a succinct "word-bite" about one aspect of the book. That way, the skimmer absorbs several different aspects of your book after just a quick read of its back cover. Keep each testimonial laser-like in its focus.

## Seven tried and true styles

Any testimonial is good, but here are some of the more effective styles:

**1. Quantify a benefit.** If yours is a nonfiction title, see if you can't get testimonials that quantify the return in reading your book. For example, someone recently emailed me with this testimonial for my book, *The Marketing Toolkit for Growing Businesses*:

> *After reading* The Marketing Toolkit for Growing Businesses, *I followed your advice. After sending only two emails, I got 4 calls back immediately, have scheduled 2 meetings to discuss new business and set up a new speaking engagement. Your method really works.*

And here's one from my second book *Stand Out from the Crowd: Secrets to Crafting a Winning Company Identity* that points out the time savings for the reader:

> *If you don't have time to get an* MBA *in marketing, read Jay Lipe's new book.*

When you use this style, the reader envisions exactly how their life will improve after reading your book.

**2. Appeal to Emotions.** This style is more commonly found in fiction, but can also work for nonfiction. Here, the testimonial works to paint a picture, at a visceral level, of the emotions a reader experiences while reading the book:

> *An edge-of-the-seat tale.*

> *Harrowing thrills …*

> *At once romantic, erotic, suspenseful—and completely unforgettable.*

**3. Create an association.** Connecting the author (or the book) to another person many times helps conjure up associations:

> *Bob Bly is to direct marketing as Mozart is to music.*

> *Alistair Cooke interprets America better than any foreign correspondent since Tocqueville.*

**4. Use a common phrase.** How about incorporating a phrase that's already part of popular culture? For example:

> *Fasten your seatbelt … a stimulating, fast-paced novel brimming with action and high drama.*

**5. Give the reader a leg up.** Anytime you can illustrate that your book provides the reader with an edge, this is powerful stuff. Here's one from a book on how to hold a successful meeting:

> *Every producer should read this before their clients do....*

**6. Cite a credible source.** Years ago I worked in marketing for a consumer goods company and we featured a testimonial from a reverend about our product. Talk about a credible source! In fact, so many people telephoned him directly to seek out his opinion that we finally had to pull his testimonial from rotation.

Seek out trusted opinion leaders in your industry for testimonials because not only does their endorsement carry more weight; they may also be willing to share your book with their universe of contacts (especially if it features their testimonial).

**7. Focus on the author.** You can get just as much mileage out of a testimonial that focuses on the author. Here's one from a book about designing websites:

> *Jakob Nielsen is entertaining, direct and not one to join the latest trend of the day....*

## Finding the right people

Before I self-published *The Marketing Toolkit for Growing Businesses*, I was fortunate enough to get 10 great testimonials. How? I asked. The truth is, if you want attention-grabbing testimonials, you'll have to ask for them. But I found that the majority of people I approached were extremely helpful (only one in twenty that I approached declined to participate).

To start, go the library and take note of who has written testimonials for books in your genre. Next, visit Amazon sites for similar books and see who has posted reviews. Then, generate a "hit list" from these two sources.

Finding addresses for these "hit list" people involves a bit more work, but if you Google a person's name and search around, you'll wind up with an address (either snail or e-mail) to approach them through.

What's the best way to approach them?

## Approaching and asking

One of the most valuable things I learned from Dan Poynter's book *The Self-Publishing Manual* was his method of approaching people for testimonials. He recommended sending a galley, a cover letter and a form which contains these sections:

I like this one:

> __ *This book has more secrets for success than the Bible. Read this book and maybe you can walk on water.*
> or
>
> __ *This book is as refreshing as a cold glass of lemonade on a hot summer day.*
> or
>
> *I can do better than that:* _____
> Signature:

As you see, you write two testimonials, position a checkbox next to each, and list them under a section called "I like this one best." Then, follow that with a section that's called "I can do better than that" and includes a blank space for them to write their own.

If the reader likes one of the testimonials you've written, they'll check the box by it, sign the form and return it to you.

If they feel moved to write their own, they can do so in the space you've provided. One thing I'll say: every time someone has written their own testimonial, it's been much better than the ones I've written.

Remember: Testimonials are a workhorse tool for your book marketing effort. Use them liberally to create awareness, establish credibility, and generate word of mouth for your book.

Jay Lipe is the author of two marketing books: *Stand Out from the Crowd: Secrets to Crafting a Winning Company Identity* and *The Marketing Toolkit for Growing Businesses.* He is also the president of Emerge Marketing, a firm that has helped hundreds of small businesses and Fortune 500 clients grow through strategic marketing.

More about his books and consulting services, as well as information about his free e-newsletter, "Marketing Tips & Tools," can be found at www.emergemarketing.com.

# Planning Author Events in Bookstores

*by David Unowsky*

BOOKSTORE AUTHOR EVENTS (readings, book talks, and signings), if done right, can be an important part of a successful plan for marketing your book. If done wrong, a lot of time and money can be wasted.

Do not make the mistake of thinking that book signings will be a financial bonanza; they won't be. Think of bookstore events as golden opportunities for marketing your book and for getting publicity and exposure.

No bookstore can guarantee either an audience or a number of books sold. The reasons for doing events in good bookstores, regardless of the number of attendees or books sold at the event, include:

**Publicity.** Events help bookstores promote a book and its author to local media as a newsworthy happening, which reaches targeted book-reading audiences. Bookstores promote the title before the event through house newsletters and pre-event displays, and afterward, as extra books inscribed at the event are often given special "Signed Copy" stickers.

**General Buzz.** Booksellers are makers of literary opinion and taste. Creating a positive impression through a good in-store reading and a lively discussion helps build an ongoing interest in you and your writings.

Remember that the best event-producing stores (the ones you want to appear at) get lots of touring national authors. You need to give them good reasons and incentives to include you and your book in their mix.

Bookstores at this level have a full-time staffer to select which authors and events to choose, from thousands seeking to use the bookstore's valuable space to promote the authors' books. I'll tell you what I do as events manager at Magers and Quinn, an independent bookstore in Minneapolis. I receive dozens of calls and emails each month from publishers and authors seeking readings or signings. I respond to each one, requesting PR material and galleys for those I'm interested in. I examine the materials, and schedule events when appropriate. I write a press release for each event, send it to a standard list, and look for special niche media for each book and author.

We list each event on our website, do an in-store display, have a printed list of upcoming events on the counter to hand customers or insert in bags, and have a sandwich board on the sidewalk to promote coming events.

On the day of the event, we move fixtures (giving up some selling space), set up chairs and microphone, introduce the author, assist in the Q&A and signing, then reassemble the area afterward.

Some stores sell signed books on their websites after the readings, thereby keeping the book and author on the web for another time period. All of these things take time, cost money, and are of value.

Clearly, everyone—author, store, and publisher—has a lot riding on making an event successful. The following lists will be helpful in preparation, performance, and follow-up, and should help maximize the benefits of author events.

## Preparing for the Event

1. Start 3–4 months before your book will be ready or before you want to make appearances. Major publishers book tours that far in advance; you are competing with all of them for a bookstore's time and space.

2. Determine which bookstores in the area that you want to visit do the best events. Consider contacting your second choices as well; you may not get your first choice for any number of reasons.

3. Contact the bookstore's event coordinator by phone or email. Explain that you are an author seeking an event; ask what the requirements are. Be prepared to send a galley or finished copy of the book, along with a press kit with material about the book and about you. Never make a cold-call visit in person; booksellers work hard and their days are usually planned out in advance.

4. It costs booksellers 300–500 dollars to put on an event. So tell (show) them what you can do build an audience and sell more

books. Three suggestions: offer an email list of friends and relatives, offer a list of organizations or college departments that would be interested, or provide your plan to get media attention for the event and for the book.

5. Don't overbook; better one good event in a town or metro area than four or five mediocre ones. If things work right, other stores in town will order the book soon enough. If you have a publisher and/or a distributor, tell them well in advance of your scheduled events.

6. Make it easy for the bookstore to order copies of the book and to return unsold copies. Make sure the bookstore makes the same percentage of profit (45–50%) on your book as it can on other books. If your book is self-published and self-distributed, agree on consignment terms with the store in advance.

7. Ask the bookstore if they have a media list and if you can get a copy of it. Send your own materials about you and the book to outlets on the list. Follow up with calls and emails seeking interviews.

8. Let the bookstore know well in advance of any special needs or equipment required: screen, projector, special sound system, flip chart, etc. While many bookstores have equipment, some do not. Do not expect the store to pay for equipment rental.

9. Discuss with the events coordinator your format and time required. Most stores set a time limit on events, as access to certain parts of the store may be limited during an event, resulting in lost sales. A thirty-minute presentation, then fifteen minutes of Q&A, followed by the signing of books is a standard expectation for in-store events.

## The Event Itself

1. Be well prepared and practiced. Know what you're going to do, say, and read. No one wants to spend time watching an author flipping back and forth in their book, trying to find the next page to read.

2. Arrive at the store at least 15 minutes before the scheduled starting time. Report to the events coordinator du jour (it may be a person other than the one you've been communicating with). Get familiar with the space and the equipment. Bring your own signing pen and beverage of choice.

3. Keep your presentation within the time frame allotted. Close by

thanking the audience for coming and the bookstore for hosting the event.

4. During the Q&A: repeat the question before answering. It's probable that many in the audience couldn't hear it. Keep your answers brief enough so that most can get their questions asked. Be prepared with extra material to offer if the dialogue slows down. End on time.

5. While signing books, keep the chatter to a minimum to allow everyone who wants to get a book signed to be able to do so promptly. Arrange to meet old friends in attendance afterward for lengthier conversations. Ask bookstore staff if they want you to sign some extra books for stock. Thank them for their work.

6. Ask the events coordinator if any pictures of the event were taken. If so, request that a copy be sent to you. Leave your contact information.

7. If there is a consignment arrangement for the books, have a clear understanding, before leaving, as to how the settlement will be made.

8. Thank everyone at the store and say good-bye.

9. Think about what you could do to make it even better next time.

## Follow Up

1. Send a card or email to the store thanking them for hosting the event.

2. If you have good pictures of the event, post them on your blog or website.

3. If it was really good, send pictures and a press release to *Publishers Weekly* and to the local media.

David Unowsky is a past president of the Upper Midwest Booksellers Association and a well-known promoter of books and literary events in the Twin Cities area, having founded Hungry Mind bookstore and the *Hungry Mind Review*, later known as *Ruminator Review*. Along with his current work as events coordinator at a Minneapolis bookstore, he is marketing manager for Scarletta Press, publisher of *The New Writer's Handbook*.

# Tips for a Well-Attended Event

*by Jenna Glatzer*

WHEN I MADE the decision to do free workshops and book signings for my latest book, *Make a Real Living as a Freelance Writer*, I thought it would be easy to draw an audience. I had, after all, done all the right things to prepare for this big event: I had a successful e-zine, AbsoluteWrite.com, sent weekly directly to my target market; I was a contributing editor at the most popular magazine for writers; had been interviewed all over writers' ezines; and had submitted articles to sites and magazines related to my primary audience (writers) and my secondary audience (those interested in working from home).

But the problem was that my audience was international. I had a workshop set up on Long Island, and more than 99% of my regular audience wouldn't be able to get there. So I had to get local attention. Through trial and error, I've come up with a system that works. I haven't had fewer than 30 people at any of my signings, and I've always sold books. I hope my tips will inspire you next time you're promoting an event.

## 1. Focus on the benefit to the attendee.

The first thing a reader should see on your promotional material is what's in it for them. A signed book is all well and good, but it'll require them to spend money. What are they getting free just for showing up? In my case, I was offering a free two-hour seminar about making money writing for magazines. What will they learn? What perks will they get? This is what appeared in big letters on my posters, with the "book signing" in small letters toward the bottom.

## 2. "Community Events" are not places to do business.

Most local newspapers have a "community events" section where they run short blurbs about local events. Submit your release at least two weeks prior to your event, with all the "who, what, where, when, why" questions succinctly answered. But after I did that and failed to place my events in local papers, I asked an ex-newspaper editor for advice.

"While I would have probably run a little blurb about your free writing workshop, I would not have run your free writing workshop combined with your book signing," she wrote. "I would invite you to pay for an advertisement because, being the jaded cynic I am, I would not give you free publicity for something from which you are profiting."

So leave your for-profit hat at home when approaching the media.

### 3. Think small.

National attention is nice, but when promoting a local event, you want to get your message to as many local people as possible. I mulled this over one day while pushing my grocery cart through a supermarket, then noticed the bulletin board filled with posters. I ran home and created my own on the computer: Colorful posters that gave all the essential information about my event in large, easy-to-read type, with pull-off tabs on the bottom that simply said "Free Writing Seminar," along with the location, date, and time. You can put these in supermarkets, as well as delis, convenience stores, libraries, and other high-traffic businesses.

### 4. Find local websites, e-mail lists, and message boards.

Many cities, counties, and regions have their own websites where people can announce coming events. You can also search for your geographic area on Yahoogroups.com to find e-mail discussion lists in your area. Write to the site owner or group moderator to request that he or she tell members about your event.

### 5. Co-promote.

When Judith Lazarus promoted her books, The Spa Sourcebook and Stress Relief & Relaxation Techniques, she asked a spa product manufacturer to provide her with samples. She used these samples to draw people to her book signing table. You might find a local business that could benefit from being featured at your event, and ask them to hang a sign about the event or include flyers in customers' bags in return. Or find someone who's promoting a complementary product or service, and agree to swap—you'll distribute postcards about their events at your table if they'll do the same for you.

### 6. Run contests and giveaways.
Similar to Judith's deal with the spa product manufacturer, see if you can get a business to donate an item for giveaway—or use one of your own products or services. On your publicity material, you can announce that one lucky attendee (or many) will win a valuable door prize. Or invite people to enter the contest beforehand, then tell each of them that you'll announce the winner/s at the event. Be sure to include the prize's monetary value on your announcements.

### 7. Use lawn signs.
If politicians can promote themselves with signs on our lawns, why can't we? Ask friends and associates to put a colorful sign on their lawn with very brief information about your event.

### 8. Be photogenic.
If this is an event you've done before, or if you have an interesting photo related to your event, send it to local newspapers with your release. You have a better shot at seeing print if you can provide a photo, and readers will be more drawn to your announcement if it's accompanied by a picture. Pick an interesting prop or a fun candid shot, not a typical headshot.

### 9. Business cards, revisited.
Although many local business don't have enough counter space to display a stack of your flyers, they may be happy to let you deposit a stack of business-card-size announcements about your event. These are easy to make on your computer, and again, should just contain an eye-catching headline and essential information about the event.

Jenna Glatzer is the author or ghostwriter of 16 books, including Celine Dion's authorized biography and several books for writers. Her latest is *The Street-Smart Writer: Self-Defense Against Sharks and Scams in the Writing World*.

Visit her at www.jennaglatzer.com.

# Focus on Niche Markets

*by Kate Bandos*

"BE ON THE OPRAH SHOW" is at or near the top of the list when most publishers and authors outline their publicity goals. For some authors and publishers this is reasonable, but for most it is a goal that wastes time, effort, and precious publicity dollars.

While stories abound about how Oprah turned an unknown book and author into a bestseller and a household name, there are many more stories about successful books that never received an Oprah "endorsement."

I have found that most publishers and authors would do well by looking beyond Oprah, the *New York Times Book Review*, and other big-name media and focusing instead on their niche markets. (Of course, if Oprah or other major media become interested, none of us would turn that coverage down!)

## Horse Sense About Sales

For example, Laura Barnes, author/publisher of the award-winning *Ernest* children's book series, sells a significant number of books through school visits, special market sales and the equestrian market—and Ernest isn't even a horse. He is a lovable miniature donkey with horse barnyard friends who co-star in the five *Ernest* books.

Schoolchildren at one particular school in New Jersey became so enamored of Ernest after Laura spoke there that they named their school buses after Ernest and his friends. Another school made Ernest their school mascot. And a parent at one of the 20–30 schools that Laura now visits annually wrote a song about Ernest that the whole school learned and sang to Laura at a big celebration. Requests for her presentations just keep growing (along with sales). In addition to securing an author-visit fee, Laura sells 40 to 100 books per visit.

As for the equine market, Laura began sending review copies to various publications. Reviews for each of the *Ernest* books in these and general-interest parenting publications have been raves, generating great direct sales through her Web site, equestrian/tack stores, and equestrian catalogs as well as the usual book markets. A popular syndicated radio show for the equestrian market has also helped spread the word through interviews and recommendations.

To support continued sales, Laura now spends around 30% of her advertising/marketing budget on the equestrian sector, 30% on the educational market, and the remainder is general. (See more about Laura's school visits and the books, which include *Ernest and Elston*, *Ernest's Special Christmas*, *Teeny Tiny Ernest*, *Twist and Ernest*, and *Ernest and the Big Itch* at www.barnesyardbooks.com.)

### Routes That Reach Parents

Another example of a publisher who has done very well without Oprah (even though he lives in her backyard in the Chicago area) is Thomas Phelan, Ph.D., author of the popular 1-2-3 *Magic: Effective Discipline for Children 2–12*. Originally published in 1990 and now in a third edition, 1-2-3 *Magic* has sold more than 925,000 copies. How? Phelan has a strong schedule of talks and workshops throughout the country that let him reach parents directly. Counselors also regularly recommend this book to parents struggling with children who are out of control.

Tom produced audio and video versions of 1-2-3 *Magic* that sell well too, and he has written five other books, most of which are also available in multiple formats. Mailings to parents and counselors, aggressive media campaigns, and conventions are other ways he gets his message to parents. Once parents try his method and get great results, word of mouth spreads excitement and sales. (See more at www.parentmagic.com.)

### Mass Merchandisers Buy from Mom

Amy Knapp, a stay-at-home mom from Kalamazoo, Mich., with a special-needs daughter, came up with a way to keep herself and her family organized. After getting questions about it from other moms she met, she decided to test the idea further with *Amy Knapp's Family Organizer*, which she produced for the first time in 1999. Promotion that first year focused on getting coverage in regional parenting publications.

That got the buzz going, helping her sell through the 3,000 copies she had cautiously printed. The 2004–2005 version of *Amy Knapp's Family Organizer* became a strong-selling calendar at both Wal-Mart and Target stores across the country, while also doing well at Borders and Barnes & Noble stores, and this trend continues. As of early 2007, more than half a million copies of *Amy Knapp's Family Organizer* have been sold.

In the fall of 2006, Sourcebooks published two titles to build on Knapp's success: *Amy Knapp's Big Grid Family Organizer* (a wall calendar), and *Amy Knapp's Family Organizing Handbook: 314 Mom-Tested Super Tips, Tricks and Secrets to Take Care of Everything with Time Left for What Really Matters* (a paperback book).

A "Mom-Tested" endorsement in *Parenting* magazine, a nice mention in Essence, and inclusion in an article in *Woman's Day* are all nice, but it is the word-of-mouth buzz and coverage in smaller publications and online that Knapp knows have helped build her ever-increasing solid sales. *The Organizer* is now available annually in several versions (including one for homeschoolers and a Christian version) and various bindings. (See more at www.thefamilyorganizer.com.)

## Make the Media Lap It Up

Sometimes successful publicity in niche markets is a matter of getting the right release to the right media at the right time. Pamela J. Vaccaro—author of *Beyond the Ice Cream Cone: The Whole Scoop on Food at the 1904 World's Fair*—timed publication of her book to coincide with the St. Louis Fair's 100th anniversary. Then a simple, fun release and selected review copies went out to food editors around the country. Also, KSB Promotions featured the book in a newsletter that went to 7,000 media nationwide, and we sent books to everybody on that list who requested one.

The various mailings generated major stories in the *Chicago Tribune, Newsday, Atlanta Journal-Constitution, The Dallas Morning News, Minneapolis Star-Tribune, Detroit Free Press, The Christian Science Monitor*, and, of course, the *St. Louis Post-Dispatch*. There was even a mention in *The New York Times*. Many other papers and magazines—more than 40 that we are aware of—also gave the book coverage, either by quoting the author or by using interesting tidbits from the book and giving credit. Also, Pam got to do many radio interviews. (See more at her website, www.beyondtheicecreamcone.com.)

What niche or submarkets might you cultivate for your book(s)? I'm sure you will find that efforts in a targeted area will be much more productive than hammering on the same door as everyone else.

Kate Bandos is a co-director of KSB Promotions, founded in 1988, which helps independent publishers of general lifestyle nonfiction books get media exposure. A veteran of more than 30 years in book promotion, she was promotions director for Globe Pequot Press and publicity director for Pelican Publishing Company, Acropolis Books, and M. Evans & Company.

For more on her consulting services, visit her website at www.ksbpromotions.com.

This article first appeared as "What's Better than Oprah?" in the *PMA Independent*, January 2005, www.pma-online.org.

# The Potential of Tips Booklets

*by Paulette Ensign*

AT LONG LAST your book is done. The cover and the contents look as terrific as you hoped they would. Your marketing plan is ready to fully launch. You're primed to make tons of money from your book, yet there's a little voice saying "But wait, there's more." What could that be?

Somewhere along the way, you remember hearing something about developing derivatives. A derivative is a product that has been distilled directly from you book. And it can be in as many formats as your imagination or other people's suggestions and interests can take you.

A tips booklet is one of those derivatives that can be created from your full-length book manuscript. It means writing your book once and making money from it over and over again in numerous ways. Tips booklets do several things. They market your book, as an appetizer to whet the appetite of the reader, guiding their hunger toward the complete entrée, your entire book.

As for a booklet being a marketing tool for your book, think of it as your marketing brochure on steroids. The tips booklet presents 3,000–5,000 words that are samples of your book content, written as action-oriented suggestions to the reader, in a format that people will pay for. Think of that, people paying you for your marketing materials! It doesn't get much better than that, does it?

The reader reads some or all of your booklet, feels great, wants more, and sees on the last page of the booklet a notice saying "For more in-depth information on this topic, you'll want to have our book *Everything You Really Wanted to Know When You Started Reading Our Tips Booklet*. You can purchase the book at our website www.TheRest OfTheStory.com or our 24-hour order line 1–800-GET-BOOK."

Tips booklets also become an income stream unto themselves.

Imagine yourself in a situation where a company, professional association, or some other organization wants to buy thousands of copies of your book. They want to use it as a promotional item for their own products, services, or cause. They then see the per-unit cost of your book. Even though they love the book, it's priced well, and they view it as an ideal match for their needs, their budget stops them in their tracks.

By also having a tips booklet available on the same topic as your book, you are immediately able to suggest their first purchase be a similar quantity of your tips booklet instead. This allows for some sale rather than no sale. It leaves your buyer feeling good about you because you gave them a workable solution. You have greatly increased the odds of this buyer (and people they know) making other purchases from you in the future. Think about all of that as you ponder the idea of creating one or more booklets from your book.

Look for obvious divisions in your book. The chapters are a good starting place. Each chapter may be grist for an individual booklet. Or, rather than going that route, you might decide to do something now called a "sampler" booklet. That means taking the 10 chapter headings from your book, and writing 10 or 12 tips under each of the chapter titles, giving the reader an opportunity to sample the entire book within a tips booklet of 16–24 pages, measuring approximately 3½ by 8½ inches.

As your reader experiences success from what they read in your booklet, your credibility increases. They want more of you and more of what you are about. The booklet gives them an opportunity to test-drive you. Remember, the booklet is not the consummate reference on everything you know about your topic. That's what the book is. The booklet will, however, often lead to the book.

Every person who reads your booklet is a ready-made marketing representative for you and your company. As a single-copy booklet buyer, they could be a decision-maker for their own company or group, and also be influential in the purchasing decisions of their colleagues, associates, suppliers, distributors, family, friends, and neighbors.

Imagine this for a moment: A company, association, or other organization that purchases a large quantity of your booklets and then your books as a promotional tool for their own purposes also promotes you and your company with each and every publication of yours that they distribute. They do this because your name and your contact information are in each booklet. Remember, they have paid you to promote you. Life doesn't get a whole lot better than that!

Your buyer may also be or know of a reporter or producer to schedule you for a print, radio, or television, or Internet interview. The reader might have contacts in another country or a community in your own country who have interest in licensing your booklet or book into another language or different physical format. You may be just the person to provide consulting or training on an issue. Or, if you are also a speaker, the group may need a series of speeches in different locations or departments within their organization. Any of that and more can and does happen from a tips booklet.

Keep in mind that the booklet is a less expensive way of accomplishing all of this, for you as the publisher, and for your buyers. Booklets will open many of these doors for you more conveniently, less expensively, and with fewer time lags than attempting to do some of the very same things using your full-length book. At the very least, you now have choices to offer people, based on their interest, budget, learning style, storage space, and desired "wow" factor.

Once your tips booklet manuscript has been developed, you will find that document can also be converted into many other products that will market your book and become their own revenue streams much in the same way booklets serve you, further expanding your product line.

When your business has a full menu of related products and services, you are able to successfully tap into what your buyers need and want, and keep your own cash flowing. The possibilities are endless when it comes to how a booklet can serve your book business.

What will your first booklet be?

Paulette Ensign has sold almost a million copies in four languages of a tips booklet, "110 Ideas for Organizing Your Business Life," without spending a penny on advertising. She has had clients achieve similar results, including many book authors.

She is Founder, CEO, and Chief Visionary of Tips Products International, in San Diego, Calif., which offers a range of products and services for all budgets to support the creation of successful tips booklets. For more, visit www.tipsbooklets.com

# Writing White Papers

*by Michael Stelzner*

WHITE PAPERS help people make decisions. The white paper can talk business or converse technically, and it can inform or influence.

The white paper's underlying strength rests on this premise: If you give readers something of value, they will give you their loyalty, and ultimately their business.

Crafting the white paper can be a rewarding and profitable experience. A single well-written white paper can propel a business to the thought-leadership position and lead to enormous business opportunities. When you author a successful white paper, its positive results are credited to your efforts.

## What is a White Paper?

Gordon Graham, an experienced white paper writer, describes white papers as persuasive essays and observes that their style rests "somewhere between a lively magazine article and a dry-as-dust academic paper." He adds that white papers are fact-driven and contain useful information, expert opinions, and ironclad logic.

White papers are tools used to create a positive image of a company in the eyes of its readership, explains Dr. Russell Willerton, a professor from Boise State University.

According to veteran writer Jonathan Kantor, white papers reveal product or service features and translate them into business advantages.

> *Detailed definition: A white paper is a technical or business-benefits document that introduces a challenge faced by its readers and makes a strong case why a particular approach to solving the problem is preferred.*

A white paper usually proposes a solution to a problem, but can also introduce a new concept or describe how to perform technical tasks. Most white papers range from 6 to 12 pages in length; however, some can exceed 50 pages. White papers are comprised of mostly text and usually very few graphics. However, diagrams, charts and illustrations are commonly included in most white papers.

The marketing aspect of a white paper is typically a very soft sell. Overt marketing messages are usually left for other documents. Often, solutions are introduced only after a significant case has been established, demonstrating a clear need.

## Why White Papers Matter

The decision to produce a white paper usually stems from the need to sell products and services. Interestingly, the same can be said of brochures, PowerPoint presentations, and case studies. What differentiates white papers is their attractiveness to specific types of audiences, including engineers, business executives, and other key decision-makers.

Often a white paper will work its way across the desks of an organization in a way that no other document could ever hope to achieve. White papers are able to fly under the radar and penetrate most organizations' anti-marketing defenses because they are sought after and brought into the organization by decision-makers. If well-written, white papers will not only reach their target, they will influence them.

White papers can be very persuasive marketing tools. When a good white paper lands in front of the right person, it is a highly effective lead-generation and sales instrument.

When asking clients how they found out about my business, the response has often been, "I registered for your white paper a few months back." In some cases, it was more than a year between when a client registered for a white paper and called to inquire about our services. Thus, white papers can have a very long shelf life and if well-written can become viral marketing documents.

In addition, white papers provide a great opportunity to introduce a new concept or show industry thought leadership. Often, professional organizations will highlight a good white paper and suggest it to their members.

## Why You Should Care about White Papers

Writing an effective and persuasive white paper for your company or client can be extremely rewarding. Often, the document becomes a foundational piece that can be leveraged for many other projects, including presentations, contributed articles, and website content.

For freelance writers, white papers represent one of the most profitable forms of writing. Word for word, there is no other type of writing that pays as well as white papers. Some experienced white paper writers charge up to $1,000 per page.

White papers can also bring significant recognition to the writer. If the white paper is well-received in your industry or goes viral, your name will be associated with the excellent ideas presented in your paper.

## How White Papers are Used

White papers are generally produced for one of three reasons: to generate leads, to demonstrate thought leadership or to help close sales.

**Lead Generation.** Most organizations will leverage their corporate website, online advertising campaigns, or white-paper syndication networks to generate leads with white papers. Additionally, many direct-mail and traditional advertisements use the white paper as a call to action.

**Thought Leadership.** Often, businesses will write white papers on concepts that are theoretical or discuss the future of an industry or technology. Thought-leadership papers are typically written to demonstrate forward thinking, to help convince existing customers to stick with a company, and to persuade the world to buy in to a future vision. These types of white papers convert nicely into trade publication articles.

**Close Sales.** White papers are often used in the later stages of a sales cycle; as a "leave behind" after a client meeting. While white papers can help close existing prospects, they are most effective for generating pre-sales leads because executives and decision-makers rely on white papers when researching solutions to problems.

Because white papers are usually educational and not hard-sell pieces, they can quickly become viral documents that spread across an organization.

White papers can be sent as responses to advertisements or when a salesperson has engaged a prospect who is asking for more information. Kantor explains their many sales uses: "White papers are used as online collateral, as handouts to support live presentations, as e-mail attachments in business correspondence, as incentive offers within advertisements and as a core ingredient within a direct mail campaign."

The vast majority of white papers are distributed as electronic documents in the form of Adobe PDF files. In the past, white papers were printed and mailed; however, the Internet has opened up new distribution models, dramatically reducing the need to print white papers.

### Who Reads White Papers?

In the past, white papers were primarily targeted at engineers and technical influencers. However, today's typical white paper reader has shifted significantly. Modern white paper readers are decision-makers and tend to be businesspeople rather than engineers.

If targeted appropriately, white papers can be valuable to literally anyone. For example, a small business owner or an investor are worthwhile recipients of white papers—just be aware that they may be more accustomed to the term guide than white paper.

### The Emergence of White Papers as Marketing Tools

Prior to the 1990s, datasheets, brochures, and presentations were the predominant forms of marketing collateral. These marketing tools were often perceived to be biased materials that were discounted by prospects early in the decision-making process.

How could marketing professionals get their complex messages in front of qualified customers? A marketing tool was needed that would be read by potential clients and work as a sales agent before contact was ever initiated.

Many businesses were submitting articles to trade publications. These articles stripped out much of the typical marketing spin and began educating readers. However, this type of marketing made businesses subject to the whim of publishers.

White papers became the solution. They were already accepted in the technology world as educational documents. They also had longer shelf lives than articles. In some cases, portions of the white paper could also be repurposed for contributed articles.

Today, most organizations either use in-house or contract writers to author their white papers, rather than subject-matter experts. Regardless of who writes them, executives and decision-makers rely heavily on white papers when researching solutions to problems.

## White Paper Standards

Despite the fact that millions of white papers have been written, there are few or no recognized industry standards. I have seen one-page advertisements and full-length books wrongly labeled as white papers. The phrase is so attractive to some industries that businesses are slapping the label on just about anything.

To help establish standards, WhitePaperSource surveyed hundreds of white paper writers. Here are some of the findings that resulted from their surveys and forum discussions. White papers should:

> Begin by addressing problems, challenges or needs, rather than the solution
> Range from 5 to 12 pages in length, on average
> Educate as a top priority
> Avoid direct selling
> Focus on benefits more than features
> Contain information useful to the reader
> Avoid the use of humor

Now that you understand what a white paper is, its value, and how it is used, it is important to [learn] how to create a well-written white paper. Even though white papers are everywhere, most are never read cover-to-cover. To ensure your paper is embraced by readers, it is critical to start with a thorough needs assessment.

Michael A. Stelzner is one of the leading authorities on writing and marketing white papers. He has written nearly 100 white papers for many prominent companies, including Microsoft, FedEx, Motorola, Monster, and Hewlett-Packard. He is author of the book, *Writing White Papers: How To Capture Readers and Keep Them Engaged*; for more on this title, see his website at www.writingwhitepapers.com. This article is condensed from Chapter 1, "A Primer on White Papers."

He also is editor of a monthly publication called *WhitePaperSource Newsletter*, and also founded WhitePaperSource.com, a unique portal site dedicated to the topic.

# Have a Positive Influence

*by Deborah Raney*

JUST BEFORE a new book is ready to hit the bookstores, most publishers send out what they call "influencers copies"—hot-off-the-press books intended to start a buzz among readers all over the country. What fun it is to send one hundred reading friends a free copy of my new novel! But often the question that follows the thank-you is, "What am I required to do as an influencer?"

Well, technically, nothing. There is no obligation whatsoever in being an influencer. If a particular book isn't your cup of tea, please pass it along to someone you think might enjoy it. But if you do like the book, there are numerous ways to help spread the word.

Not everyone will feel comfortable or have the means to drop leaflets while parachuting from an airplane, but on the list below, you'll find at least one thing that will be a perfect fit with the ways God has gifted you. And I guarantee your efforts, large or small, will bless the author.

> Write a review for the book on online bookstores such as:
>> www.amazon.com
>> www.barnesandnoble.com
>> www.christianbook.com
> Write a review at one of the many online book review sites, including:
>> www.acfw.com/bookreviews.html
>> www.faithfulreader.com/wom/wom.asp
>> www.epinions.com
> At www.christianbook.com, you can recommend books via an email link that will take your friends right to the page of the book you're promoting.
> Recommend the book as a featured title for an area book discus-

sion group. This is especially appropriate if the book has discussion questions in the back.

> Start a discussion about the book on your blog or on email loops you're a part of.
> If you have a website or write a newsletter, consider featuring novels you've read and enjoyed.
> Add the book to your list of favorites on Myspace, Facebook, or other online communities.
> After reading and reviewing the book, give it away as a prize in a drawing on your website or blog.
> If you have a unique perspective—for instance, personal experience with the book's topic, a man offering a male perspective for a women's fiction book, etc.—offer your insights in venues that might not ordinarily hear about the book.
> Donate your influencer copy to your public library or church library when you're finished reading it. Better yet, share your copy in other ways and buy a second copy for the library.
> Print out a review you've written—or other reviews of the book— and give them to your public or church librarians for consideration.
> Offer to distribute bookmarks and/or postcards for the author or publisher. Public libraries, church libraries, bookstores, and gift shops are usually happy to have giveaways on their counters.
> Ask your church if you could tuck postcards or bookmarks in the morning service bulletin some Sunday.
> Place bookmarks or postcards about the book at each place setting as favors for a luncheon or banquet.
> Hang out in your local bookstore and "hand sell" the book by talking it up to customers shopping in the fiction department.
> Talk to the clerks in any bookstores and libraries you visit and ask if they carry the book. If not give them a short book report and recommend they order a few copies.
> When visiting bookstores, do a little creative rearranging to turn the book face out on the shelves. Use good judgment and don't hide one book to promote another. Also keep in mind that in some stores front-table space is paid for by the publisher, so don't "steal."
> Offer to write a book review for your church newsletter, neighbor-

hood newspaper, or any other printed source that might reach readers.

> At your next women's retreat, volunteer to organize a book table, where you will feature the book.

> Offer to organize a blog tour for the author, setting up a week when numerous blogs will feature the book and interviews with the author.

> When you're finished with the book, tuck it into a gift basket for someone who is ill or in the hospital, or take it to your next dinner party as a hostess gift.

> Leave the book in a waiting room where someone with a few extra minutes might start reading it.

> Prison ministries are always looking for wholesome books to distribute. Check out groups like Prison Book Project: www.nbbd.com/npr/PrisonBooks/index.html.

> Word-of-mouth is still probably the number one way books hit bestseller lists, so simply start conversations about the book. Tell your friends and family what you've been reading and why you enjoyed it so much.

Using any one (or more) of the ideas above, you can have a profound influence on the life of a book—and its author.

Deborah Raney is at work on her 17th novel. Her books have won the RITA Award, the HOLT Medallion, the National Readers' Choice Award and the Silver Angel from Excellence in Media. Her first novel, *A Vow to Cherish*, inspired the World Wide Pictures film of the same title. She serves on the advisory board of American Christian Fiction Writers, and lives in Kansas. Her website is www.deborahraney.com.

This article appeared in Terry Whalin's *Right Writing* newsletter in the January 26, 2007 issue.

# INTERNET SKILLS

# Your Author Website: Five Tips

*by Patrice-Anne Rutledge*

If you're an author, you need a website. A website is the core and starting point of any online book promotion campaign. Despite the current popularity of blogs, podcasts, and ezines, your website is still your primary online "home" for information on your book. To create a profitable site that generates results, you need to do several things:

## 1. Determine What Drives Your Site.

When you plan the structure and content of your site, one of the first things to determine is what drives your website.

> On a personality-driven site, the author is the draw. This is most common for fiction writers or authors of creative nonfiction in which who you are is more important to readers than the specific subject matter you cover.

> A platform-driven site is most common with nonfiction authors who are experts in a particular niche and offer a book (or a series of books) on this topic in addition to related products and services such as consulting, speaking engagements, audio CDs, and special reports.

> A book-driven site is appropriate for authors who have written a single book or multiple books on unrelated topics. In this case, the book itself is the draw.

Determine what your driver is and then build your site around this focal point.

## 2. Focus on Your Audience.

Any book website has at least two audiences: your readers and the media. Be sure to design a site that meets the needs of both. For your main site content, develop a profile of your target reader, and focus your site on this profile. Are you targeting new parents, travelers to Italy, or fans of romantic suspense? Think about what your target audience is looking for and meet that need.

### 3. Establish Site Goals.

Establishing site goals is important if you want to profit from your website. Are you primarily interested in selling books? Or do you want to sell other products and services as well? Are you hoping to garner major media coverage or establish yourself as a professional speaker? Write down specific goals and keep these in mind as you plan your site.

### 4. Remember that Content is King.

Now that you've determined what drives your site and have a clear idea of your target audience and the goals you want to achieve, it's time to start thinking about your content. The right content can make the difference between a high-traffic site that drives the sale of books, products, and services and a site that receives few visitors.

The following are several tips for creating quality web content:

> Before even starting any site design, map out your page content.
> Determine the goal for each page on your site and create content that supports that goal. For example, you may have pages that are informational and others there to generate sales for your books and products. Truly informational pages usually take on a more journalistic tone, but sales-oriented pages should have a call to action.
> Remember that you're writing for the web, not another medium. If you're not an experienced web copywriter, consider learning more about writing for the web.
> Keep in mind that the design supports the content; the content doesn't support the design.

### 5. Encourage Action.

Before creating your site, decide what action you want your site visitors to take. Do you want them to buy your book? Purchase additional products? Sign up for your classes, coaching services, or ezine? Hire you as a speaker? For each specific action you'd like a visitor to take, you need to create a call to action, web copy that encourages a website visitor or email recipient to take a desired action, such as purchase a product or sign up for an ezine.

By doing some upfront strategic planning, you can create a site that generates results—and profits.

Patrice-Anne Rutledge is the bestselling author of 24 books, a successful technology journalist, and an expert in online book promotion. She is the author of *The Web-Savvy Writer: Book Promotion with a High-Tech Twist* (Pacific Ridge Press, 2006), which shows authors how to profit from the latest techniques in online book promotion.

Her website is www.websavvywriter.com.

# Creating an Online Portfolio

*by Moira Allen*

ONE OF the questions most often asked about sending e-mail queries and submissions is "how do I send clips?" Most editors don't want to receive clips as attachments (e.g., as Word or PDF files), and stuffing clips into the body of an e-mail can make your message cumbersome and unprofessional.

One solution is to develop an online portfolio—an author Web site where you can post your "clips." Then, you can simply refer editors to that page for samples of your work. (Always give them the option, of course, of requesting clips by surface mail as well!)

An online portfolio works very much like a physical portfolio. It should be attractive, easy to peruse, and representative of your best work. If you know a little HTML, it is easy to create such a page yourself; if you don't, you'll find a number of services online that will create a low-cost author page from a set of standard templates.

In the past, many authors turned to free or inexpensive web-hosting sites to post their author pages and portfolios. While these are certainly an option, today it looks far more professional to have one's own domain name, particularly if you hope to achieve more recognition for that name. The simplest type of domain name is simply your own—e.g., "www.maryjones.com."

The problem, of course, is that if you have a relatively common name, chances are that the domain has already been taken. You can also try variations; besides using ".net" and ".org" suffixes, consider hyphenating your name (e.g., "www.mary-jones.net" or "www.mary_jones.org").

If you focus upon a particular area of writing, you might also consider taking out a domain name that reflects your expertise, such as "www.thepetwriter.com." Avoid overly "cute" domain names, however, such as "www.thestarvingwriter.com" or "www.theperfectpoet.com."

These days it costs around $20 per year (or less) to register a domain name. To find a place to host your website, check sites like Find An ISP (www.findanisp.com), HostSearch (www.hostsearch.com/), or Find-MyHosting.com (www.findmyhosting.com).

Most clip sites open with an attractive home page that includes the name of the author, a brief bio, perhaps a photo, and links to the clips themselves. Some authors include a more extensive bio page or even a resume or curriculum vitae. If you include more than a paragraph of biographical material, make this a separate page. The site should also include contact information.

Many authors use portfolio sites not simply to show off a range of clips, but to demonstrate their expertise in a particular area. For example, someone who writes about pets might develop a site not just to showcase his or her pet articles, but to serve as a general pet information resource on the Web. The advantage to creating a "resource" (rather than just a portfolio) is that you'll be able to encourage other sites on related topics to link to you—and thus possibly attract the attention of editors in that subject area even before you send them a query!

Here are some things to keep in mind when posting clips:

1. Make sure that you have the right to post the material. If you've sold all rights to a piece, or all electronic rights, or exclusive electronic rights, you may not "own" the right to post the material on your own site. While selling all rights to an article doesn't preclude you from *mailing* a clip, posting that material on a Web site is often considered a form of "publication," which your contract may prohibit. Some publications (print or electronic) make exceptions for personal Web sites, but others don't. If you have any doubts, check with the editor or publication that originally published the piece.

2. Post only your *best* material. Don't ask editors to wade through a mass of unrelated articles, and don't post everything you've ever written since that first essay in your high-school newsletter. Think about the types of clips you'd select to mail to an editor; those are the clips you want on your site!

3. If possible, post the material in HTML format. Try to post an electronic version of the *edited* article—i.e., the version that was actually published, rather than your original manuscript. The published

article may have been significantly changed from your original submission. If you don't have an electronic file of that version, ask your editor; often, the editor will be able to send you the final, published file. (A final alternative, of course, is to retype the clip from the published version.)

4. If you must scan a clip, save it as a PDF file rather than as a JPEG. Such a file enables the editor to see the clip just as it was published. An editor can choose to download the file to read it, or click on it to view it through a browser just like an HTML file. In addition, once you've scanned a clip and saved it as a PDF file, this will enable you to send it as an attachment if an editor requests that you do so. Most scanners have the ability to save a file directly as a PDF file.

5. Link to clips that are posted on other sites. If your work has been published online, either by an e-zine or by a print publication that posts or archives material on the Web, consider linking to that publication directly rather than posting the clip on your own site. By doing so, you enable the editor to view the clip in context—i.e., within the publication in which it actually appeared.

6. Provide full publication details for every clip. List the publication in which the clip appeared, and the date. You might also wish to include a link to the publication, if it has a Web site.

7. Include copyright information on every clip page. Each page should clearly state that the material on the page is copyrighted (in your name) and cannot be used or reprinted without your permission. Make sure that anyone interested in reprinting your materials can contact you easily.

8. Organize your clips by subject or category. Consider what types of editors you might be referring to your clip page, and organize your clips accordingly. Create a table of contents for each category, and a master table of contents that links to the various categories. If you have only a few clips in each category (or only a few categories), your master table of contents could include both the categories and the titles of the clips.

Finally, keep in mind that a clip site should be just that: a site that displays your previously published work. Don't waste your time posting unpublished articles in hopes that an editor will surf by and decide to buy them; it rarely happens. In the first place, editors receive more than enough material through ordinary channels and don't feel the need to go out hunting for more. In the second place, most editors aren't going to be interested in articles that you've written with no particular market in mind; they want to know that you've reviewed their publication and targeted their audience specifically.

Articles posted "for sale" on a Web site clearly don't meet that criteria. Most importantly, your portfolio should be the place where you publicize your successes, not your lack of them!

Moira Allen, editor of Writing-World.com, has published more than 350 articles and columns and seven books, including *How to Write for Magazines*; *Starting Your Career as a Freelance Writer*; *The Writer's Guide to Queries, Pitches and Proposals*; and *Writing.com: Creative Internet Strategies to Advance Your Writing Career*.

Allen is a contributing editor for *The Writer*. She also hosts the travel website TimeTravel-Britain.com, the Pet Loss Support Page, and the photography website Allen-Images.net.

An earlier version of this article originally appeared in *The Writer* magazine.

# Why Aren't You Blogging?

*by Lani Voivod*

I HAVE five minutes to write this post.

However ...

I have hours upon hours—days, really!—of pent-up energy on the subject of why you should be blogging. I'm sitting on the equivalent of a massive nuclear weapon here, or the cure for cancer, and no one's really understanding the implications....

Ever have one of those dreams when you're doing everything you can to run at a full sprint, but it feels like your legs are thigh deep in black tar? Or you're trying like heck to shout a very important message to someone you love, like "Get out of the way! The train's coming!" or "Watch out! There's a giant shark fin right behind you!!" but all that comes out is strained, laryngitis-ized hot air?

This is what's happening in my life right now. I sit across from friends and business associates, talk with entrepreneurs and small business owners, and share strategy sessions with larger companies and corporations, and I mention the possibility of them blogging. There's a universal glazed look, often followed by a shrug, or a nose crinkle. "Eh, I don't see the point," or "Yeah, I thought about that...."

I know it's my job to just let it go, and I do, because every business person knows the "I'm not ready to talk about this" look. Oh, but it's killing me! Because if you're serious about your business, career, or professional reputation, there is absolutely no reason for you not to publicize your interest and expertise in the form of a blog.

1.  A blog is conversational. It comes alive with *your* distinct voice, style, and proclivities. It dies if it's fueled by the dreaded corp-speak, stiff language, or totally self-conscious and "safe," play-by-the-rules drivel.

2. A blog is *free*. (Or extremely low-cost, depending on how you go.) I mean, come on, what else is *free* these days?!

3. A blog is a mirror. It's an organized trail of your ideas, experience, and hints at your vision. It's *also* a living, breathing organic organism that grows as you grow. It's like one of those "smart" computers that develops its own life and personality over time.

4. A blog is search-engine friendly. It's *proof* you know your industry or subject matter. It's *proof* you're active in your business and niche.

5. A blog is a way to connect with other like-minded professionals. When you comment on someone else's blog, or when they comment on yours, it's like a quick, manly nod that says, "Hey. Saw your post. Liked it. Peace out."

6. A blog is a simple, searchable content management system. Why, oh why, are you hoarding all of your industry knowledge to yourself? Are you saving it for posterity? Do you think St. Peter will give you extra points for having a huge collection of inaccessible folders on your computer?

7. A blog is *fun*, darnit! It's a chance to just be you, and even see and experience your own voice and priorities over time.

Sure, a lot of blogging gurus say there are "rules"—like, "you should blog at least three times a week!" or "be strategic" or "keep posts short; avoid long tangents!" (like this one). And a lot of PAGs (that's People Against Blogging) say no one reads them, or they're a waste of time, or all of the above. But to this I say, *who cares*?!

No one's reading your darn internal folders, or going through your file cabinets, but you still throw articles and information in there!

Why not claim your intellectual territory and put a select and steady amount of information, opinions, photos, and energy *out there* to be discovered by one or more of the proverbial masses, if and when they come looking for you or the information, knowledge, products, or services you have to offer?

God didn't just not bother with Antarctica because he figured no one would ever find the frigid continent, right? And now, with advances in technology, we get to watch fine films like *March of the Penguins*, *National Treasure*, and *The X-Files Movie*.

If you have a passion, specialty, niche, mission, or business (and you gotta have at least one of those things, unless you're a corpse ... or Paris Hilton), then *start blogging*. Don't worry about traffic. Don't worry about the nit-picky stuff.

Do it imperfectly. Find your voice. Discover your flow. Loosen up. Be bold. Get yourself out there.

And if you refuse, please answer me one question in the comment field. *Why?*

Lani Butler Voivod is a creative consultant and co-owner and "Chief Creativity Evangelist" of Epiphanies, Inc. She also leads a local writers' group, Wild Quills. This article (January 2007) comes from the A-Ha! blog (www.epiphaniesinc.com/blog). She lives in New Hampshire.

# Fundamentals of Blogging

*by Steve Weber*

BLOGGING is a relatively easy way for you to publicize your book and even improve your writing while you're at it. If you can write an e-mail, you can write a blog—it's the easiest, cheapest, and perhaps best way for authors to find an audience and connect with readers. Blogging is an informal, intimate form of communication that inspires trust among your readers.

For the same reasons that traditional advertising is usually ineffective for selling books, a blog can be highly effective for book promotion. People interested in your topic seek out your message.

## What is a blog?

Put simply, a blog is a Web site with a few interactive features. You don't have to call it a blog unless you want to. It's possible that within a few years, nearly every Web site will have interactive features, and people simply won't call them blogs anymore.

You needn't know anything about computers to blog. Simply type into a form, and presto—the whole world can see it. Your blog is a *content management* system—a painless way to build and maintain a platform where readers can discover and enjoy your writing.

A blog can be a part of your Web site, or it can be *the* Web site. The main thing that distinguishes a blog from a plain old Web site is that a blog is frequently updated with short messages, or *posts*. Readers often chime in with their own comments at the bottom of each post. This free exchange of ideas is what makes blogs a revolutionary tool for authors: A successful blog is a constant stream of ideas, inspiration, perspective, and advice—it's a real-time, global focus group.

## Why blogs are better

Some authors who already have a book for sale resist the idea of blogging and the "extra work" it entails. Their reasoning is, "Why create more deadlines when your book is already finished?" Well, blogging can help you maximize the effectiveness of things you're probably already doing, like answering e-mails from your readers.

Compared with other types of Internet publicity content such as static Web sites or e-mail newsletters, blogs provide three big advantages:

> Blogs are easy to start and maintain.
> The short, serialized content of blogs encourages regular readership, repeated exposure to your books, and more sales.
> Blogs rank high in search-engine results from Google and other providers, making them easy to find.

Why do blogs get so much traffic from search engines? First, blogs are topical. When you're writing about the same topics and ideas day in and day out, your site becomes packed with the keywords your audience is searching for. Stay at it awhile, and it becomes nearly impossible for your target audience to miss you, thanks to Google and the other search engines. Most new visitors will find your site by using a search engine, after looking for words and topics contained in your Web pages.

Another reason blogs are so easy to find is that search engines usually rank them higher than other types of Web sites. Thus your links can show up at the top of search results, which is where most people click.

Google and the other search engines give extra credit to blogs for a couple of reasons:

> Blogs are updated frequently, and the assumption is "fresh" content is more valuable.
> Blogs tend to have many links from other Web pages with similar content. The assumption is that because other bloggers and Webmasters have decided to link to your content, it's probably valuable.

Your visibility in search results is key, since about 40 percent of your new visitors will likely arrive via a Web search. If your site ranks highly in Web searches for the keywords related to your book, you'll have a constant source of well-qualified visitors and likely book buyers.

## Breathing the blogosphere

Step 1 in becoming a blogger is to consume some blogs yourself. Reading other blogs gives you a quick feel for what works, what doesn't, and the techniques you'll want to apply to your own blog.

There are millions of blogs, and finding ones that suit you can be like searching for a needle in a haystack. There's no easy way to filter out low-quality blogs—you've just got to sample what's out there.

A good place to begin is by browsing for blogs about your hobbies, pastimes, and passions. You can find a list of the most popular blogs here:

www.Technorati.com/pop/blogs

You can drill down deeper into niche territory by browsing www.Technorati.com/blogs, where you'll find a menu of subjects on the left. You can also search blogs by keyword at these sites:

www.Blogsearch.Google.com
www.Feedster.com
www.IceRocket.com

Once you've found a few blogs of interest, it's easy to find more. Bloggers tend to link to one another, both within their blog posts, and often within a side menu of links known as a *blogroll*.

A handy tool for keeping track of all your blogs is a *newsreader* or *aggregator*, which saves you the trouble of poking around the Web, looking for new blog posts. Instead, your newsreader gathers and displays updates for you. One free, easy-to-use reader is:

www.Bloglines.com

You'll quickly learn which blogs you've subscribed to are must-reads, and which can be ignored or deleted.

## Connecting with readers

It's natural to be apprehensive about starting a blog. When you first begin, it may feel like being on stage without a script or a view of the audience. Don't worry, feedback will come soon enough. Remember, there's no right or wrong way to blog. The only rule is your target audience must find something worthwhile.

One way to ease into blogging is to start with a temporary blog at www.Blogger.com, where you can set up a free practice blog in five minutes. Take a dry run for a week or two, then make your blog public when you're ready.

Good blogs are addictive, which is one reason they're so effective for authors. Many book buyers must be exposed to a title six or seven times before deciding to buy. With a good blog, getting repeated exposure won't be a problem.

A lively blog is like a focus group and writing laboratory rolled into one: It provides you with constant feedback, criticism, and new ideas. Your blog readers will pepper you with comments and e-mails. When you've struck a chord, you'll know immediately from the response. When you lay an egg, you'll know that too, from the silence.

Just as theater companies try out new productions in the hinterlands before storming Broadway, authors can fine tune their material on their blog, says technology writer Clive Thompson:

> Ask writers who blog regularly—like me—and they'll tell you how exciting it is to be wired in directly to your audience. They correspond with you, pass you tips, correct your factual blunders, and introduce you to brilliant new ideas and people. The Internet isn't just an audience, it's an auxiliary brain. But you have to turn it on, and it takes work. You can't fake participation and authenticity online.

Indeed, the true power of blogging is the momentum created by your audience. Once your blog has 100 frequent readers, it has critical mass. It may take six months or a year to get there, but from there it's all downhill. Members of your core audience begin competing to hand you the most useful, compelling ideas by writing comments on your blog and e-mailing you directly. That's when your blog becomes electric, a magnet attracting new readers. Your core audience swells as word of mouth goes viral.

### Your blog's angle

A nonfiction author's blog can approach the topic from several directions:

> New developments.
> New products or services.

> Hot-button issues of the day.
> What other blogs or media are saying.
> Reviews of new books in the field.

You can publish a blog in the style of a perpetual newsletter, an aggregation of interesting tidbits about your book's topic. As you notice new things and write about them, each post is stacked on top, and with each new post added on top, one of the older posts is bumped from the bottom and sent to your archives.

Let's imagine you're writing a blog on the topic of *Organic Strawberries*. Your blog could serve as an information clearinghouse covering every conceivable angle and trend of organic strawberry growing, cooking, and consuming. You'll constantly monitor consumer and trade media for the latest news on organic growing, interpret this material for your audience, and link to the source material, adding your own commentary.

Your blog could include:
> Questions from your blog readers on organic fruit, along with your answers.
> Guest articles from experts on organic strawberry gardening.
> New books and magazines on the topic.
> Strawberry dessert recipes.
> The best places to grow organic strawberries.
> Listings and maps of markets offering organic strawberries.
> Reviews of cookbooks addressing natural, organic, fruit and dessert preparation.

Fiction authors have even more freedom, but a bigger creative burden. They can write about themselves, or even from the point of view of a fictional character. A story from their book can continue on the blog, veering off in new directions, experimentally, in response to suggestions from readers and other writers

## Writing your blog posts

The essential ingredient of a blog is its short entries, or posts. They're arranged in reverse chronological order, with the newest at top.

Posts can be a few sentences long, or many paragraphs long, and often link to outside information like blogs, newspaper stories, or multimedia clips hosted elsewhere on the Web. Nearly any tidbit of information relevant to your audience can be spun into a blog post of some type:

**Informational.** A news-oriented blurb. A new development.

**Question/Answer.** Easy to write, and fun to read. Reliable material, even if you have to make up the question.

**Instructional.** Can be a longer post, a tutorial that explains how to do something related to your niche.

**Link posts.** Find an interesting blog post elsewhere. Link to it and add your own spin.

**Rant.** Let off some steam, and let it rip. Interesting blogs don't play it safe, they take sides.

**Book review.** Review a book related to your field. It can be a new book or a classic that newcomers haven't heard of.

**Product reviews.** The word "review" is a popular search term. Give your frank opinion, and encourage your readers to chime in with their own views.

**Lists.** Write about the "Top 5 Ways" to do a task, or the "Top 10 Reasons" for such-and-such. Readers love lists. If someone else publishes a list, you can summarize it or critique it on your own blog.

**Interviews.** Chat with someone in your field. Provide a text summary on your blog. You can also add a transcript or even an audio file.

**Case studies.** Report on how so-and-so does such-and-such. You don't have to call it a "case study," just tell the story.

**Profiles.** Profiles focus on a particular person, a personality. The person profiled can be someone well known in your field, or perhaps a newcomer nobody's heard of.

Most blogs are conversational and informal, but that doesn't give authors a license to be sloppy. Readers expect clear writing from an author, and that requires attention to detail—not to mention beginning your sentences with capital letters and ending them with periods. It's worth proofreading and spell-checking your posts before publishing. Keeping your paragraphs short will minimize your rewriting chores.

## Selecting your blog publishing tool
Most bloggers don't have special blogging software installed on their

PC, but work on their blog from within a Web browser. Here are the most popular blogging services:

**Blogger.com.** Owned by Google since 2003. It's free and easy. There's an add-on program enabling you to post to your blog from Microsoft Word. You can use Blogger's free Web space, Blogspot.com, but it's best to keep your content on a domain you control, like Your-BookTitle.com. Do this by using Blogger's FTP feature. For instructions: http://Help.Blogger.com/bin/topic.py?topic=8917.

Other blogging systems have similar options: You can publish free on their Web space, or publish on your own domain.

**TypePad.com.** TypePad is a flexible and professional-looking platform, but takes a bit longer to learn than Blogger. Still, you'll have many options for personalizing your blog without having to learn HTML computer code. Basic service costs $4.95 a month; the Plus level costs $8.95 a month and gives you up to three blogs hosted on your own domain. A 30-day free trial is available.

**WordPress.com.** Set up a free blog, or upgrade to a fuller-featured service. All that's required to begin is a user name and e-mail address.

Steve Weber is a veteran of the U.S. Air Force and a former newspaper reporter with a degree in journalism from West Virginia University. He lives in the Virginia suburbs of Washington, D.C. Since 2000, he has been a successful online book dealer, specializing in hard-to-find fiction and nonfiction. In 2005, Weber wrote and published *The Home-Based Bookstore* through his own press, Weber Books (www.weberbooks.com).

This article is excerpted from his newest book, *Plug This Book: Online Book Marketing for Authors* (Weber Books, 2007) from a chapter on blogging. His own blog for this book can be found at www.PlugYourBook.com.

# 10 Tips on Writing the Living Web

*by Mark Bernstein*

SOME PARTS of the web are finished, unchanging creations—as polished and as fixed as books or posters. But many parts change all the time:

> News sites bring up-to-the-minute developments, ranging from breaking news and sports scores to reports on specific industries, markets, and technical fields;
> Weblogs, journals, and other personal sites provide a window on the interests and opinions of their creators;
> Corporate weblogs, wikis, knowledge banks, community sites, and workgroup journals provide share news and knowledge among co-workers and supply-chain stakeholders.

Some of these sites change every week; many change every day; a few change every few minutes. Daypop's Dan Chan calls this the Living Web, the part of the web that is always changing.

Every revision requires new writing, new words that become the essence of the site. Living sites are only as good as today's update. If the words are dull, nobody will read them, and nobody will come back. If the words are wrong, people will be misled, disappointed, infuriated. If the words aren't there, people will shake their heads and lament your untimely demise.

Writing for the Living Web is a tremendous challenge. Here are ten tips that can help.

## 1. Write for a reason.

Write for a reason, and know why you write. Whether your daily updates concern your work life, your hobbies, or your innermost feelings, write passionately about things that matter.

To an artist, the smallest grace note and the tiniest flourish may be matters of great importance. Show us the details, teach us why they matter. People are fascinated by detail and enthralled by passion; explain to us why it matters to you, and no detail is too small, no technical question too arcane.

Bad personal sites bore us by telling us about trivial events and casual encounters about which we have no reason to care. Don't tell us what happened: tell us why it matters. Don't tell us your opinion: tell us why the question is important.

If you don't really care, don't write. If you are a student and everybody is talking about exams and papers and you simply don't care, let it be. If your job bores you, it will bore us. (If you despise your job with a rich, enduring passion, that's another thing entirely!) Write for yourself; you are, in the end, your most important reader.

If your site belongs to a product, a project, or an enterprise, you must still find a way to represent its passion and excitement. If you do not understand why your product is compelling or comprehend the beauty of your enterprise, find the reason or find a new writer.

Write honestly. Don't hide, and don't stop short. When writing about things that matter, you may be tempted to flee to safe, familiar havens: the familiar, the sentimental, the fashionable. Try to find the strength to be honest, to avoid starting the journey with passion and ending it with someone else's tired formula. The work may be hard, it may be embarrassing, but it will be true—and it will be you, not a tired formula or an empty design. And if you can be satisfied with that tired formula, you aren't writing for a reason.

Never, for any consideration, publish a statement you know to be false.

Though you write with passion about things that matter greatly, always remember that it's a big world, filled with people and stories. Don't expect the world to stop and listen. Never expect any individual (or, worse, any quantity of individuals) to read your work, for they may have other things to do. At the same time, steel yourself to expect the unexpected visitor and the uninvited guest; the most unlikely people may read your work. Your mother, who never uses a computer, may read your intimate weblog one day in the library. To be honest with the world, you may need to be honest with your mother; if you cannot face your mother, perhaps you are not ready to write for the world.

## 2. Write often.

If you are writing for the Living Web, you must write consistently. You need not write constantly, and you need not write long, but you must write often. One afternoon in grad school, I heard B. F. Skinner remark that fifteen minutes a day, every day, adds up to about book every year, which he suggested was as much writing as anyone should indulge. You don't need to write much, but you must write, and write often.

If you don't write for a few days, you are unfaithful to the readers who come to visit. Missing an update is a small thing—rudeness, not betrayal—and readers will excuse the occasional lapse.

If you are inconsistent, readers will conclude you are untrustworthy. If you are absent, readers will conclude you are gone. It's better to keep religiously to a once-a-week, or once-a-fortnight schedule, than to go dark mysteriously.

If you cannot write for a time, and the reason for your absence is interesting, write about it. Your honeymoon, your kidney transplant, your sister's gubernatorial inauguration—all these can be predicted and worked into the fabric of your writing so that the interruption, when it comes, seems natural. But avoid, if you can, sudden cryptic pronouncements: "I'll be unable to post for a while" gives us nothing we can use or learn from.

Don't assume that you will find something to say every morning. The day will come, sooner or later, when you need inspiration and find you have none. Store topics, news items, entire articles for slow times. Carry a notebook or a PDA and jot down reminders. You cannot have too many notes saved up, but you can easily find yourself with too few.

Since you write often, use good tools. Select them to fit your hand and voice. Learn to use them well.

## 3. Write tight.

Omit unnecessary words.

Choose a visual design that fits your voice. Unless the design is the point of your site, select colors and visual elements that support without dominating. Resist the temptation to add features, for it is often best to use only those few technical and design elements that support your mission. Don't rush to replace a good design: you will grow bored with it long before your readers do.

Read your work. Revise it. Don't worry about being correct, but take a moment now and then to think about the craft. Can you choose a better word—one that is clearer, richer, more precise? Can you do without a word entirely?

Omit unnecessary words.

## 4. Make good friends.

Read widely and well, on the web and off, and in your web writing take special care to acknowledge the good work and good ideas of other writers. Show them at their best, pointing with grace and respect to issues where you and they differ. Take special care to be generous to good ideas from those who are less well known, less powerful, and less influential than you.

Weblog writers and other participants in the Living Web gain readers by exchanging links and ideas. Seeking to exchange links without ideas is vulgarly known as blogrolling. Begging high-traffic pages or famous writers to mention you is bothersome and unproductive

Instead of begging, find ways to be a good friend. All writers thrive on ideas; distribute them generously and always share the credit. Be generous with links. Be generous, too, with your time and effort; A-list sites may not need your traffic, but everyone can use a hand.

Many prominent web writers travel a lot—to conferences, meetings, trade shows. Sooner or later, they'll come to your corner of the world. Offer to feed them. Invite them to parties. Offer to introduce them to interesting people. They might be too busy. They might be too shy. But the road can be a lonely place, and it's always interesting to meet thinking people.

Small, thoughtful gifts are nice. Share books you love, or that you've written. If you're a photographer or an artist, prints and sketches can be unique and memorable. (Include permission to reproduce them on the web.) Join their cause. Donate to their charity.

Friends are vital for business sites as well, but business and friendship can be a volatile mix. Your prospects, customers and vendors are obvious friends, but both they and your readers will understand that your friendship is not disinterested. Unlikely friends, including your competitors, may prove more convincing.

## 5. Find good enemies.

Readers love controversy and learn from debate. Disagreement is exciting. Everyone loves a fight, and by witnessing the contest of competing ideas we can better understand what they imply.

Dramatic conflict is an especially potent tool for illuminating abstract and technical issues, whether in software engineering or business planning. At times, choosing a communications protocol or adopting an employee benefits plan may seem an abstract task, barely related to the human crises that daily confront us. If each alternative has a determined, effective advocate, however, it may reveal the source of the conflict and to remind us of the consequences of the choice.

To make an abstract or difficult point more real, identify and respond to an advocate who holds a different position. Choose your opponent with care. If you choose a rival who is much less powerful than you, readers may see you as a bully. If your rival is a business competitor, you may seem unscrupulous. The best enemy, in fact, is often a friend—a writer you cite frequently and who often cites you, but with whom you disagree on a specific questions.

A handful of individuals seemingly live for controversy and seek out ways to create and inflame disputes. These so-called trolls are chiefly the bane of discussion groups but occasionally find their way into the Living Web. Never engage them; you cannot win. (Trolls, when ignored, will usually retire. If they cause danger or damage that cannot be ignored, the police and the courts will assist you.)

When beginning a debate, always have in mind a plan for ending it. Ill-planned arguments can drag on, lost in a mass of boring detail or irrelevant side-issues. Worse, the personalities of the advocates may become more engaging than the issues, obscuring your purpose entirely. Have in mind, from the outset, an idea of how long you want to engage the issue and how you expect the exercise to end (or reach a resting point). Plan a conclusion before firing the first salvo. You might devise an event—a final meeting, a live debate or online poll—that will provide a sense of closure. Write a joint communique for your readers or your management, summarizing the outstanding issues and highlighting progress. Then archive both sides of the exchange—perhaps

THE NEW WRITER'S HANDBOOK 2007

with annotation from a neutral authority—so future readers may enjoy and benefit from the conflict.

When it's over, try to make good friends with good enemies.

## 6. Let the story unfold.

The Living Web unfolds in time, and as we see each daily revelation we experience its growth as a story. Your arguments and rivalries, your ideas and your passions: all of these grow and shift in time, and these changes become the dramatic arc of your website.

Understand the storyteller's art and use the technique of narrative to shape the emerging structure of your living site. Foreshadowing hints at future events and expected interests: your vacation, the election campaign, the endless midnight hours at work in the days before the new product ships. Surprise, an unexpected flash of humor or a sudden change of direction, refreshes and delights. Use links within your work to build depth, for today's update will someday be your own back story.

People are endlessly fascinating. Write about them with care and feeling and precision. Invented characters, long a staple of newspaper columnists, are rarely seen on the Living Web; creating a fascinating (but imaginary) friend could balance your own character on your site.

When the star of the site is a product or an organization, temper the temptation to reduce the narrative to a series of triumphs. Although you don't usually want to advertise bad news, your readers know that every enterprise faces challenges and obstacles. Consider sharing a glimpse of your organization's problems: having seen the challenge, your readers will experience your success more vividly.

Interweave topics and find ways to vary your pacing and tone. Piling tension on tension, anger on rage, is ultimately self-defeating; sooner or later, the writing will demand more from you than you can give and the whole edifice will collapse in boredom or farce. When one topic, however important, overshadows everything else in your site, stop. Change the subject; go somewhere new, if only for a moment. When you return, you and your reader will be fresher and better prepared.

## 7. Stand up, speak out.

If you know your facts and have done your homework, you have a right to your opinion. State it clearly. Never waffle, whine, or weasel.

If you are not sure you are right, ask yourself why you are writing. If you are seeking information or guidance from your readers, ask them. Don't bore them (and discredit yourself) with a hesitant, unformed opinion. If you are writing in order to discover your mind or to try out a new stance, continue by all means—but file the note in your desk drawer, not on your website.

If you believe you are right, say so. Explain why. It doesn't matter that you are young, or unknown, or lack credentials, or that crowds of famous people disagree. Don't hesitate or muddy the water. The truth matters; show us the right answer, and get out of the way.

Never lie about your competitors, and never exult in your rival's bad news.

Try, if you can, to avoid inflicting unnecessary pain and humiliation on those who have the misfortune to be mistaken. People err, and you too will be wrong tomorrow. Civility is not mere stuffiness; it can be the glue that lets us fight for our ideas and, once we recognize the right answer, sit down together for drinks and dinner.

## 8. Be sexy.

You are a sexual being. So are all of your readers (except the Google robot). Sex is interesting. Sex is life, and life is interesting. The more of yourself you put into your writing, the more human and engaging your work will be.

If your writing is a personal journal, and if it is honest, you will have to write about things that you find embarrassing to describe, feelings you might not want to share, events that you wouldn't mention to strangers (or, perhaps, to anyone). Decide now what you will do, before it happens.

Undressing, literally, figuratively, or emotionally, has always been a powerful force in personal sites and web logs. Pictures don't matter in the long run; what matters is the trajectory of your relationship with the reader, the gradual growth of intimacy and knowledge between you.

### 9. Use your archives.

When you add something to the Living Web and invite others to link to your ideas, you promise to keep your words available online, in their appointed place, indefinitely. Always provide a permanent location (a "permalink") where each item can be found. Do your best to ensure that these locations don't change, breaking links in other people's websites and disrupting the community of ideas.

The promise to keep your words available need not mean that you must preserve them unchanged. In time, you may find errors you want to correct. The world changes, and things that once seemed clear may require explanation.

Today, this permanent location is often a chronological archive, a long list of entries for a particular week or month. These archives are useful and easy to make. Many popular tools build chronological archives automatically. But chronological archives are limited: you might someday want to know what you wrote in May of 1999, but why would anyone else care? Topical summaries and overviews are much more helpful to new readers and to regulars alike, and if they require a modest additional effort every day, that effort pays dividends that grow as your archives expand.

New tools like Six Degrees and Eastgate's Tinderbox can make it easier to keep track of categories, to find where new things fit and to find old things that need new links. Topical archives are Google's natural friend. Remember that your old pages will often be read by visitors from search engines; introduce yourself on every page, and be sure that every page, however obscure, has links to tell people:

> Who you are, what you want, and why you're writing
> Your email address
> Where to find your latest writing

Link to work you've already written—especially to good work that you wrote long ago. Don't be shy about linking to yourself: linking to your own work is a service, not self-promotion.

### 10. Relax!

Don't worry too much about correctness: find a voice and use it. Most readers will overlook, and nearly all will forgive, errors in punctuation and spelling. Leave Fowler and Roget on the shelf, unless they're your old friends. Write clearly and simply and write quickly, for if you are to write often you must neither hesitate or quibble.

Don't worry about the size of your audience. If you write with energy and wit about things that matter, your audience will find you. Do tell people about your writing, through short personal email notes and through postcards and business cards and search engines. Enjoy the audience you have, and don't try to figure out why some people aren't reading your work.

Don't take yourself too seriously.

Do let your work on the Living Web flow from your passion and your play, your work life and your life at home. Establish a rhythm, so your writing comes naturally and your readers experience it as a natural part of their day or their week. But if the rhythm grows onerous, if you find yourself dreading your next update or resenting the demands of your readers, if you no longer relish your morning web routine or your evening note-taking, find a new rhythm or try something else. Change the schedule, or voice, or tone. Switch topics. Try, if you can, to resist the temptation to drop things entirely, to simply stop.

Don't worry about those who disagree with you, and don't take bad reviews to heart. The web is filled with caring and kindness, but thoughtless cruelty can and does cloud every writer's spirit from time to time. Ideas matter, but name-calling doesn't, and petulant critics wrap tomorrow's virtual fish.

Mark Bernstein is chief scientist at Eastgate Systems, publishers of Tinderbox (www. eastgate.com/Tinderbox), a "personal content management assistant" that helps users store and organize notes, ideas, and plans on their computers, and helps them share ideas through Web journals and web logs.

# Your Email Signature

*by Linda Formichelli*

RECENTLY I DECIDED to update my email signature line. For the last few months it had read, "Hire me to write your stuff! I'm swell." It got positive comments from clients, but I became tired of seeing it. So my husband Eric and I spent longer than we should have today playing with ideas like:

> Writing since 1997. Walking upright since 1970.
> I write. You buy.
> Good writing; est. 1997.
> I write words and paragraphs.

I finally settled on (for now) "Making editors smile since 1997."

When I first started using the Internet as part of my freelancing career, my sig line listed the magazines my work appeared in that month. The problem was that I had to change my sig whenever I found out that I was in a new magazine. Also, I'm sure that no clients went racing to the newsstand every month to look up my latest work; really, it impressed other writers more than potential clients. Then I went with the usual: a list of my books. When I started my 8-week e-course on getting published in magazines, I put that in my sig line instead.

I don't remember what made me switch to a more light-hearted sig, but I like making people laugh, and I'm not afraid to take risks to do so—like the risk that a client will think I'm a freak and not work with me. If someone is highly offended by a slightly humorous sig line, I'm not sure I'd want to work with that client anyway.

Although I do break a few rules when it comes to content, I pay attention to other rules of sig-line netiquette, such as the McQuary limit, which states that sig lines should max out at four lines, with fewer than 80 characters per line. Sig lines should also be plain text only—no HTML, no images. They're sometimes delimited from the body of the message by two hyphens followed by a space and a return, so that the receiver's software can automatically remove the sig line if the receiver chooses to do so.

Your sig line is a little sales pitch for you and your services; you want to entice the reader to click on the link to your site (and hire you and pay you gobs of cash). My upbeat sig has gotten nice comments from editors, and probably garnered more click-throughs than the one boasting of many publication credits. You can also try a testimonial from a happy client, or some benefit of working with you, such as, "My writing will give you a whiter smile and fresh breath."

What does your sig line say? Does it get a lot of response? Have you experimented with different styles, lengths, etc., and if so, what were the results?

Linda Formichelli is the co-author of *The Renegade Writer: A Totally Unconventional Guide to Freelance Writing Success* and *The Renegade Writer's Query Letters that Rock!* This piece is drawn from an entry on her Renegade Writer blog, December 18, 2006.
Her website is www.lindaformichelli.com.

# LITERARY INSIGHTS
# & LAST WORDS

# How to Speak a Book

*by Richard Powers*

EXCEPT FOR brief moments of duress, I haven't touched a keyboard for years. No fingers were tortured in producing these words—or the last half a million words of my published fiction. By rough count, I've sent 10,000 e-mail messages without typing. My primary digital prosthetic doesn't even have keys.

I write these words from bed, under the covers with my knees up, my head propped and my three-pound tablet PC—just a shade heavier than a hardcover—resting in my lap, almost forgettable. I speak untethered, without a headset, into the slate's microphone array. The words appear as fast as I can speak, or they wait out my long pauses. I touch them up with a stylus, scribbling or re-speaking as needed. Whole phrases die and revive, as quickly as I could have hit the backspace. I hear every sentence as it's made, testing what it will sound like, inside the mind's ear.

Like all good Jetson futures, speech recognition is really a memory. Speak the thing into being: as dreams go, that's as old as they get. Once, all stories existed only in speech, and no technology caused more upheaval than the written word. In the *Phaedrus*, Socrates—who talked a whole lot but never, apparently, wrote a word—uncorks at length about how writing damages memory, obscures authority and even alters meaning. But we have his warning only through Plato's suspect transcript.

For most of history, most reading was done out loud. Augustine remarks with surprise that Bishop Ambrose could read without moving his tongue. Our passage into silent text came late and slow, and poets have resisted it all the way. From Homer to hip-hop, the hum is what counts. Blind Milton chanted *Paradise Lost* to his daughters. Of his 159-line "Tintern Abbey," Wordsworth said, "I began it upon leaving Tintern ... and concluded ... after a ramble of four or five days.... Not a line of it was altered, and not any part of it written down till I reached Bristol." Wallace Stevens used to compose while walking to work, then dictate the results to his secretary, before proceeding to his official correspondence as vice president of the Hartford insurance company. (I've tried dictating to my tablet while rambling; traffic and birdsong make it babble.)

Even novelists, working in a form so very written, have needed to write by voice. Stendhal dictated *The Charterhouse of Parma* in seven weeks. An impoverished Dostoyevsky had just six weeks to deliver the manuscript of *The Gambler* or face complete ruin. He hired a stenographer, knocked the book out in four weeks, then married the girl.

Not that efficiency has always been dictation's prime selling point: in dictating his own last few baggy monsters, Henry James perfected such fluid elocution that, according to Edith Wharton, he couldn't even ask directions without releasing a torrent of "explanatory ramifications." James grew so accustomed to his sonatas for voice and typist that the sound of his secretary's Oliver, when the workhorse Remington was in the shop, threw him off his speaking rhythm.

Dickens reportedly acted out his characters while looking in a mirror. In the final hours of his life, Proust re-dictated the death of Bergotte, supposedly claiming that he now knew what he was talking about. Once, while dictating *Finnegans Wake* to Beckett, Joyce is said to have answered a knock on the door; Beckett dutifully jotted down his "Come in." Surprised by the transcript, a delighted Joyce let it ride.

The all-time champion of Xtreme Dictation, though, must be Thomas Aquinas. Witnesses report how he could relay four different topics to four secretaries at once, and even (Maritain writes) "lay down to rest in the midst of the dictation to continue to dictate while sleeping." That's what I really want from my tablet; I trust that technicians are working on the problem.

Why all this need for speech? Long after we've fully retooled for printed silence, we still feel residual meaning in the wake of how things sound. Speech and writing share some major neural circuitry, much of it auditory. All readers, even the fast ones, subvocalize. That's why so many writers—like Flaubert, shouting his sentences in his gueuloir—test the rightness of their words out loud.

What could be less conducive to thought's cadences than stopping every time your short-term memory fills to pass those large-scale musical phrases through your fingers, one tedious letter at a time? You'd be hard-pressed to invent a greater barrier to cognitive flow. The 130-year-old qwerty keyboard may even have been designed to slow fingers and prevent key jamming. We compose on keys the way dogs walk on two legs. However good we get, the act will always be a little freakish.

The faster I speak, the better my tablet PC transcribes. It won't choke, even at bursts over 200 w.p.m. The real hitch remains accuracy. When in the groove, my speech software is remarkably precise, far more accurate than most typists. But no machine makes phonetic distinctions as fine as humans do, and my software's recognition engine doesn't model meaning. So where my fingers might stop at changing "sign" to "sing," my tablet can turn my words hallucinatory without limit.

This machine is a master of speakos and mondegreens. Just as we might hear the Beatles sing how "the girl with colitis goes by" or the Psalms avow that "Shirley, good Mrs. Murphy, shall follow me all the days of my life," my tablet has changed "book tour" to "back to work" and "I truly couldn't see" to "a cruelly good emcee." Legend claims that the astoundingly prolific William Vollmann once tried speech recognition software while suffering from repetitive stress injury. He sat down to write his folks. "Dear Mom and Dad" came out as the much more Vollmannesque "The man is dead."

A greater barrier to computer dictation is the huge cognitive readjustment involved, especially after decades of straitjacketing keyboards. I needed weeks to get over the oddness of auditioning myself in an empty room, to trust to the flow of speech, to learn to hear myself think all over again. So what do I get from the trade-off?

For one, I can write lying down. I can forget the machine is even there. I can live above the level of the phrase, thinking in full paragraphs and capturing the rhythmic arcs before they fade. I don't have to queue, stop, batch dispatch and queue up again. I spend less mental overhead on orthography and finger mechanics and more on hearing my characters speak themselves into existence. Mostly, I'm just a little closer to what my cadences might mean, when replayed in the subvocal voices of some other auditioner.

Writing is the act of accepting the huge shortfall between the story in the mind and what hits the page. "From your lips to God's ears," goes the old Yiddish wish. The writer, by contrast, tries to read God's lips and pass along the words, via some crazed game of Telephone, to a further listener. And for that, no interface will ever be clean or invisible enough for us to get the passage right. As Bede says of Caedmon, scrambling to transcribe the angelic hymn dictated to him in a dream: "This is the sense, but not the words themselves as he sang them in his sleep; for however well composed, verses cannot be translated out of one language into another without much loss of beauty and loftiness."

Everything we write—through any medium—is lost in translation. But something new is always found again, in their eager years. In Derrida's fears. Make that: in the reader's ears.

Richard Powers is a novelist whose works explore the effects of modern science and technology. He is the author of nine novels, including *Operation Wandering Soul*, nominated for a National Book Award in 1993. His novel *The Echo Maker*, which he wrote primarily using voice-recognition software and speaking into his computer, won the 2006 National Book Award. Set in Nebraska during the Platte River's massive spring migrations of sandhill cranes, this novel "explores the power and limits of human intelligence."

Powers has received numerous other honors including a MacArthur Fellowship, a Lannan Literary Award, and the James Fenimore Cooper Prize for Historical Fiction. He lives in Illinois.

This essay appeared on January 7, 2007, in the *New York Times*.

# Books as a Gateway Drug

*by L.J. Schmidt*

ACCORDING to Wikipedia, a gateway drug is "using one 'soft' non- or only slightly addictive drug will lead to the use of other 'harder' drugs and the associated criminal and social consequences—the first drug used is thus described as a gateway to further abuse." The term, however, can be applied to anything that introduces you to a taste, sensation, or idea which you will gradually follow up to higher levels. Pinot Noir could be the gateway drug to darker, deeper reds. Hershey's could lead you into Godiva and then to Moonstruck.

With books, it is often the big-name, popular types that act as the gateway to get people to read. Dan Brown—for all the flack he gets—got a lot of people voluntarily reading again, and not just his books. People who picked up *The Da Vinci Code* moved on to read *Angels and Demons,* sure, but they also might have branched out to *Holy Blood, Holy Grail* or other fictional conspiracies like *The Eight* by Katherine Neville. These same people might now be reading *Atlantis* by David Gibbons, *Mary, Called Magdalene* by Margaret George, or *A History of God* by Karen Armstrong. Although it was only a work of fiction, *The Da Vinci Code* opened up many avenues of reading to those who may have been hesitant before.

Author as gateway drug can also work in a different fashion when a well established author jumps genres or from fiction to nonfiction. The loyal audience follows (sometimes knowingly, sometimes not) and a certain number of those might like what the find. Suddenly they might be open to trying other things in this genre or area of reading that they wouldn't have thought of before. I have to wonder how many of John Grisham's readers who like *An Innocent Man* will turn to other true crime writers now that they've been introduced. Will Ann Rule, Gregg Olsen, and others benefit from their need to read other real life tales?

Perhaps too often, though, we turn to these big name authors to act as the gateway drugs to our friends when a more subtle approach would do. Haven't we all dealt with the friend that we know would just love books X, Y, and Z if they would give them a try, but they won't because name recognition tells them that they belong in genre S?

"Ewww, I'd never read fiction/mystery/romance/sci-fi/fantasy/true crime/fill in the blank," they cry. "Don't you have something good?"

Now you can either explain that X, Y, and Z are good until you run out of air, or you take a step back and regroup. Days later you dig out a nondescript paperback with a kickass story line; something subtle enough that it won't tip your friend off until they're fully drawn into the characters and situations. You then gush to said friend, leaving out any tip-off words or phrases and emphasize how crazy, wonderful this book is.

It must be crazy, wonderful in some way, otherwise it won't work.

And once they are truly sucked in and have devoured the author's whole backlist, you move them up, feed them the books that have a little "more" of whatever defines that genre until you've got them hooked on a three book a day habit and they've destroyed their library card with over-use.

At which point, if you were me, you would sit back and cackle, but I'm evil, so you might just get a warm, fuzzy feeling.

Or you might not have experienced this sensation at all.

What books, famous, infamous or other have used to hook others on your genre drug of choice? Do the famous types or those still building their fan base work better? What was your gateway drug?

Hey, there's a reason I call booksellers knowledge dealers.

L.J. Schmidt is a bookseller and blogger under the name Bookseller Chick. Her blog can be found at: www.booksellerchick.blogspot.com. This blog entry is from November 2006. She lives in Oregon.

# Time Traveling by Words, Music, & Art

*by Robert Gray*

*Another instance—*
*time as a verb.*

These are the concluding lines of a poem in Daniel Berrigan's new collection, *Beyond Alchemy*. The chapbook was just published by Arrowsmith Press, an extraordinary, limited-print-run, labor-of-literary-love-and-madness venture undertaken by Askold Melnyczuk and Alexandra Johnston.

On Saturday, December 2, at Friends Meeting House in Cambridge, Mass., I had the privilege of witnessing a place in time where the paths of Father Berrigan and Arrowsmith Press crossed briefly, a place where words, written as well as spoken, still reflect action. It was an extraordinary day that marked the beginning of an extraordinary week.

A week in which words and spirit and time meshed; a week in which I felt like a time traveler.

I won't tell you everything about it because it is mine. I'll tell you some.

At Arrowsmith's post-reading reception, I was asked to sit next to Father Berrigan and keep him company while he (graciously and patiently) signed books for a long line of ... the best phrase that comes to mind is comrades in linked arms. So many stories of past meetings, so many expressions of admiration and gratitude.

I've sat in "the chair beside the author" many times as a bookseller. I know the drill. I know how to be invisible while still keeping an author from feeling abandoned. I did my job, but I also watched Father Berrigan, who at 85 displayed remarkable grace, resilience, and focus, engaging his devoted audience one by one while scribbling his name on proffered items (including, oddly enough, a baseball).

He seemed to be—and there are few people in the world I can say this about—the person I'd always imagined he might be. That was his gift to me.

Later that evening, I read his poems, including "The Prisoner, The Cave," which begins:

*Ancients are writing with pencil stubs*
*scriptures in a cave.*

Time, verb that it is, sent me on my way, and I spent the rest of the week in New York. The Berrigan event soon began to feel like an overture to a magical stretch of time in which I encountered, again and again, words and their meanings, sounds and their variations, icons and their spiritual calls.

Time, you see, cannot destroy everything.

It tries.

At the Metropolitan Museum of Art, I wandered among anonymous, weatherbeaten apostles and kings in an exhibition titled *Set in Stone: The Face in Medieval Sculpture*. Many of these relics were "survivors" of a frenzied post-French Revolution iconoclasm that essentially drove men to "cleanse" the cathedral at Notre-Dame of its royal and religious icons by beheading statues. Men may have struck the first blows to these limestone icons, but time and weather had tried hard to finish the job over the succeeding decades.

Yet here, in this quiet hall, the busts continued to speak to us, their in-human "destroyers" long dead and forgotten.

Afterward, I revisited *Brush and Ink: The Chinese Art of Writing*, an exhibition I'd seen before. Again I was entranced by the abstract pleasures of writing as art, of visual and verbal blending seamlessly in graceful brush strokes from a thousand years ago.

Marking time.

And I made a new discovery on this trip. I had not fully explored the calligraphy of contemporary Chinese artists that hung near the end of the exhibition before, having been more intrigued by the ancient works.

Now, however, I found a pair of hanging scrolls by Xu Bing titled, "The Song of the Wandering Aengus." Drawing with ink on paper, mixing the artistic tradition of the east with the literary tradition of the west, Xu Bing had transcribed a poem by William Butler Yeats into calligraphy. Not a translation, but a re-imagining, the letters of each word cleverly rearranged to resemble Chinese characters. The poem about love and aging, about elusive time, spoke to me through an old technique given new form:

*Though I am old with wandering*
*Through hollow lands and hilly lands*

My pilgrimage that day next took me to The Frick Collection, where an exhibition of 18th-century artist Domenico Tiepolo's *New Testament* drawings made ancient words appear as visions.

And later, after darkness fell, I moved back further in time to the 16th century for a concert at St. Thomas Episcopal Church on 53rd Street and Fifth Avenue. The Tallis Scholars stood at the foot of an awe-inspiring altar and performed choral works by Renaissance masters, including Phillipe de Monte, Giovanni Pierluigi da Palestrina, and John Taverner. The centerpiece of the evening was Christopher Tye's "Missa Western Wynde," but the group began with a brief work by their namesake, Thomas Tallis. Spiritually-charged Latin words echoed throughout the Gothic church and seemed as abstract, and as meaningful, to me as Chinese calligraphy.

*Loquebantur variis linguis apostoli, allelluia*

Then the translation in my program brought me back to words again:

*The apostles were speaking in different tongues, alleluia.*

The following night, I saw George Bernard Shaw's *Heartbreak House* at the American Airlines Theatre on Broadway. Shaw wrote the play in 1920 to depict the spiritual bankruptcy he despised among his countrymen, which he believed had drawn them into the horrifying glories of World War I. The play's contemporary reference points were sledgehammers, however, and I left feeling that words had let me down this time. Lady Utterword says:

*The important thing is not to have the last word,*
*but to have your own way.*

No, m'lady. The important thing is to know what words can do and what they cannot do.

*Time as a verb*

Time travels.

We ride along and, if we're very lucky, never feel that we've arrived. Read. See. Listen.

Robert Gray is a writer, bookseller, and publishing consultant. He writes a weekly column about bookstore Web sites for *Shelf Awareness*, a daily online newsletter covering the publishing industry. Through his own company, Fresh Eyes Now, Gray helps agents, authors, and publishers establish direct connections with booksellers nationwide.

He holds an MFA in Writing & Literature from Bennington College. Gray was a full-time bookseller at the Northshire Bookstore (Manchester, VT), an influential independent, for nearly 14 years. He still works weekends at the Northshire.

This blog entry is from Fresh Eyes: A Bookseller's Journal (www.fresheyesnow.com) from December 2006.

# Literary Fiction

*by Rachel Donadio*

THE PRIDE AND JOY of publishing, literary fiction has always been wonderfully ill suited to the very industry that sustains it. Like an elegant but impoverished aristocrat married to a nouveau riche spouse, it has long been subsidized by mass-market fiction and by nonfiction ripped from the headlines. One supplies the cachet, the others the cash.

The divide between sales of literary and commercial fiction has always been vast—the 345,000 copies that Marilynne Robinson's Pulitzer Prize-winning 2004 novel *Gilead* sold in hardcover and paperback is an impressive figure, but not when compared with the more than 18 million copies of *The Da Vinci Code* in print in North America, and more than 60 million worldwide. These days literary fiction has to contend with two factors that are increasingly central to the publishing process: timing and volume. In a market dominated by the big chain stores, if a novel doesn't sell a healthy number of copies in the first two weeks after its publication, its chances of gaining longer-term momentum are slim.

"The whole system is set up for impatience," said Drenka Willen, an editor at Harcourt whose authors include Umberto Eco and José Saramago. That "system" also favors the familiar name over the new voice.

"In the post-9/11 world, we've found it has, until very recently anyway, been more difficult than previously to get the common reader to take a chance on new writers," said Jonathan Galassi, the president and publisher of Farrar, Straus & Giroux, which publishes Jonathan Franzen and Nadine Gordimer, as well as Marilynne Robinson. "The pressures on literary books are growing, as an ever smaller number of books continues to sell more and more broadly."

Indeed, in 2005, almost half of all sales in the literary fiction category came from the top 20 best-selling books, according to Nielsen

Bookscan, which tracks sales in 70 percent to 80 percent of the domestic retail market. The three top sellers in literary fiction were *The Curious Incident of the Dog in the Night-Time*, by Mark Haddon (640,000 copies in Bookscan's sampling); *Memoirs of a Geisha*, by Arthur Golden (560,000 copies, including the movie tie-in); and *The Known World*, by Edward P. Jones (274,000 copies).

This top-heavy pattern makes promoting literary fiction a challenge. "You need 15 things to happen in the right order on time," said Bill Thomas, the editor in chief of Doubleday-Broadway, whose recent successes include *The Curious Incident*, as well as Jonathan Lethem's *Fortress of Solitude* and, yes, *The Da Vinci Code*. Those things include drumming up enthusiasm inside the publishing house, spreading the word to booksellers and reviewers by sending out manuscripts months before publication, and securing a front-of-store display at Barnes & Noble and Borders and prominent placement on Amazon.com. To show booksellers you're serious, Thomas said, you have to ship a minimum of 20,000 copies to stores at the time of publication.

But literary novels rarely sell that many copies in hardcover, and the need for a high print run sets up expectations that can be difficult to meet. Printing 20,000 copies off the bat also requires the commitment of the entire publishing apparatus. To get "in-house support" for a book, editors vie against one another to win over the marketing and art departments so the book gets advertising dollars and the best jacket possible. That means literary fiction editors are increasingly called upon to become businesspeople and lobbyists. "The stereotype of the introverted book editor scribbling away in a dimly lit office may have once been true, but now if you're that way, your books fail," said Geoff Shandler, the editor in chief of Little, Brown, which publishes Rick Moody and David Foster Wallace.

Today, "it's a zero-sum game and the publisher knows they can only push so many titles per season," said Eric Simonoff, a literary agent at Janklow & Nesbit whose clients include Jhumpa Lahiri and Edward P. Jones. "There's an enormous amount of internal triage that goes on. Rarely is a publisher surprised at the success of a work of fiction." That doesn't mean their best efforts always bear fruit. "A lot of preplanned successes turn out to be flops," Galassi said. Benjamin Kunkel's *Indecision* sold 19,000 copies from its release last August through the end of April, according to Bookscan—a respectable figure for a first literary novel, but disappointing for such a heavily promoted title (though it was much discussed in literary circles, which to some is the true measure of success).

After the internal lobbying, publishers turn to winning over the single most powerful person in American literary publishing. No, not Oprah, but a woman you've probably never heard of: Sessalee Hensley, the one literary fiction buyer for Barnes & Noble. (Other buyers handle romance, mystery and additional genres.) Publishers are reluctant to talk about Hensley on the record, for fear of jeopardizing their rapport with the gatekeeper to a company with 799 stores and 17 percent of the United States book market. But most say they respect her judgment, even if they sometimes complain she has middlebrow taste. Hensley can decide whether to place a book on an attention-grabbing front table and often advises publishers to change a book jacket. (The company wouldn't make her available for an interview.)

It's a delicate dance: buyers use a writer's past sales to determine how many copies of a new novel to order; publishers try to convince buyers that a book has potential even if they can't justify spending the money to promote it the way they would a commercial title. Publishers frequently argue for the bottom quarter of their list—the books that get the least marketing support and often sell the fewest copies. That's "where the major writers of the future usually start," Galassi said. "It's where much of the best writing is, the work of the odd, uncooperative, intractable, pigheaded authors who insist on seeing and saying things their own way and change the game in the process. The 'system' can only recognize what it's already cycled through. What's truly new is usually indigestible at first."

With so many factors in play, it's hard to know what makes a book take off. "When I started, I used to think it was 80 percent hard work on the part of your author and 20 percent luck," said the literary agent Nicole Aragi, whose authors include Jonathan Safran Foer and Monica Ali, young writers who have broken out of the pack. "Now, I think it's 50 percent hard work and 50 percent luck." To promote novels, publishers often seek "nonfiction hooks" to draw readers in. *The Plot Against America*, by Philip Roth, a major literary event when it appeared in 2004, has sold extremely well—412,000 copies so far in hardcover and paperback, according to Bookscan—in part because it was seen as an oblique commentary on the Bush administration. (The normally reclusive

Roth also made his first American television appearances since 1968, on the *Today* show and PBS's *Newshour*.) It's not enough to say a book is "beautifully written and ambitious and wonderful," said Janet Silver, a vice president and publisher of adult trade books at Houghton Mifflin, which publishes Roth. You have to find "different ways of talking about a book that go beyond its intrinsic merit."

Publishers will often use a writer's background to promote a book. But taken to the extreme, this places more value on the writer's pedigree than on the quality and originality of the prose. Consider the case of *How Opal Mehta Got Kissed, Got Wild, and Got a Life*, a first novel whose intense marketing strategy emphasized that the author, Kaavya Viswanathan, was a photogenic 19-year-old Indian-American Harvard sophomore. It was pulled from stores last month by its publisher, Little, Brown, after Viswanathan was accused of recycling from multiple sources. It soon emerged that the book had been delivered to Little, Brown by a packager who encouraged Viswanathan to aim for broad commercial appeal. But these days, even established editors have been known to advise literary novelists to tailor their plots and characters to the presumed appetites of the public.

It can become a vicious circle: publishers lament that literary fiction has trouble finding a foothold—then flood the market with over-hyped and often derivative work in the hope of meeting some vague idea of reader expectations. In the end, what will rescue literary fiction from the crushing commercial demands of publishing today is exactly what has always sustained it: the individual writer's voice.

There is, after all, a difference between a reader and a market.

Rachel Donadio is a writer and editor at the *New York Times Book Review*. This essay first appeared as "Promotional Intelligence" in the *New York Times*, May 21, 2006.

# Thank You for Hating My Book

*by Katha Pollitt*

ACTUALLY, this is good," my editor said when my book got panned. "It's a long review by a well-known person. It's on a good page. It's even got a caricature of you."

True, the drawing made me look like a demented chicken—a fat demented chicken—but as he explained, art meant space and space meant respect and respect meant attention. As my former husband put it, quoting Dr. Johnson as is his wont, "I would rather be attacked than unnoticed." Even in the 18th century, it seems, there was no such thing as bad publicity.

Unless, of course, it's your own. In the days that followed, I discovered something interesting about my writer friends. Here I had thought of them as anxious and sensitive, taking to their beds, or the phone, or both, when professional setbacks came their way. How often had I had the conversation about the culture editor with a grudge dating back to the reign of Tiberius, the clueless reviewer, the publicist who stops returning your phone calls and the publisher who suggests you consider another line of work?

But that was them. My bad review was something else again: my writer friends thought it was great. It was an opportunity, a platform, a megaphone, a lemon about to be transmuted into the most ambrosial lemonade. The very things that made it bad made it good: its frivolity displayed my depth, its confusion threw into relief my steely logic, its snark showed all too clearly who the real wit was.

"Yes, it was pretty negative, and your arms looked like tree stumps," said one friend, helpfully. "But so what? That just means you're a star!"

"All the review did was tell the world you have a new book out," said another friend. "It's attention. Just watch your Amazon numbers soar." I reminded her that she hadn't been so cheerful when her novel was panned by that Romanian diplomat. "Oh, that," she explained. "That was different." Her bad review was written by an ignorant nobody. My bad review was written by a mini-celebrity. The reviewer's semi-fame would enhance my own. Gee, I suggested, maybe I should be sending her flowers.

Of course, like every writer, I had been obsessively monitoring the sales ranking on my Amazon.com page since well before publication, ignoring the advice of my friend the historian. ("Don't look at Amazon, whatever you do! After they dredged up that Welsh farmer to review my book, it was like watching Enron stock implode.") By judiciously purchasing one book an hour—something I was going to do anyway, I have free shipping and a lot of relatives—I had managed to raise my rating from 101,333 at 2:25 on June 17 to 6,679 at midnight—a staggering advance of 94,636 places at a cost of only $110.60.

Skillfully timed additional purchases—I have a lot of friends as well—kept things simmering in the 4,000s. When I clicked on my number for the previous day, I could even see what books were selling like my own. On June 28, for example, when, inexplicably, my book had plummeted to 55,777, it was sandwiched between *Postcolonialism: A Very Short Introduction* and *Calligraphy Alphabets Made Easy.* Fortunately, I found an old Rolodex with the addresses of a whole bunch of people I used to know in Canada—what better way to reconnect than to send them a book!

"Mom," my daughter said in that stern way she gets sometimes. "Stop it. Those numbers don't mean anything."

"Well, I don't know the precise algorithm, nobody does, but the ratings aren't totally meaningless."

"No, Mom, I mean your numbers don't mean anything. You're raising them by buying the book yourself."

Well, technically, yes. But nobody who visited my page knew that. They would just see that only 6,515 books were selling more copies than my own—and most of them were written by Dan Brown.

Would the bad review help my book? By 6 P.M. that Sunday it had reached 2,087 ("See?" my novelist friend emailed. "Just wait!" The author of a new book on crime wrote: "I'm jealous. Why can't my book get panned?")

By 8 P.M. my ranking had reached a stratospheric 1,520. I basked in the knowledge that at least six people had figured out that only a truly wonderful book would get such a terrible review.

"You see?" my editor said on Monday morning. "Length, placement, caricature. Works every time." I didn't have the heart to tell him I had already drifted back down into the 3,000s.

"Oh, well, it's Fourth of July weekend," said my novelist friend, consolingly. "A lot of people are away."

Apparently there is such a thing as bad publicity, and that's bad publicity that people don't know about. That problem though, I could fix. I wrote up an e-mail message describing my new book, with a comical lament about my bad review and a link so people could read it for themselves, and I sent it off to my entire address book. Then, just to get the ball rolling I ordered a copy for a friend of my father's who lives in Hawaii and one for a Legal Aid lawyer I'd met on the train. Sure enough, by the end of the day I had advanced to 1,314. If you take out Dan Brown, I was practically a best seller.

And all it took was $256.68—and a really bad review.

Katha Pollitt is the author, most recently, of *Virginity or Death! And Other Social and Political Issues of Our Time* (Random House, 2006).

This op-ed piece appeared July 12, 2006, in the *New York Times*.

# The Origin of Names

*by John Clayton*

As a child, I was fascinated by surnames. Was someone named King descended from royalty? How did Carl come to have so many sons? Then I moved to a small town, where the issue is not so theoretical.

Among my friends, for example, are Greg The Plumber and Tom The Guy Who Does The Maps. There's Lee From The Movie Theater and Lee Who Does The Juniper Furniture. Curt, who tries to work as little as possible, is thus known not by occupation but as Curt Of Curt And Carol.

Scott and Elizabeth seem such a perfect match that each has gained the last name, Of Scott And Elizabeth. There's Glen, Who's Married To Heather The Realtor, and Tim, Katie's Brother, Who Goes With Joy From The Bank.

The girlfriend of Andy From Outward Bound is Amy, Emily's Sister. Emily, of course, is known as Emily, Amy's Sister. It helps that both sisters are rabid Utah Jazz fans with bright red hair. If somebody didn't know Emily's husband, Jim The Baker, one might give Jim this alternative last name: "You know, Emily and Amy, with the red hair. Emily's husband. There's Amy and Andy From Outward Bound. And there's Emily and Jim." Sure, it's a mouthful, but it's a lot more meaningful than some surname passed down from somebody's father, who almost nobody here has met.

Some are known by physical characteristics. Little Robbie is well, small. Big Dave is a giant. One day Big Dave's bride met some of his basketball buddies in a non-basketball setting. She tried to explain who she was, using Dave's last name. Nobody knew it. "You know, Dave, from basketball," she kept saying. She kept getting blank looks until finally someone said, "Oh! Big Dave!" Everyone laughed and understood. "Now," she says, "I've realized my name is Mrs. Big Dave."

Occasionally someone's first name is enough, and we get small town versions of Madonna or Twiggy. The combination of a unique first name and unique personality means that when it comes to people like Anner or Verlynn, either you know them or you don't. Any surname would be extraneous. I think my friend Lexy is headed for this status: You Know Lexy—Everybody Knows Lexy.

The new last names can make for interesting "families." Daryl The Pepsi Guy and Dean The Pepsi Guy are related only through occupation. Jim Who Has The Little Paper and Lou Who Has The Little Paper not only weren't related but ran competing publications. Meanwhile, who could figure out that Rigger The Chocolate Sauce Guy and John Who Runs The Boys And Girls Club are (biologically) brothers? When small-town surnames collide with "real" surnames, complications ensue. For example, after a Boys and Girls Club meeting, John Who Runs The Boys And Girls Club said to me, "The kids want to get somebody named Rebecca Nesbitt (as a mentor). You have any idea who that is?"

"Sure," I said. "That's Rebecca From The Brewery." His face fell. "She'd be perfect," he said. "But I didn't approve it during the meeting because I'd never heard of this Nesbitt character."

Circumstances were reversed recently when I had to get my house painted. I decided to use Tracey The Painter, whom I've seen around town for years, though I've never known him well. I happen to know his "real" last name because his sister works at the newspaper. Of course, she's known as Shelley From The News (indeed, if she calls me on the phone, she says "Hi, John, this is Shelley From The News"). But her byline, for some reason, features her "real" last name. So I looked it up in the phone book, where I found her brother listed as well.

Tracey and I traded messages, then finally spoke directly. "John Clayton..." he mused at one point. "I could tell from your message that you knew me, but I'm embarrassed to say I can't place who you are."

"Oh, you know me," I said, and tried to describe myself. "Tall, skinny, brown hair. I hang out at the coffeeshop a lot." There was a pause; I could picture him shaking his head on the other end of the line. Then, as if a lightbulb went off above his head, he said, "John The Writer?"

Subconsciously, I guess, I'd wished for something flashier, say, John the telemark skier, but you can't choose your last name in a small town, any more than you can choose your parents. "Yup," I told Tracy The Painter, who probably has similar unfulfilled identity fantasies. "That's me."

John Clayton writes on Western history, environment, and literature, as well as advanced management communications techniques, for clients ranging from National Geographic to Harvard Business School publishing. He is the author of *The Cowboy Girl: The Life of Caroline Lockhart* (University of Nebraska Press, May 2007) and is a contributor to Writers on the Range (www.hcn.org). He lives and freelances in Red Lodge, Montana.

His website is www.johnclaytonbooks.com.

# Discovering Home Ground

*by Barry Lopez*

SOME OF US in the United States can trace our family lines back many generations to, say, the Green Mountains of western Vermont, the urban hills of the San Francisco peninsula, or the sandhills of western Nebraska; to small towns along the Mississippi River or a red-earth farm in Alabama. Many of us have come from ranching, farming, or logging families, and might have listened with a measure of envy while a grandparent spoke of these places of origin, using a language so suited to the place being described it fit against it like another kind of air. A language capable of conveying the most evanescent of the place's characteristics.

Today, the majority of us raise our families, go to school, find employment, and locate much of our inspiration in urban areas. The land beyond our towns, for many, has become a generalized landscape of hills and valleys, of beaches, rivers, and monotonous deserts. Almost against our wills the countrysides of our parents' and grandparents' generations—the Salinas Valley we might have once pictured reading John Steinbeck, images of Sarah Orne Jewett's Maine or the barefoot country of Eudora Welty's stories, of Willa Cather's Nebraska and New Mexico—almost without our knowing it, the particulars of these landscapes have slipped away from us. Asked, we might still conjure them, but we probably could no longer still name the elements that make them vivid in our memories.

It has become a commonplace observation about American culture that we are a people groping for a renewed sense of place and community, that we want to be more meaningfully committed, less isolated. Many of us have come to wonder whether modern American life, with its accelerated daily demands and its polarizing choices, isn't indirectly undermining something foundational, something essential to our lives. We joke that one shopping mall looks just like another, that a housing development on the outskirts of Denver feels no different to us than a housing development outside Kansas City, but we are not always amused by such observations. No more than we are amused when someone from the rural countryside implies that his life is spiritually richer than ours because the place we've chosen to live is Park Slope in Brooklyn or the South Side of Chicago.

What many of us are hopeful of now, it seems, is being able to gain—or regain—a sense of allegiance with our chosen places, and along with that a sense of affirmation with our neighbors that the place we've chosen is beautiful, subtle, profound, worthy of our lives.

It is with these thoughts, about the importance of belonging, of knowing the comfort that a feeling of intimate association with a place can bring, that we began work on *Home Ground*. We wanted to recall and to explore a language more widespread today than most of us imagine, because we believed an acquaintance with it, using it to say more clearly and precisely what we mean, would bring us a certain kind of relief. It would draw us closer to the landscapes upon which we originally and hopefully founded our democratic arrangement for governing ourselves, our systems of social organization, and our enterprise in economics. If we could speak more accurately, more evocatively, more familiarly about the physical places we occupy, perhaps we could speak more penetratingly, more insightfully, more compassionately about the flaws in these various systems which, we regularly assert, we wish to address and make better.

It had come to me as a fourteen-year-old reading *Moby-Dick*, a moral drama set in an intensely physical place, that this seemingly unfettered, nearly unmeasureable American landscape I had become acquainted with (Colorado's fourteeners, Appalachia's Carolina bays, Manhattan's tidal races, a complex landscape, robust with suggestions of freedom, power, and purity) it came to me that this particular landscape had distinctively stamped the long line of American literature, starting with Cooper and Hawthorne and coming up through Twain, Cather, and Steinbeck, through Stegner, Mary Oliver, and Peter Matthiessen, through Wendell Berry and Gary Snyder. In fact, it is striking the degree to which the work of so many American writers is informed by sentences of wonder, meditation, and confoundment, of intimacy, alienation, and homage, inspired by the features—plowed land, deep woods, mountain streams—of American landscapes. In *Inheritance of Night*, William Styron writes: "You look out once more at the late summer landscape and the low sorrowful beauty of the tideland streams, turgid and involute and secret and winding through marshes full of small, darting, frightened noises and glistening and dead silent at noon except for a whistle, far off, and a distant rumble on the rails."

Whatever their styles and emphases, many American poets and novelists have recognized that something emotive abides in the land, and that it can be recognized and evoked even if it cannot be thoroughly plumbed. It is inaccessible to the analytic researcher, invisible to the ironist. To hear the unembodied call of a place, that numinous voice, one has to wait for it to speak through the harmony of its features—the soughing of the wind across it, its upward reach against a clear night sky, its fragrance after a rain. One must wait for the moment when the thing—the hill, the tarn, the lunette, the kiss tank, the caliche flat, the bajada—ceases to be a thing and becomes something that knows we are there.

...

It is a language that keeps us from slipping off into abstract space.

Barry Lopez is an essayist, author, and short-story writer who has been described as "the nation's premier nature writer" by the *San Francisco Chronicle*. His writings address the relationship between nature and culture. He is the author of *Arctic Dreams* (1986), winner of the National Book Award, *Of Wolves and Men* (1978); a National Book Award finalist, and eight works of fiction, including *Light Action in the Caribbean*, *Field Notes*, and *Resistance*. His collected essays include *Crossing Open Ground* and *About This Life*, and have appeared in many anthologies, including *Best American Essays*, *Best Spiritual Writing*, and collections from *National Geographic*, *Outside*, and *The Paris Review*.

He is a recipient of the Award in Literature from the American Academy of Arts and Letters, the John Hay Medal, and other honors. He lives in Oregon.

His website is www.barrylopez.com.

This piece is excerpted from his introduction to *Home Ground: Language for an American Landscape*, co-edited with Debra Gwartney (Trinity University Press, 2006). For this landmark work of language, geography, and folklore, the editors brought together 45 poets and writers to write more than 850 eloquent definitions for terms like cutbank, flatiron, yazoo, monadnock, hollow, kiss tank, gulch, birdfoot delta, detroit riprap, swale, trace, and paternoster lakes.

More about *Home Ground* can be found at www.homegroundproject.com.

# Into the Light

*by Mick Silva*

*The more lucidly we think, the more we are cut off: the more deeply we enter into reality, the less we can think.*
—C.S. Lewis, "Myth Became Fact," in *World Dominion*

In a sense, we fiction writers should love this quote. I know it's true that the more reality I have to stomach in a given day, the less I'm able to think, really think, like this lucid way he's suggesting.

And conversely, I know what it's like to feel cut off after emerging from the vacuum chamber of a story, bleary-eyed and squinting at the light as I try to acclimate.

But I don't think that's what he's intending here. The context is of the deeper reality, the one beyond this physical world. In the spiritual world no human rationality or intellect can serve. It's similar to the alternate world I create as a fiction writer, but wholly different. Heaven provides inspiration in how dissimilar it is to my waking reality, though I can't claim to know it fully—or even partially. It's a world only imagined beyond words.

And the greatest hope I have is that that place I've never seen is waiting for me to wake up to it, hoping I'll remember as I strive on in my daily business. There are times I feel such strong hope for that spiritual reality, I want to disappear and wake up there, as though I'd never left. If it didn't exist, I wouldn't want to write.

For me, that other reality is the point. Writing is a way for me to try to bring something of that world back, to capture what little spark of it I can before it disappears again and we all have to get up and go about our busy lives. Like an addict, the more time I spend seeking it, the more I want to escape to that deeper reality.

But I can't just stay there. I have to bring what I know of the struggle to bear on my writing as well. It's that struggle between this dirty place and that real one that makes me know I'm alive. The contrast is an inspiration in itself: that inescapable pull between light and dark. That's where we live and die as humans and as writers. Either we see it and we render it, or we ignore it and forget it's there.

It's only when I'm seeing both this world and the evidence of that greater one that I feel the weight of my calling and the gravity of my existence.

And it's at that moment, right then, when I have to write and write into the empty space, filling it with all my alternately stinking, shining words, trading my life and my world for the deeper one until everything melts away and my mind grows quiet and my senses grow stronger, and it's only the flying stream of words that's stopping me from disappearing.

Mick Silva is an editor for Waterbrook and runs an independent blog, discussing issues of literature and Christianity today, at www.yourwritersgroup.com. This piece is from that blog, February 2006.

# On Being a Minor Writer

*by Bruce Holland Rogers*

I LIKE being a minor writer, and so should you.

I have my grandiose fantasies, but I do know that it's all pretend. Even if *Steam* has the sort of success that I'm hoping for, I won't be a major writer. Anne Lamott isn't a major writer, either. Nor, I'm willing to bet, are you. Not if even William Shakespeare can't be assured of the title.

That takes off some of the pressure of measurement, of trying to figure out where we stand in the literary hierarchy.

Admittedly, the publishing world is a world of measurement. What were the numbers for your last book, your print run, your sell-in, your sell-through? These numbers matter. They help to determine the publishing budget for your next book.

On the other hand, we are writers, not profit centers. We live in the world of numbers, but we can choose to remember that the world of numbers is all made up. It's one way of seeing things, but not the only way. It may even be the view of most people, but we're not most people. We're writers, the people hired for their imaginations.

We can choose where our focus is. Jesus said, "Be in the world, but be not of it." Buddhism instructs us to be awake, but to live without attachment. Other great religions remind us of this same thing. We must do our business in the marketplace, but not confuse the marketplace with the Supreme, with our ultimate purpose.

Measurement, comparing one degree of success with another, keeps us apart. If I think that my publishing numbers and your publishing numbers matter, then I may take the difference between those numbers to mean that we're different. But we're not so different, whether we've made the bestseller list or are still seeking our first sale. We're all of us minor writers. Our measurements don't matter nearly as much as our immeasurable contributions. Measuring keeps us from living in full communion with one another and the world.

Preoccupation with measuring, with seeing how your career stacks up, steals time from making your contribution. Making your contribution, your deepest offering to readers, means that you don't try to impress, but only to reveal the impressive thing beneath your work: the language, the subject matter, or whatever it is that you love. Love something, and then get out of the way so that from the side you can point to what you love. That's how you contribute.

If you take nothing else from this essay, take that. To write like a hero, love something, and get out of the way so that you can point to what you love.

Writing is not about you. It's about something, or some things, much bigger than you.

If you're a minor writer, you don't have a major reputation to risk. You can dare to be authentic and genuine.

You're free to follow your heart and write things that only you can write.

Bruce Holland Rogers lives in Eugene, Oregon. His writings range from literary and experimental fiction to science fiction, fantasy, and mystery genres. His stories have won a Pushcart Prize, two Nebula Awards, the Bram Stoker Award, two World Fantasy Awards, and have been nominated for the Edgar Allan Poe Award and Spain's Premio Ignotus.

He is also author of *Word Work: Surviving and Thriving as a Writer* (2002), about the challenges of full-time fiction writing. A motivational speaker and trainer on creativity and problem-solving for corporate clients, he is also on the faculty of the Whidbey Writers Workshop MFA program in creative writing.

This piece is excerpted from his essay "On Being a Minor Writer—and Why All Writers are Minor Writers"; the full text is available as a downloadable essay from Amazon. com.

# Writing a New World

*by Mary Pipher*

In my thirty years of being a therapist, I have never seen Americans more stressed. If the news were a weather report, every day it would be the same: Black clouds overhead. Tornado warning!

We live together in an era of what Anthony Lewis, a columnist for the *New York Times*, has called "existential blindness." *Tech Tonic*, a publication of the Alliance for Childhood, reports that the average American can recognize over a thousand brand names but is unable to identify ten indigenous plants or animals. We understand many facts about the world, but we cannot discern their meaning or their implications for action. Our world needs leaders, and yet people everywhere feel helpless and lack direction.

While we call our time the Age of Information, wisdom is in short supply. Language, which maps the way we think, is often just another marketing tool. Style trumps substance. War is called peace, while destruction is called development. Environmental devastation is footnoted or ignored. Hype and spin trivialize and obscure the truth. My favorite example of fuzzy language is George Tenet's line during congressional hearings in spring 2004. When questioned on inaccurate government information regarding weapons of mass destruction, he said, "The data do not uniquely comport with policy decisions." Parse that.

Sometimes language itself is a weapon. In urging a crackdown on asylum seekers, people who have fled their countries without valid documents, James Sensenbrenner, a congressman from Wisconsin, said that he wanted to "stop terrorists from gaming the asylum system." He failed to mention that no asylum seekers have been identified as having links to terrorists. And, clearly, he does not know the asylum seekers I know—Tibetan monks fleeing Chinese soldiers, human rights advocates escaping repressive governments, some of

America's greatest friends who are leaving countries where rulers fear democracy.

Language is weaponized when it is used to objectify, depersonalize, dehumanize, to create an "other." Once a person is labeled as "not like us," the rules for civilized behavior no longer apply. The phrase "illegal alien" is an obvious example. Both the word "illegal" and the word "alien" separate us from the person being described. Indeed, America treats illegal aliens quite badly. The truth is that no person is illegal and no person is an alien.

Progressives as well as conservatives have their way of dehumanizing. They hurl stones when they use terms such as "fundamentalist," "rednecks," or "right-wing conservatives" in derisive ways that allow no room for nuances, individual differences, or empathy with their adversaries' points of view.

I am not interested in weapons, whether words or guns. I want to be part of the rescue team for our tired, overcrowded planet. The rescuers will be those people who help other people to think clearly, and to be honest and open-minded. They will be an antidote to those people who disconnect us. They will de-objectify, rehumanize, and make others more understandable and sympathetic. They will help create what philosopher Martin Buber called I-thou relationships for the human race.

Buber distinguished between "I-it" and "I-thou" relationships. In I-it relationships, we deal with living creatures in one-dimensional ways. An "it" exists merely to serve our own purposes. A bank teller is essentially a nonperson who gives us our money; an old growth forest is lumber waiting to be harvested. In an I-thou relationship, the bank teller is a person like us, with desires, dreams, and loved ones. And an old-growth forest has a purpose far greater than our wish for lumber. When we deal with the teller or the forest in I-thou ways, we show respect. We are entering into a relationship.

Once the concept of otherness takes root, the unimaginable becomes possible. We don't want to look at the faces of the homeless as we walk past them; when we do, they become people, and it becomes harder to keep walking. During the Vietnam War, our GIs called the Vietcong "gooks"; in Iraq, our soldiers call the insurgents "rats" and their trails "ratlines." Psychologically, humans can kill rats much more easily then they can kill hungry, tired, frightened young people much like themselves.

With connection comes responsibility. Without it, decent Americans can vote for government policies or support businesses that leave villages in India or Africa without drinking water. We do this by erasing from our consciousness any awareness that our actions have hurtful consequences for people whose names we do not know. Labels help. It's easy to erase "civilians," "peasants," "insurgents," "enemy combatants," even "protesters." Once we have a label that doesn't fit us, we can ignore the humanity of the labeled.

A writer's job is to tell stories that connect readers to all the people of the earth, to show these people as the complicated human beings they really are, with histories, families, emotions, and legitimate needs. We can replace one-dimensional stereotypes with multidimensional individuals with whom our readers can identify, creating a world of I–thou relationships.

Dr. Mary Pipher is a psychologist and writer, with a Ph.D. in Clinical Psychology from the University of Nebraska. She was awarded the American Psychological Association Presidential Citation in 1998.

Her writings look at how American culture influences the mental health of its people. Three of her books, *Reviving Ophelia*, *The Shelter of Each Other*, and *Another Country* were *New York Times* bestsellers. *Reviving Ophelia* was on the *NYT* list for 154 weeks and number one for 27 weeks. Dr. Pipher travels all over the world sharing her ideas with community groups, schools, and health-care professionals.

This piece is excerpted from *Writing to Change the World* (Riverhead Books, 2006). This excerpt also appeared in the *UU World Magazine*, Fall 2006.

# APPENDICES

# Editor's Afterword

*by Philip Martin*

THIS 2007 EDITION, first in an annual series, offers an eclectic mix of advice and thoughts about writing well. Most is recent, from the last year or so. In compiling the selection, however, I did find a few older but useful pieces to round out some topics; in some cases I contacted authors to ask for an update.

I have tried to cover a lot of bases, from the sublime to the practical, from craft to career, from polished prose to more spontaneous blog thoughts. You may notice a few more religious-oriented pieces than appear in most published works on writing. For some reason, these materials are often overlooked in collections that speak to all writers. I've drawn on authors who range from Christian to Buddhist to (my own denomination) the eclectic Unitarian Universalist. Quick joke: How do you tell a Unitarian? Ask if he'd rather go to *heaven* ... or ... (as his eyes light up!) ... go to a lecture *about* heaven.

My religious belief can be summed up by: I'm guessing it's all connected. I mention this only because it is also my editorial philosophy: I think it's all connected. Everything from grammar to good thoughts to gosh-knows-what-else. To be a successful writer, you need to do lots of diverse things. Some you're naturally good at. For others, you need to stretch and listen and practice and consider new ideas.

In the end, writing skills are mostly absorbed, not learned. Like learning to speak as a native speaker, learning to write well is not just learning a set of rules or techniques. It's a huge, messy body of deep knowledge, inspired by bits of readings, conversations, incidents; it's affected by how you were taught and where you live and who you want to become. For every convention, there is another way that may work better. For every rule, there are mavericks who succeed by flaunting it. There's no right or wrong way to write, no ten easy steps. There are no initiation rites to take you into the dark hut and reveal the magic chants and secret knowledge. It's not secret; quite the opposite. It's mostly confusing if you try to listen to all of it.

The way to learn is the same as to master a language, to understand an eco-system. Immerse yourself, stick around and be part of it, listen to others with experience, look for a place to fit in, find your niche. And learn to live with messy contradictions. Writing isn't logical, it's a part of life.

I've looked for articles that might surprise you, that might make you stop and think, whatever sort of writing you do. I want to introduce new ideas—a batch each year—to help you advance your skills. That might be techniques for writing haiku or sex scenes or white papers, or thoughts about messy desks or why to re-read Dr. Seuss or why blogging is useful, not just lots of fun. I'm not sure exactly what will help you most, but I do know that all this, and more, goes into being a good writer.

Books of writing advice should come with a caveat: your actual results may vary. The only advice I would have said is constant is what Jane Yolen named in her recent book, *Take Joy*, the BIC principle: Butt in Chair. But here, an article by Richard Powers on "speaking a book" offers a variant: he composes out loud, using a voice-recognition software. He enjoys doing this most of all in his bed.

I might need to do some rethinking.

Writing is a gift. We should try to use it for good things, like helping and inspiring others. And because writing is meaningful and we take ourselves so seriously in our agonies to create it, it is also often funny. We might as well learn to laugh at ourselves and enjoy the company of each other and that fool we see in the mirror each morning. So I've also chosen a few pieces that tickled my funnybone.

Mostly, I want you to find some things mind-stretching and some practical here. I hope you find ways to write better and express your amazing thoughts and bring your stories to life and, yes, succeed. Perhaps just one article here will make a difference.

Sometimes the best new ideas comes from left field. Often we keep company only with those who think as we do. But cross-disciplinary reading is good; it is fuel for the brain and heart to listen and talk to those who are different from us.

Feel free to send me ideas for next year's edition, either pieces you or others you have written and you'd like me to consider.

And we'll keep at it, writing, together.

I'll leave you with a practical bit: keep writing. Don't let anything get in your way.

Good writing comes from great passion and personal dedication. Let's believe not just in ourselves and our own success but also in the goodness and success of those around us. As writers, we can and do make a difference. We do that every day.

*Philip Martin*

# Publication Credits

Abrahamson, Eric (interview with)
see McLaughlin, Michael

Adams, Linda
"Running a Critique Group" is © 2006 by Linda Adams and is reprinted by permission of the author. Her website is www.hackman-adams.com.

Allen, Moira
"Creating an Online Portfolio" is © 2007 by Moira Allen and is reprinted by permission of the author. Her website is www.writing-world.com. An earlier version of this piece appeared in 2003 in *The Writer*.

Backes, Laura
"What Dr. Seuss Can Teach Us" is © 2007 by Laura Backes and is reprinted by permission of *Children's Book Insider*. This article appeared in the March 2007 issue of *Children's Writing Update*, an e-zine published by *Children's Book Insider*.

Bandos, Kate
"Focus on Niche Markets" is © 2007 by Kate Bandos and is reprinted by permission of the author. Her website is www.ksbpromotions.com. An earlier version of this piece appeared in the January 2005 issue of PMA *Independent*, newsletter of the Publishers Marketing Association, and can be found online at www.pma-online.org.

Bertrand, J. Mark
"Beyond Showing & Telling" is © 2006 by J. Mark Bertrand and is reprinted by permission of the author. The passages come from his blog, Notes on Craft, which is found at his website www.jmarkbertrand.com.

Bernstein, Mark
"10 Tips on Writing the Living Web" is © 2002 by Mark Bernstein and is reprinted by permission of the author.

Block, Marylaine
"My First Rule of Information" is © 2007 by Marylaine Block and is reprinted by permission of the author. An earlier version of this material appears on her website at www.marylaine.com.

Bridges, Judy

"Snappy Introductions" is © Judy Bridges and is reprinted by permission of the author. Her website is www.redbirdstudio.com.

Carroll, Jonathan

"Ingredients" is © 2006 and © 2007 by Jonathan Carroll and is reprinted by permission of The Richard Parks Agency. The passages come from his blog, which is found at his website, www.jonathancarroll.com.

Carlson, Linda

"How Authors Can Help Publishers with Marketing" is © 2007 by Linda Carlson and is reprinted by permission of the author. Her website is www.lindacarlson.com. An earlier version of this piece appeared in the November 2004 issue of *PMA Independent*, newsletter of the Publishers Marketing Association, and can be found online at www.pma-online. org.

Clark, Roy Peter

"The Line between Fact & Fiction" is © by Roy Peter Clark and is reprinted by permission of the author. This is excerpted from a longer version of an article that appeared in Issue #16 of *Creative Nonfiction*, the text of which can be found at www.creativenonfiction.org.

Chi, Lu

see Hamill, Sam (translator)

Clayton, John

"The Origin of Names" is © 2003 by John Clayton and is reprinted by permission of the author. His website is www.johnclaytonbooks.com. The piece originally was written for the Writers on the Range series distributed by the *High Country News*.

Coulter, Brenda

"How To Write a Query Letter" is © Brenda Coulter and is reprinted by permission of the author. The article appears on her website, www. brendacoulter.com.

Donadio, Rachel

"Literary Fiction" is © 2006 and is reprinted by permission of the *New York Times*. The essay was originally published with the title "Promotional Intelligence."

Ensign, Paulette

"The Potential of Tips Booklets" is © 2004 by Paula Ensign and is reprinted by permission of the author. The article appears as "Unleash the Potential of Booklets to Sell More Books and Enhance Your Cash Flow" on her website at www.tipsbooklets.com.

Franklin, Lynn

"Psychological Action in Nonfiction" is © 2007 by Lynn Franklin and is reprinted by permission of the author. The passages are drawn from discussions posted on the WriterL listserv, which is found at www.writerL. com.

Formichelli, Linda
> "Getting the Tough Interview" is © 2007 by Linda Formichelli and is reprinted by permission of the author. This piece appeared in *Writer's Digest* in January/February 2007.
>
> "Your Email Signature" is © 2007 by Linda Formichelli and is reprinted by permission of the author. The piece is based on an entry from her blog, The Renegade Writer, December 18, 2006, found at www.therenegade writer.com.

Gaiman, Neil
> "Instructions" is © 2000 by Neil Gaiman and is reprinted by permission of the author. This is an excerpt from that poem, which was first published in *A Wolf at the Door*, anthology edited by Ellen Datlow and Terri Windling. Neil Gaiman's website is www.neilgaiman.com.

Getlen, Larry
> "Recreating Nonfiction Scenes" is © 2007 by Larry Getlen and is reprinted by permission of the author. This piece appeared in *Writer's Digest* in January/February 2007.

Glatzer, Jenna
> "Tips for a Well-Attended Event" is © by Jenna Glatzer and is reprinted by permission of the author. The article appears on her website at www. jennaglatzer.com.

Gray, Robert
> "Time Traveling by Words, Music, & Art" is © 2006 by Robert Gray and is reprinted by permission of the author from his blog, Fresh Eyes: A Bookseller's Journal, which can be found at www.fresheyesnow.com.

Gudding, Gabriel
> "The Cultivation of Mindstates" is © 2007 by Gabriel Gudding and is reprinted by permission of the author. The passages come from his blog, Conchology, which is found at www.gabrielgudding.blogspot. com.

Hamill, Sam
> Excerpt from "Choosing Words," from *The Art of Writing: Lu Chi's Wen Fu*, translated by Sam Hamill (Minneapolis: Milkweed Editions, 2000). Translation copyright © 1991, 2000 by Sam Hamill. Reprinted with permission from Milkweed Editions, www.milkweed.org.

Joiner, Whitney
> "The Blind Pitch" is © 2003 by Whitney Joiner and is reprinted by permission of the author.

Jong, Erica
> "All Writer's Are Vain" is © 2007 by Erica Jong and is published by permission of the author.

Kiernan, Kristy

"How Many Writers?" is © 2007 by Kristy Kiernan and is reprinted by permission of the author. It appeared first as a comment on a blog for mystery writers, The Good Girls Kill for Money Club, at www.good-girls-kill.com. It was posted February 9, 2007, in response to questions posed in an interview by Tasha Alexander with author Robert Gregory Browne.

Kleinman, Jeff

"Nonfiction Proposals" is © 2007 by Jeff Kleinman and is reprinted by permission of the author. It appears on the website of his literary agency, Folio Literary Management, www.foliolit.com.

Lipe, Jay

"How To Get Great Testimonials" is © 2007 by Jay Lipe and is reprinted by permission of the author. His website is www.emergemarketing.com. An earlier version of this piece appeared in the March 2004 issue of *PMA Independent*, newsletter of the Publishers Marketing Association, and can be found online at www.pma-online.org.

Lippi, Rosina

"Lyricism in Sex Scenes" is © 2004 by Rosina Lippi and is reprinted by permission of the author. The passages come from her blog, a current version of which is found at her website, www.rosinalippi.com.

Lopez, Barry

"Discovering Home Ground" is © 2006 by Barry Lopez and is reprinted by permission of the author. It is an excerpt from his introduction to the book *Home Ground: Language for an American Landscape*, co-edited with Debra Gwartney (Trinity University Press, 2006).

Martin, Gregory

"The Treadmill Journal" is © 2007 by Gregory Martin and is reprinted by permission of the author. It first appeared in the April 2007 issue of *The Writer*.

"A Checklist for Character & Conflict Revision" is © 2007 by Gregory Martin and is reprinted by permission of the author.

Martin, Philip

"Where Do Ideas Come From?" is © 2007 by Philip Martin and is reprinted by permission of the author. A version of this piece appears in his book, *A Guide to Fantasy Literature* (Crickhollow Books, 2007).

"Working with a Small Press is © 2007 by Philip Martin. An earlier version appeared in *The Writer* in 2002.

"Editor's Afterword" is © 2007 by Philip Martin and is published by permission of the author.

Meyers, Theresa

"Your Press Kit" is © Theresa Meyers and is reprinted by permission of the author. It is excerpted from a longer article, "Beginning your Publicity Plan," that appears on her website at www.bluemooncommunications.com.

McConnell, Sheri

"Developing Intuition" is © 2006 by Sheri McConnell and is reprinted by permission of the author. A longer version of this article appears on the website of the National Association of Women Writers, www.naww. org.

McLaughlin, Michael

"The Benefits of Messiness" (interview with Eric Abrahamson) is © 2007 by Michael McLaughlin and is reprinted by permission of the author. It is an excerpt from a longer interview in the March 2007 issue of the e-newsletter, *Management Consulting News*, found at www.management consultingnews.com.

Mooney, Paula

"How To Pitch your Stories to an Editor" is © 2007 by Paula Mooney and is reprinted by permission of the author.

Morris, Evan

"Glamour & Grammar" is © 2006 by Evan Morris and is reprinted by permission of the author. It first appeared in his online newsletter, *The Word Detective*, May 2006, which can be found at www.word-detective.com.

Palumbo, Dennis

"The Three Cosmic Rule of Writing" is © 2007 Dennis Palumbo and is reprinted by permission of the author. His website is www.dennis palumbo.com.

Park, Linda Sue

This article © 2007 by Linda Sue Park and is reprinted by permission of Curtis Brown, Ltd. It first appeared in *Keystrokes* online magazine, 1999, and also is posted on her website at www.lspark.com.

Pearson, Ridley

"The 3-Act Structure" is © 2007 by Ridley Pearson. It appeared in the April 2007 issue of *Writer's Digest* under the title, "Getting Your Act(s) Together," and is reprinted here by permission of the author. His website is www.ridleypearson.com.

Pipher, Mary

"Writing a New World" is © 2006 by Mary Pipher and is reprinted by permission of Riverside Literary Agency. This is an edited excerpt drawn from her book, *Writing To Change the World* (Riverhead, 2006). This excerpt also appeared in *UU World Magazine*, Fall 2006.

Pollitt, Katha

"Thank You for Hating My Book" is © 2007 and is reprinted by permission of the *New York Times*.

Powers, Richard

"How To Speak a Book" is © 2006 and is reprinted by permission of the *New York Times*.

Raney, Deborah

"Have a Positive Influence" is © 2007 by Deborah Raney and is reprinted by permission of the author. Her website is www.deborahraney.com. This piece appeared in the January 2007 *Right Writing* newsletter.

Reichhold, Jane

"Haiku Techniques" is © 2000 by Jane Reichhold and is reprinted by permission of the author. It is an excerpt from a longer version originally published in *Frogpond*, the journal of the Haiku Society of America, Autumn 2000.

Reissenweber, Brandi

"The Art of the Start" is © Brandi Reissenweber and is reprinted by permission of the author. This piece originally appeared in *Letterpress*, her newsletter on fiction writing, and also is posted on the Gotham Writer's Workshop website.

Roe, Paula

"Perfecting your Live Pitch" is © Paula Roe and is reprinted by permission of the author. It appears on her website at www.paularoe.com.

Rogers, Bruce Holland

"On Being a Minor Writer" is © Bruce Holland Rogers and is reprinted by permission of the author. This is an excerpt from his essay, "On Being a Minor Writer." His website is www.sff.net/people/bruce.

Rutledge, Patrice-Anne

"Your Author Website: Five Tips" is © Patrice-Anne Rutledge and is reprinted by permission of the author. Her website is www.websavvy writer.com.

Sands, Katharine

"Pitching your Book to an Agent" is © 2007 by Katharine Sands and is reprinted by permission of the author. This piece is drawn from her several articles in her book, *Making the Perfect Pitch* (The Writer Books, 2004).

Schmidt, L.J.

"Books as a Gateway Drug" is © 2006 by L.J. Schmidt and is reprinted by permission of the author. The piece appeared on her blog, which can be found at www.booksellerchick.blogspot.com.

Silva, Mick

"Into the Light" is © 2006 by Mick Silva and is reprinted by permission of the author. The passages come from his blog, Your Writers Group, which can be found at www.yourwritersgroup.com.

Stelzner, Michael

"Writing White Papers" is © 2006 by Michael A. Stelzner and is reprinted by permission of the author. This piece is drawn from the first chapter of his book, *Writing White Papers* (2006).

Tapply, William G.

"The Invisible Writer" is © 2005 by William G. Tapply and is reprinted by permission of the author. It first appeared in the November 2005 issue of *The Writer* under the title, "Don't Be a Show-Off." His website is www.williamgtapply.com.

Unowsky, David

"Planning Author Events in Bookstores" is © 2007 by David Unowsky and is reprinted by permission of the author.

Viehl, Lynn (Kelly, Sheila)

"Strange Fruit" is © 2007 by Sheila Kelly and is reprinted by permission of the author. It appeared on her blog, Paperback Writer, which can be found at www.pbackwriter.blogspot.com.

Voivod, Lani

"Why Aren't You Blogging?" is © 2007 by Lani Voivod and is reprinted by permission of the author. The piece comes from her "A-Ha!" blog at www.epiphaniesinc.com.

Weber, Steve

"Fundamentals of Blogging" is © 2007 by Steve Weber and is reprinted by permission of the author. It is excerpted from his book, *Plug this Book: Online Book Marketing for Authors* (Weber Books, 2007).

Whalin, W. Terry

"Join a Critique Group" is © 2006 by W. Terry Whalin and is reprinted by permission of the author. His website is www.right-writing.com.

Yolen, Jane

"Writing Rhythms" is © 2006 by Jane Yolen and is reprinted by permission of Curtis Brown, Ltd. It is drawn from her online journal at www.janeyolen.com.

Yudkin, Marcia

"M-Factors: Qualities that Help You Break into Major Magazine" is © 2007 by Marcia Yudkin and is reprinted by permission of the author. An earlier version can be found on her website at www.yudkin.com.